From the Potomac to the Etowah

From the Potomac to the Etowah

THE LETTERS OF
REV. ALONZO HALL QUINT
TO THE CONGREGATIONALIST;
VOLUME 1 - 1861 & 1862

———

Edited by
Jonathan C. Lane

Bonney 4 Joplin Press

BonneyJoplin Press
P.O. Box 539
Oxford, MA 01540

© 2017 Jonathan C. Lane
All rights reserved.

ISBN-13: 9780692899557
ISBN-10: 0692899553

For Mom and Dad – who gave to me the gift of life, the love of learning, and the passion to share what I know.

Table of Contents

Acknowledgments · ix
Preface · xi
Alonzo Hall Quint 1827 – 1896 · xvii

1861 · 1
The 2nd Massachusetts Volunteer Infantry in 1861 · · · · · · · · · · · · · · · · · 3
September 20, 1861 · 7
October 4, 1861 ·12
October 11, 1861 ·17
October 18, 1861 ·23
November 1, 1861 ·29
November 15, 1861 ·38
November 29, 1861 ·45
November 29, 1861 ·50
December 20, 1861 ·56
December 27, 1861 ·62

1862 · 67
The 2nd Massachusetts Volunteer Infantry in 1862 · · · · · · · · · · · · · · · · ·69
January 10, 1862 ·75
January 31, 1862 · 80
February 21, 1862 ·85
February 28, 1862 · 90
March 14, 1862 · 97

March 21, 1862	102
March 28, 1862	107
April 11, 1862	113
April 11, 1862	120
April 25, 1862	125
May 9, 1862	132
May 23, 1862	138
May 23, 1862	142
June 6, 1862	147
July 18, 1862	155
July 25, 1862	161
August 1, 1862	170
August 8, 1862	176
August 22, 1862	180
August 22, 1862	190
September 12, 1862	194
September 19, 1862	200
September 26, 1862	207
October 10, 1862	214
November 21, 1862	220
December 5, 1862	226
December 5, 1862	232
December 12, 1862	239
December 26, 1862	246
December 26, 1862	252
Index	255

Acknowledgments

As with any project, there are many people to whom the author is indebted. Vincent Golden, Curator of Newspapers and the Reader's Services staff at the American Antiquarian Society provided me with unparalleled service and advice in utilizing the Society's collection of newspapers. Keith Vezeau and Brigadier-General Leonid Kondratiuk at the Massachusetts Military Museum and Archives likewise provided me aid and support in the use of the original records of the 2nd Massachusetts Infantry. I also appreciate Melissa Arndt for her efforts on the book's cover and all her graphic arts savvy.

I cannot understate the gratitude I have for Douglas Ozelius, William Sherburne and Robert Carney for their enthusiasm and support for this project, their generosity of time and treasure to visit many of the places mentioned in this volume, as well as for their long-standing friendship and companionship. I am likewise indebted to Thomas J. Keenan whose kindness, camaraderie, and guidance is valued beyond measure and to whom I could never adequately express my appreciation.

I acknowledge my love and gratitude towards my sister Kate Lane Van Sleet who encouraged and nurtured this project as well as acting as my *ad hoc* editor in her copious free time; to my sister Elizabeth Murdock whose unfailing generosity and emotional support was always there to be drawn upon; and to my brother Frederick S. Lane whose own published efforts are an inspiration to me.

I am grateful to my boys, Jonathan and Thomas who are willing accomplices in my explorations of Civil War battlefields, historic sites, as well as my disciples in the "Did you know…?" Society. I love you both and I am proud of you.

Lastly, to my wife Allison, I will exclaim that I am humbled by your love for me, your faith in me, and by all the blessings you have brought into my life.

Preface

ON 3 JUNE 1875 AT the North Congregational Church in New Bedford, Massachusetts Charles Edward Benton and Harriet Maria Drown stood up before Alonzo Hall Quint, pastor of the Congregational Church, to pledge their troth to one another. Charlie was a Civil War veteran and farmer from Dutchess County, New York and Harriet was the only child of a New Bedford merchant and ship owner. The couple met at a house party in Sharon, Connecticut near where Charlie, a widower, worked a small farm. Harriet had traveled out to Sharon from her home in New Bedford to meet a friend from her days at Vassar College. Remarkably, when Harriet and Charlie stood up before her minister that day, despite his being from New York, Charlie also knew the Reverend Quint. In fact, the last time they had seen each other was in a field hospital in Kingston, Georgia during General William T. Sherman's Atlanta campaign in 1864.

After the wedding, Charlie and Harriet moved back to Charlie's farm in Connecticut until 1891 when they returned to New Bedford to live with Harriet's widowed mother. By this time the Reverend Quint had moved on from his New Bedford flock, accepting a post first at the Broadway Church in Somerville, Massachusetts and then a new parish in Allston, Massachusetts. Despite their passing like ships in the night, Charlie and Alonzo Quint renewed their acquaintance through their mutual participation in the Civil War Veteran's association, known as the Grand Army of the Republic. In fact, according to Charlie Benton's recollection, he relied upon the Reverend Quint's advice when working upon his reminiscence, entitled *As Seen from the Ranks*, as well as the regimental history of the One Hundred and Fiftieth New York Infantry, and they remained friends until Alonzo's death in 1896.

Among Charlie's library that has trickled down to his descendants is a first edition copy (1864) of Alonzo H. Quint's book entitled *The Potomac and the Rapidan*. This book was among the first historical retrospectives of the war up to that point. The work is an edited reprinting of Quint's letters which he wrote to a religious newspaper called the *Congregationalist*, then being printed in Boston by Galen James & Co. The letters of Alonzo Quint to the Congregationalist along with those of Horace James, Chaplain of the 25th Massachusetts Infantry and the mysterious Washington correspondent "Spectator," are among the highlights of the paper during the war years. The American Antiquarian Society in Worcester, Massachusetts hold a complete run of the *Congregationalist* and allow historians to read Quint's letters as they originally appeared in print.

What became clear when the 1864 book was compared to the letters printed in the *Congregationalist* was that Quint heavily edited the letters for their publication in *The Potomac and the Rapidan*. While we cannot know for certain the reasons behind Quint's editorial excises, evaluation of the material can provide some clues. Some of the material was probably considered too personally connected to members of the 2nd Massachusetts to be of interest to a wider and more national book audience. Similarly, some of Quint's writing played up the virtues of the Massachusetts regiments at the expense of other regiments within the army. These sentiments may have played well within a regional audience (the bulk of the readers of the Congregationalist being in Massachusetts) but presumably would have attracted unnecessary criticism upon the author.

However, it is Quint's references to General McClellan that stand out as the most glaring topic excised from his publication. The acrimonious 1864 Presidential election pitting the former Union Army General against the incumbent, Abraham Lincoln was likely the motivation for Quint's editorial choices. Quint believed, as many soldiers in the East did, that McClellan was the best of the Union Generals and that Lincoln was mistaken to remove him from command. Quint's unceasing support for McClellan, continuing well into 1864, brought letters to the newspaper chastising him for his admiration of the man who stood opposed to President Lincoln. Quint defended himself in an 1864 editorial entitled "Who shall we vote for" in which he states that while he believes that McClellan was a great military leader, his adherence to the Democratic party, its platform of a negotiated peace and his Vice Presidential running mate George Pendleton,[1] an outspoken peace advocate, made support of the McClellan candidacy untenable for anyone who had enlisted and fought for the Union cause.

In addition to the material that Quint or his editors decided to cut from his original letters as printed in the Congregationalist, there were 11 full letters and another seven editorials or sermons written after his return home that remained in print only in the newspaper. Most of the letters concern events after Quint's return to the regiment after shepherding those soldiers who had reenlisted to and from Massachusetts for their two-week furlough. These late narratives follow the trials and tribulations of the 2nd Massachusetts from their departure from Tennessee right up through the battle of Resaca, Georgia. The editorials, all of which were written in 1864 and 1865, deal mostly with events leading up to the election and the decision of the voters of how to prosecute the war from that point. While not "letters from the battlefield," these are included these in this publication because it helped to clarify some of Quint's opinions regarding General McClellan as well as Quint's lukewarm support for the administration. He was not the only New Englander to feel this way.

Several editorials appeared after Lee's surrender and President Lincoln's assassination and they reveal a fascinating aspect of Quint's theology. While he decried bringing wholesale vengeance upon the south Quint was in favor of applying harsh punishment to the leaders of the Confederate cause and the entire Southern aristocracy. Quint's rebuttal to the "turn the other cheek" argument was that, in his opinion, God's desire for his followers to forgive

---

[1] George Hunt Pendleton (1825 – 1889) was a graduate of Cincinnati College and the University of Heidelberg. Pendleton was a leader among the anti-war Democrats in the House of Representatives and was not reelected during the election of 1864 when Pendleton was on the Presidential ticket with George B. McClellan. In 1869 Pendleton served as President of the Kentucky Central Railroad, a position he kept until he was elected to the U. S. Senate in 1879. Pendleton was married to the daughter of Francis Scott Key. "Pendleton, George Hunt;" *Biographical Dictionary of the United States Congress*;

those who wronged them was applicable only to private or personal wrongs and did not apply to governments dealing with traitors. For them, Quint says, God demands justice.

Given the prevalence of digital printings of Quint's original work, now well within the public domain, it may seem superfluous to reprint his previously published writings. However, the material which was edited out of Quint's book, now restored as written to the editors of the *Congregationalist*, as well as the previously unprinted material, only enhances what is previously known about Quint's work. He had an eye for detail and for understanding military strategy. Quint wrote extremely detailed and engaging narratives for a populist publication, and his work remains one of the premier primary sources for the campaigns of the 2nd Massachusetts Infantry and XII Corps, life as a volunteer army chaplain, as well as the privations and Herculean efforts of the men who fought and died in the American Civil War.

The letters are reproduced exactly as found in the newspapers with the spelling and grammar kept as it appeared in print. The italicized dates at the head of each letter represent he date the letter appeared in print in *The Congregationalist*.

Jonathan C. Lane   May 2017

Officers of the 2nd Massachusetts Infantry Regiment in camp at Camp Andrew on Brook Farm, West Roxbury, Massachusetts.
(Image courtesy of the Massachusetts Historical Society)

Alonzo Hall Quint 1827 – 1896

"No regiment from this or any other State has been more favored in its Chaplain than the Massachusetts 2d. When it left our city for the seat of war, on the eighth of July, 1861, Chaplain Quint went with it; -- and no thinning of its ranks – no loss from it of dear friends – not even the loss of his own health, and urgent appeals from family, and from church, have yet induced him to leave it. Besides ministering with ability, zeal, and tact to its spiritual and temporal wants in camp, on the battle-field, and in the hospital, he is writing a history of it which will descend to posterity as one of the most graphic records of this war."[2]

THE REVEREND ALONZO HALL QUINT was born 22 March 1828 in Barnstead, New Hampshire to George Quint, a machinist at the Cocheco mills, and his wife Sally Hall. Alonzo lived most of his youth in Dover, NH where he prepared for college at Franklin Academy. At the age of 16 he entered Dartmouth College as a member of the sophomore class and graduated as the youngest member of the class in 1846. For three years following, Quint divided his time between working with his father as a mechanic's mate and studying medicine in his hometown of Dover. These years of unstructured study would stand him in great stead during the Civil War, though neither of these employments satisfied his soul.

---

2 *Boston Daily Advertiser*; "Letters to the Editors;" September 1, 1863.

In 1849, Alonzo entered Andover Theological Seminary in Andover, Massachusetts and he completed his studies in 1852, though he continued on one more year at Andover for post-graduate study in 1853. The Seminary instructed Quint in the traditional or orthodox form of Congregationalism. While Quint identified readily with the Pilgrim Fathers and the early Massachusetts Bay Puritans as the forefathers of his faith, he was of a more liberal temperament as befitted his time. Quint was very much a "commonsense" Congregationalist who saw his faith as one that guided his parishioners along the right path of life, rather than one that was an unyielding and unforgiving religion. Quint's Congregationalism also recognized the Christian spirit present in those ministers of the gospel who worked in other Christian denominations and he was a great advocate for cooperation between faiths against societal ills such as drunkenness and the abuse of the Sabbath day.

Quint's writings exhibit the depth and breadth of his education, both spiritually and scholastically. He quotes with ease both scripture and popular literature and frequently illustrates his sermons with quotations and descriptions from the works of Dickens, Jules Verne, Robert Burns, and other popular writers of his age. However, it was from his own life experiences, particularly his time in the army, which Quint used to illustrate his Christian teachings, turning chance encounters and events great and small into parables for his congregations.

His Chaplaincy with the 2nd Massachusetts was a tree that bore much fruit in his later years as he used illustrative stories to draw pictures of the everyday Christianity he encountered while at the "seat of war." Quint relates a story in one of his sermons about going past the picket line with Colonel (later General) Gordon to visit a local Virginian farmer who had invited them to dinner. As dinner was prepared Col. Gordon grew increasingly agitated because he and his staff (including Quint) were well away from the regiment with only their side-arms and Gordon was afraid he had allowed himself to be drawn into a trap which would result in his capture. Only when the farmer said grace before dinner did Col. Gordon relax his heightened anxiety and gave as his explanation to Quint "when the old man made such a prayer, I knew he was honest and couldn't mean any treachery." Quint used this incident to remind his audience that "real praying is a test of character," and that "communion is the channel by which the graces come."[3]

Similarly, Quint relates a story that took place at the headquarters of General Alpheus Williams during the Atlanta Campaign. Gen. Williams had asked Rev. Quint to come speak to a condemned man who was, in Gen. Williams' opinion, feigning stupidity in hopes of avoiding his sentence of death. Quint spoke to the man and divined that the convicted soldier has been raised Catholic. Using images of the crucifix and Roman Catholic teachings, Quint got the man to acknowledge his fate. What Quint drew from this was an admiration for the way in which the Roman Catholic church instructed its followers from the cradle to the grave and how the rote learning of the doctrine stayed with the parishioner when all other knowledge failed them. Quint viewed this as a model for Congregational churches to adopt as a way to grow the faith. While a sleeping baby may not understand the words that are spoken in Christian prayer, yet there is a parallel for a child to be "in a good spiritual atmosphere," as it is "being in a healthful, material atmosphere."[4]

On December 7, 1853, Alonzo Quint was ordained as the first pastor of the Mather Church (now the Central Congregational Church) in Jamaica Plain, Massachusetts. The congregation had been founded the previous February by twenty-one families and numbered just over 100 people, with 157 children in Sunday School.[5]

During his early pastorate Quint became actively involved in the General Association of Massachusetts, an association "designed to promote brotherly harmony and intercourse among the ministers of Christ; - to obtain religious information relative to the state of their churches; - and to cooperate with one another, and with other ecclesiastical bodies, in the most eligible measures for advancing the cause of truth and holiness;" throughout Massachusetts but with strong national influence and ties. The Rev. Quint held many offices

---

3 Quint; *Commonsense Christianity*; p. 49
4 Quint; *Commonsense Christianity*; p. 73
5 American Congregational Association, et al... *The Congregational Quarterly*; vol. 1; 1857; p.71

within this organization through his many years of membership but he was the longest serving Secretary of Statistics keeping track of the number of Congregational parishes and the numbers of families and children they were serving.

In 1854, Quint married Miss Rebecca Page Putnam of Salem, the daughter of Captain Allen Putnam, a sea captain, ship-owner, and surveyor of customs (in which post he replaced the author Nathaniel Hawthorne). They went on to have four children; George Putnam Quint, who died young; Clara Gadsden Quint (1858), who died just prior to her father; Wilder Dwight Quint (1863) named for Rev. Quint's companion-in-arms killed at the Battle of Antietam; Katherine Mordannt Quint (1867), who went on to receive the first post-graduate degree awarded to a woman from Dartmouth College; and John Hastings Quint (1868) a graduate of Bowdoin who, like his father, became a Congregational minister.

At the outbreak of the war Quint delivered a sermon to his congregation entitled "A Christian Patriot's Present Duty," detailing the reasons God-fearing Northerners should go off to war and support the Union cause. Quint instructed his congregation that warfare by the government in support of the government was not only permitted by scripture, with a just cause it was sanctioned by God. As with many contemporary writers in support of the Union cause, out of the four reasons espoused by Quint for supporting the war effort, all of them began with the phrase "The war is to sustain a government;" and only the last one makes mention of slavery when he writes "The War is a war to sustain a government imbued with the spirit of liberty against a rebellion which is the child of slavery."[6]

It must be noted that Quint himself admits in a letter from March of 1862 that he never voted for a Republican ticket and that when the war began he could not be counted an anti-slavery fanatic. In reading "A Christian Patriot's Present Duty" one gets that sense that Quint's objections to slavery only began at the borders of Massachusetts, or perhaps the Mason-Dixon line, where the slave-holders held sway over the liberties of the Northern citizen. "We never asked to meddle with slavery," Quint writes, "we only asked it

---

6 Quint; *The Christian Patriot's Present Duty*; p. 15.

should not meddle with us." He rails against the "compromises" made by the North for the sake of peace which required to them to fully participate in the slave culture by upholding the Fugitive Slave law. The Anthony Burns and Shadrach Minkins cases seem to be at the forefront of his mind, particularly the Burns case which resulted in an unprecedented military display in order to prevent Burns from being spirited away by the anti-slavery citizens of Boston. While the outbreak of war may be regrettable, Quint argued that it was of some relief to New Englanders since the result for them was that "the chain is off our limbs; the padlock off our lips; the iron off our hearts."[7] No longer would residents of the north stand silently by while their southern cousins held other men in chains.

So many friends and neighbors enlisted for service in volunteer regiments that Reverend Quint sought to go with some of them as regimental chaplain. Quint knew from his historical lessons the value of religion in an army of men away from the moderating influences of home. He invoked the name of Oliver Cromwell's Ironsides regiment, known for their singing of psalms before battle; and, General Henry Havelock who held regular Bible study classes with any of his regiment who expressed interest. Both regiments achieved great fame through valor inspired by faith. Filled with his own patriotic fervor and a desire to inspire patriotic valor amongst his fellow New-Englanders, Quint met with Col. Gordon, one of his parishioners, then recruiting for the first "3 years or the war" regiment, which was to be known as the 2nd Massachusetts Volunteer Infantry. On 20 June 1861, the Reverend Quint was commissioned regimental chaplain of the 2nd Massachusetts.

Quint undertook his duties while the regiment was still encamped at Brook Farm in West Roxbury, preaching sermons in a hollow near the camp. Brook Farm, a former transcendental community, belonged to another noted minister, James Freeman Clarke who had offered it to the Government of Massachusetts free of charge as a suitable place to gather and instruct troops. On 8 July 1861, Quint and the rest of the 2nd Massachusetts packed up their tents and prepared to join the Union Army in Williamsport, Maryland. Just prior to departure from Camp Andrew, the Reverend Quint was presented

---

7 Quint; *The Christian Patriot's Present Duty*; p. 19.

with a horse and "all the necessary equipments" from his parishioners in Jamaica Plain.[8]

Quint's service as a regimental chaplain brought him more than an accumulation of experiences from which he drew upon for a lifetime of sermons. The war was a transformative Christian experience for Quint. During his time in the army he saw first-hand the societal ills of intemperance, blasphemy, desecration of the Sabbath, as well as slavery and its feverish grip over Southern society. Quint considered slavery the original sin for which the Civil War was the punishment of the nation. To counter-balance these blemishes on a Christian life, Quint also saw many ministers and men of faith laboring to combat the worst sins in and around the army camp. Sons of Temperance chapters were prevalent and greatly encouraged as was the distribution of religious texts and morality reading material. Religious and secular organizations such as the U. S. Christian Commission, the Sisters of Charity, and the U. S. Sanitary Commission were welcome aids in Quint's mission to minister and supply succor to the men of his regiment. The success or failure of these efforts greatly depended on the support, active or passive, of the men in command, not all of whom could be claimed to be moral or Christian pillars of the military community.

Quint's war-time ministry is detailed in his letters home to the *Congregationalist*, though less is said of his regimental sermonizing than a historian might desire. The reader of his letters does enjoy a fuller picture of the work beyond the pulpit that fell to the chaplain in his efforts to bring the comfort of religion and home to the boys in the field. Quint spends a great deal of time looking after the wounded, collecting and delivering the mail, writing letters home and answering letters from home as well as arranging for such special supplies as the regiment may find itself in need of.

In August of 1861, the Young Men's Christian Association of New York sent out a circular to chaplains in the field to discover what, if any, material needs the regiments might have. Quint reported in October of 1861 that the regiment was well fitted with supplies because of their regimental fund, but he needed some publications, particular "good Catholic books" for the

---

8 *Boston Traveller*; 8 July 1861; p.2

Romanists in the regiment. He reports that his men "are a reading set" and read avidly any material they can lay their hands upon. He doesn't spend a great deal of time writing letters for the men because most of them were literate. When asked if the officers of the regiment were pious, Quint replied that it was "Hard to decide, as the piety is reality;" but he went on to add that only one officer helps him with the prayer meetings held on Wednesday evening. When asked to detail the number of pious men in the regiment Quint replied, "I think about 100; but numerous others are backsliders; and 300 Catholics."[9]

Quint went on to report that there was no drunkenness in the regiment and very little in the way of vice. Sabbath services were held on Sundays at 3:30 P.M. and everyone attended except the sick and those on guard duty. The only obstacle to Sunday service was being on the march or bad weather, particularly since they did not have a regimental church tent. Quint was pleased to say that he had "every opportunity which officers could possibly give," and that his work was pleasant and "attended with good results." One wonders how his answers would have change had he answered this questionnaire in January of 1864.[10]

After the battle of Antietam, in September of 1862, Quint accompanied the body of Major Wilder Dwight home for burial. Though the regiment was still in active service, the recently dismissed regimental band joined Reverend Quint for Dwight's funeral which included a touching graveside eulogy by Reverend Quint. It was not Quint's first funeral duty for a regimental brother, but it is certainly the one death in the regiment that affected him more than any other.

Through his letters, Alonzo Quint makes it plain that he intended to serve the entirety of the war with his regiment, even though it placed a financial burden upon his family. This is supported by the fact that Quint returned home on furlough in January of 1864 with the contingent of men who had signed their re-enlistment papers. He was a participant in the reception of the regiment by Governor Andrew and General Ambrose Burnside at Faneuil Hall on the 20th of January. Newspapers reported that during this trip home

---

9 Brainerd; *The Work of the Army Committee;* p.36
10 Brainerd; *The Work of the Army Committee;* p.37

Quint resolved to publish a record of the service of the 2nd Massachusetts Regiment up to that point. Notices for *The Potomac and the Rapidan* were being published as early as January of 1864 with hints at a second publication detailing the men and officers of the Regiment.

Also during his sojourn home, Quint took the opportunity to once again show his support of public education by making an address at the State Normal School at Salem, where his family had been living during his service in the army. While visiting his family he also participated in a reception by the town authorities of Salem and a community supper and levee as well as many other special events, religious services and programs held in support of the returning veterans.

In March of 1864 newspapers announced that Rev. Quint was offered the pastorate of the North Congregational Church of New Bedford and by the middle of April, Quint had accepted. Founded in 1807, this was the second oldest Congregational parish in the city. The North Congregational Church was built in 1833 in the center of a wealthy neighborhood filled with merchants, ship owners and their families. The congregation was almost triple that of his Jamaica Plain flock, numbering 372 with almost an equal number in Sunday School. Quint took to his post on the 21st of July, 1864.[11]

After his war-time service, Quint renewed his activity with the Massachusetts General Association, a Congregational church affiliation, and the National Council of the Congregational Churches of the United States. At one point, he sat on four standing committees of the Council and was a leading force in their deliberations concerning reconstruction efforts in the South as well as the restoration of relations with the Congregational churches in Great Britain. These were both controversial topics which arose from the debates of the National Council at their meeting in Boston, held in June of 1865. By their own reckoning, the National Council meeting of 1865 represented only the fourth synod of Congregational churches since the founding of Massachusetts Bay Colony in 1630, although the previous synod had been held in 1852 in Albany, New York.

---

11 American Congregational Association, et al... *The Congregational Quarterly*; vol. 7; 1864; p.71

The topics for this synod included the work of evangelization, particularly in the South and the West as well as statements of Congregational church polity and the possibility of issuing a declaration of the Christian faith held in common by the churches. These topics and others were to be discussed and debated, with the overriding caveat that one of the fundamental tenets of Congregationalism was that the local church "is the only organized and authoritative ecclesiastical body established by Christ and his apostles…and with an authority that cannot be delegated." Therefore, they resolved, "The National Council….is wholly destitute of any power or authority whatever over individuals, churches, or other organizations."

The National Council began their week long synod with a service in the Old South Meeting House, chosen by the Boston Council for "its association with the sacred memory of the elders" of Congregationalism in America. Following some brief organizational motions, the synod agreed to reassemble the next day for an opening sermon at the Mt. Vernon Church in Ashburton Place, near Beacon Hill. There were 532 attendees to the National Council meeting, sixteen of them from England, France and Canada and not a single minister from the South.

On the sixth day, a discussion arose debating the civil rights of the former rebels. The Reverend Truman M. Post of Missouri reported that he was tasked with subjoining several resolutions to the report from the "State of the Country" resolutions which had been presented the day before. Among these was a resolution that the National Council of Congregational Churches

> "extend to the inhabitants of the late revolted States who have been snared into this rebellion through ignorance, surprise, or overbearing violence of public sentiment, or forced by the power of a merciless conscription, our sympathy and commiseration, and our readiness to welcome them back to civil fellowship and fraternity under the old flag."[12]

---

12 National Council of the Congregational Churches *Debates and Proceedings*; p. 259

This resolution was promptly responded to by Rev. Quint, who rose and stated that he desired to change the resolution because he found it "a little strong." Quint states that he is "not prepared to now welcome back those people who have fought against us, to full fellowship." Rev. Quint felt that "Persons so easily snared through ignorance are not the persons to be welcomed back immediately to full civil rights," because, as Quint said, "they will again become tools of those leaders, again to be snared in the same way." Quint believed that "They are unfit for civil rights until they are a little more enlightened and intelligent."[13] Quint called for many years of repentance before Southern Congregationalists be allowed full fellowship in the National Council, in fact, Quint stated publicly that "it goes terribly against my grain to see one of those scoundrels under the old flag again."[14]

On the Seventh day, a formal response to the greetings given by the delegates from foreign Congregationalist societies and churches, specifically from England, Scotland, Wales and France, was drafted and read. The outline of the response was drafted by Rev. Henry Ward Beecher, but the response was written out by Rev. Leonard Bacon from Connecticut. The response began as a recitation of the long and ancient ties that American Congregationalists had with their brethren across the Atlantic, but quickly diverted into an expression of the "pang like that which any man might feel when some friend whom he loved and trusted has suddenly become his enemy."[15] Beyond the open hostility found in many segments of British society, the authors remarked with disappointment with the silence of their fellow Congregationalists in England and Wales in support of the Union cause.

Quint agreed with this report and motioned for its acceptance, acknowledging in a three-minute speech his relief at the hard stance the report took, since the foreign delegates had been received with great fanfare earlier in the week. In a speech supporting the adoption of the report in response to foreign delegates Quint took the British delegates to task by arguing that they were "always ready to crush the weak; robbing in India, plundering in Ireland, and

---

13 National Council of the Congregational Churches *Debates and Proceedings*; p. 250
14 National Council of the Congregational Churches *Debates and Proceedings*; p. 251
15 National Council of the Congregational Churches *Debates and Proceedings*; p. 324

in connection with our [Civil War] affairs, worse than that. Further on Quint said to great applause,

> "When I was in the service of my country, and saw my comrades fall; when I saw friends from Wisconsin, Indiana, and New York, fall side by side, I knew that they fell by British bullets, from British muskets, loaded with British powder, fired by men wearing British shoes, and British clothing, and backed by British sympathy."[16]

As he felt about the residents of the American South, Quint argued that he did not feel "responsible for any fraternal fellowship;" towards the British, "but when they express their repentance for the past, it is different."[17]

Quint never seems to have relinquished his animosity towards Britain that he harvested from his service with the 2nd Massachusetts, if indeed that is the original basis for his ire. In an oration celebrating the Emancipation Proclamation held at New Bedford in August of 1867 Quint spoke these words about England's abolition of slavery in 1833;

> "England, always selfish, would not [emancipate the slaves] until its advocates found that freedom would pay more money than slavery.... The negro race owed nothing to Great Britain for that act, for during the rebellion large portions of the succor which the Southern armies received came from Great Britain, and the war was lengthened mainly from and furnished by the rebels by England."[18]

The fact was, said Quint, that the negro owed his thanksgiving only to God, the God who got President Abraham Lincoln to promise to emancipate the slaves as a matter of military necessity, and the God who created all men equally.

---

16 National Council of the Congregational Churches *Debates and Proceedings*; p. 327
17 National Council of the Congregational Churches *Debates and Proceedings*; p. 328
18 "Emancipation Celebration at New Bedford;" *Boston Journal*;

Quint enjoyed a great deal of post-war notoriety based on his letters to the *Congregationalist*. In 1866 the Massachusetts Legislature chose Quint to deliver their annual election sermon. True to Quint's nature and his fascination with statistics, he began by drafting a list of all previous ministers who had been called to deliver the annual election sermon and the text they used for the basis of their sermon. Quint took as his theme Deuteronomy, iv. 33; "Did ever people hear the voice of God speaking out of the midst of the fire, as thou hast heard, and live?" Quint's thesis was again driven by his experiences during the war and his belief that "the people, in great peril and trial, have proved themselves capable of maintaining their distinctive institutions." Quint argued that a Democratic people raised an army, trained it, fought a war, supported it through taxation and private efforts and after the enemy was defeated, returned to its peaceful existence.[19]

Even though the Reverend Quint was greatly esteemed for his sagacious and pious sermons and for the care and concern given to his parishioners, it was as an advocate for fellow veterans where Quint stood tallest. Quint was involved with the Grand Army of the Republic movement for many years, almost from the outset of the organization, and served as Chaplain-General at the 1868 & 1869 National encampments. As a new pseudo-military organization, rules and rituals were needed to support the meetings and celebrations of the membership as well as to attract new members. Rev. Quint was appointed to the committee to determine the appropriate rituals for the organization, specifically the services surrounding installation and burial services.

With Quint's involvement in the National G.A.R. Association, it is no surprise then that Rev. Quint was a member of G.A.R. Post No. 1 of Massachusetts named for William Logan Rodman in New Bedford. At the first Encampment of the Massachusetts G.A.R. At New Bedford, May 7 1867, Quint spoke of the fact that "the Soldiers owe it to society, as to themselves to be industrious and sober citizens; and they do ask the privilege of being such, but do not always have it accorded to them." Quint illustrates his point with the story that "a few

---

19 Quint; *A Sermon Delivered*. p. 13

instances have come to my personal knowledge of discrimination in the hiring of workmen, exercised against them because they were soldiers."[20]

From his post as Chaplain in Chief of the Massachusetts G.A.R. Quint continued his efforts to support the causes of veterans as he iterated during his 1869 Memorial Day address in New Bedford. Following the Memorial Day parade and the decoration of veteran's graves in various cemeteries throughout New Bedford, about a thousand people assembled on New Bedford common to hear Rev. Quint's address for which he took as his theme the three principles of the Grand Army of the Republic organization, fraternity, loyalty and charity. "Everywhere we take each other by the hand in …. common service," said Quint, "High or low, rich or poor, an old comrade is a brother." For the maimed, widows and orphans, Quint argued, "we have pledged…. the cheering word, the hearty hand and the open purse." Beyond that, Quint swore that "By the flag which waves over us we have pledged ourselves to an undying loyalty to our country." It was not just for the men of their generation that Quint holds to that pledge, but Quint also promises to his listeners that "we shall educate our children to take our places when we too lie in the ground."[21]

Quint also spoke of the Cincinnati-like transformation of an industrious and peaceful people who are called "in defense of their national flag against treason;" and "that contrary to all predictions…the soldiers of that great army, at the close of the war, peacefully, quietly settled down in their homes, returned to their business and their trades…and gave one grand example to the world that disbanded soldiers can be as loyal to law in peace as they were true to the sword in war."[22]

The reasons, says Quint, for this "memorable transformation" were twofold. First the cause for which he fought was just and holy, and the second was that the veterans proved themselves worthy of that cause and as such, ceased to fight once the cause was finished. The last duty of these peace-loving men was remembrance, from which duty came about the Memorial Day holiday.

---

20 *Boston Herald*; 14 August 1904; p. 38
21 Grand Army of the Republic; *The National Memorial Day*; pp. 252 - 257
22 Grand Army of the Republic; *The National Memorial Day*; p.252

In 1875, Rev. Quint resigned his pastorate at the North Congregational Church in New Bedford because his ill health derived, in part, from his time as regimental chaplain during the Civil War. While Quint may have been seeking a respite from the daily requirements of maintaining a large and active parish, he was a continuing influence on the Congregationalist faith and he began a long and fruitful relationship with his hometown newspaper, the *Dover Herald*. By the time of his death Quint had written over 800 historical and genealogical articles for the paper. Quint had long been interested in genealogy and history, having been elected a member of the Massachusetts Historical Society, the New Hampshire Historical Society and the New England Historical and Genealogical Society.

In addition to his writing and historical and genealogical studies, Quint continued to lecture and speak widely, particularly on Memorial Day and at the dedication of monuments. In 1877, Quint as Chaplain-in-Chief of the Grand Lodge of Masons of Massachusetts delivered the prayer of consecration over the Army and Navy monument built on Boston Common. In his prayer, he referenced the "trial by fire" laid upon the Union by a God who saw it as necessary and that the monument stood not "to perpetuate remembrance of fratricidal strife" but to honor "the memory of patriotic devotion to the flag." Moreover, Quint said, the monument stood in honor of the mothers, wives, and children who encouraged, supported and lost loved ones; the men and women who cared for those who were sick, hurt or dying, as well as the men, living or dead, who served their nation. Quint prays that future generations will "be inspired to know that honor is more than wealth, right is more than peace, and heroic death is more than life."[23]

In November of 1896 Dr. Quint died after a short illness. His obituary in the *Congregationalist* stated that Rev. Quint's death marked "the closing of an important epoch in Congregational life."[24] Considering the years he spent as publisher of the *Congregational Quarterly*, a director of the American Congregational Association and the Massachusetts General Association of Congregational churches he was without question one of the pillars of the

---

23 Boston City Council; *Dedication of the Monument*; p. 102
24 "In Memory of Dr. Quint;" *The Congregationalist*. p.782

Congregational faith in New England. His death notice in the Andover Theological Seminary report for that year noted that Quint was more than a minister of the gospel. "As a wise student of church history and of the word of God he saw and seized his opportunity, and never faltered in his devotion to it."[25] The Grand Army of the Republic Bulletin said when the listed Rev. Quint in the "mustered out" section of their report that Quint "held to a sturdy old-fashioned Puritan faith, tempered by his wide intercourse with society and by a wealth of experience such as but few men are fortunate enough to have."[26] Quint believed in the tenets of the old Congregational church, that it was a fellowship rooted in the teachings of Christ, but he was also a thoroughly modern man who believed that while the underlying principles may be ancient, the tools and means used to support those principles must be modern.

The memorial addresses published by the organizations with whom Dr. Quint maintained a life-long association, including his alma maters, Dartmouth College and Andover Theological Seminary, the Grand Army of the Republic, the Grand Masonic Lodge of Massachusetts, the New England Historical and Genealogical Society, the New Hampshire and Massachusetts Historical Societies, as well as the Congregational Quarterly and the *Congregationalist* newspaper, tell the whole story of Quint's life. He was a man devoted to education of the young, remembrance of the fallen, the shared brotherhood of his fellow man, honoring the past and the preservation of the Congregational faith. All those who knew him, mourned him, and each felt lessened by the loss of his wisdom and guiding hand, but during his life he had helped each of them reveal their founding and bedrock principles. True to his nature, Quint believed that these principles were a far better guide to the future than any one man, even one who was a patriot, a theologian, a historian, a loyal friend, a loving family man and a mighty counsellor.

---

25 Andover Theological Seminary; "Alonzo Hall Quint;" *Necrology*; p.259
26 Grand Army of the Republic; "Mustered Out;" *Thirty-First Annual Encampment*; p.103

1861

The 2nd Massachusetts Volunteer Infantry in 1861

THE SECOND MASSACHUSETTS VOLUNTEER INFANTRY began their Civil War iteration on the 15th of April, 1861 when George H. Gordon was given authorization to raise a regiment for three years by Massachusetts Governor John A. Andrew. Gordon, a graduate of the United States Military Academy at West Point was ably seconded by Wilder Dwight who encouraged the recruitment as well as the raising of a regimental fund. Dwight was so successful in his fundraising that before the end of April he had raised $30,000. These two men were joined by George L. Andrews, another West Pointer and it was settled between them that Gordon would be Colonel, Andrews, Lt. Colonel, and Dwight, Major. Traditionally, the company officers of a Massachusetts regiment elected their own field officers, but as a "professional" soldier, Gordon thought this tradition was absurd, and as the regiment was being raised specifically for federal service, the question of officer election, he believed, was moot. On the 25th of April, the newspapers announced the opening of regimental recruiting offices at no. 20 State Street in Boston. The Second Massachusetts was the first of the three-year Massachusetts regiments raised for service.

Company A, the "Abbott Grays," was the first company of men to inhabit "Camp Andrew" on the site of Brook Farm in West Roxbury, Massachusetts. They arrived May 11, 1861 in their cadet grey uniforms and were followed by Company C, Captain Cogswell's "Andrew Light Guard" on May 14, 1861. These two were followed by Company B, under Greely S. Curtis, Company D under Captain James Savage, Company F under Charles R. Mudge, Company G, commanded by Richard Cary, Company H, led by Francis H. Tucker,

Company I, recruited by Adin B. Underwood, and Company K, headed by Richard C. Goodwin.

Brook Farm, in West Roxbury, Massachusetts, was once an experimental transcendentalist community owned by James Freeman Clarke, who offered his property to the Governor of Massachusetts for the training and recruitment of Union forces. The large working farm had several structures that were used as officer's quarters, kitchen, hospital and quartermasters store room. Once the 2nd Massachusetts Volunteers took command of the property they renamed it "Camp Andrews" after Major General Samuel Andrews, commander of the First Division of the Massachusetts Militia. Lt. Col. George L. Andrews and Colonel Gordon led the drill and learning of the company officers, drilling them and demanding recitations of their lessons daily. The enlisted men were initially drilled by a Sergeant Collins of the United-States Sappers and Miners.[27]

As with many of the early regiments raised in the state of Massachusetts, Colonel Gordon and his officers were able to procure a regimental fund to purchase uniforms, buy food and supplies as well as to purchase arms. Most of these expenses would later be reimbursed by the state, but as a result of the regiment providing the funds for their own equipage, Gordon had a large influence on the supplies the men received. Their uniform was on the army pattern of a dark blue broadcloth sack coat and light blue flannel trousers rather than the Massachusetts militia uniform of grey. For hats, they wore a black "Kossuth" or slouch hat, with the left side turned up with a blue band around the crown and blue plumes in the upturned flap. Gordon was also insistent on the regiment having rifled muskets as their weapon and with some effort more than a thousand Enfield rifles were purchased. The regiment was

---

[27] Edward Collins (1824 - 1905) was a native of Milton, Massachusetts who enlisted in the Army in 1846 in the Corps of Engineers, also known as "The Sappers and Miners." Collins saw service in the Mexican-American War, following which he helped to survey a railroad route from the Mississippi River to the Pacifica Ocean through Yellowstone Park. In May of 1861, Collins left Massachusetts to accept a commission in the 17th U. S. Infantry. After the Civil War Collins saw service on the frontier in the wars against the American Indians. *Our Paper*; Massachusetts Reformatory.

also provided with twenty-five wagons for camp equipage, along with four horses to pull each wagon.

J. Lothrop Motley, the diplomat and historian, came to Camp Andrew on the 26th of June, 1861 and presented a set of national colors to the Regiment. The flag was 6' x 9' and made of silk. The stars were gold bullion, embroidered on a blue field. The staff had a solid silver eagle, gilded, at the top of the staff and though the staff was broken and the eagle lost and the flag shot through in many places, yet the flag survived to be returned to the Massachusetts State House.

On the first of July, the regiment was presented with the gift of a new state flag. Hundreds of Bostonians ventured to Camp Andrews for the presentation, which was made on behalf of some ladies of Boston by Mr. George Hillard, a former law partner of Senator Charles Sumner. The flag was constructed with a blue field rather than white, the official field color of the state, and on one side was the state arms and state motto, while on the other side was a solitary pine tree in a frame surmounted by a liberty cap and the words of Rufus Choate, "We carry the flag and keep step to the music of the Union."

On July 8, 1861, the 2nd Massachusetts departed their camp early in the morning and took the train to Boston. Once in the city they formed up and marched in column with their regimental band and their wagons and horses for Boston Common. They had intended to march through much of the downtown area, but the day was oppressively hot and a shorter route was chosen for the comfort of the men. Once on the Common, arms were stacked and a meal was shared with friends and family as goodbyes were shared and tears were shed. The regiment left the state by way of the Boston and Providence railroad, which went as far as Groton, Connecticut, where they caught a steam ferry for New York City. From there, the regiment was sent to Maryland where it remained until December of 1861. Few events broke their camp routine, though they were called down to Edward's Ferry in the aftermath of the Ball's Bluff debacle, but they were sent to winter camp in Darnestown, Maryland without entering combat.

ALONZO H. QUINT
TO THE
CONGREGATIONALIST

September 20, 1861

From the Army
Camp Near Darnstown, MD., Sept. 10, 1861
A Chaplain's Post

Still waiting orders to march. Still keeping three days' rations ready cooked. Still drilling twice or thrice a day. While I now write, our regiment is engaged in their afternoon battalion drill. I hear, from my tent, the rapid words of command. The music of some other regiment of our Division, subdued by distance, floats to my ear. The thunder of artillery practice rolls in from miles away. Sharp-rifle vollies are echoing through the valley – in similar practice. The tents of our General sit queenly upon an opposite hill. Whichever way I look, are cities of camps, which will soon, as evening comes on, be lighted up in a scene of gorgeous fascination. Even here and now, reveries of home steal over the mind; but not in lamentation – only in love.

    I wrote to you, last week, of a chaplain's opportunities. Yesterday, we compared notes, -- we, the chaplains. We established our "Monday Chaplains' Meeting." The thoughts of some of us went back to its model in Boston, but how different, you need only imagine. For the crowded, confined city, substitute these beautiful fields and shady woods; for the dark and dingy lane, our wide camp streets; for the brick chapel, a canvas tent, -- only ten feet square, but with its sides gracefully looped up until only the light roof remains; for the carpeted floor, the turfed ground; for the brothers of like name and hear home, brothers of five denominations and linking

Wisconsin, New York, Pennsylvania and Massachusetts, in fellowship. Yet while so unlike, similar prayers (but more of them) ascend to God; similar experiences of the Gospel; similar faith and trust in the Holy Spirit, were there. A Methodist offered the first prayer – a Congregationalist followed, -- but which was which, it were hard to tell, for both prayed as Christians. We gave in turn, "an account of the Sabbath's work," less formally, and more as if thawed out of conventional stiffness. A Universalist began; start not at that; he was welcomed to the Chaplain's Meeting; if he could improve us, well; if we could improve him, well. An Old School Presbyterian followed. Then a Congregationalist. Then a Baptist. Then a New School Presbyterian pastor of a Congregational church. Then a Methodist. Then an Old School Congregationalist. And I thought that perhaps some account of texts as well as of times and meetings, might be pleasant to you – only they will not come in the above order.

One preached from the words, "We love him, because He first loved us." In addition to the intrinsic excellence of God as a spring of our love, he declared the wonderful love of God to us, greatest and dearest in the sacrifice of Jesus for our salvation.

A second took as text, "So fight I, not as one that beateth the air." The aim and method of a soldier's work, was his theme.

A third, "If they hear not Moses and the prophets, neither will they be persuaded through one rose from the dead;" – the sufficiency of the Scriptures.

A fourth. "O God the Lord, the strength of my salvation, thou hast covered my head in the day of battle;" – true manliness comes from communion with God.

A fifth, "He heard the sound of the trumpet and took not warning;" – the inevitable destruction of those who neglect warnings to "flee from the wrath to come."

These give you specimens of the themes in camp. Diverse, and yet aimed at the one central theme.

And then we delineated our times of meetings.

In one regiment, sudden orders had put by the customary Sabbath morning service, an evil we can never wholly avoid in a life so changeful as this. But, not to lose his day, the chaplain announced personally to each company an impromptu meeting in the afternoon, to be held immediately on the notice. A hundred attended. After his part of the service, others spoke; several backsliders confessed their long forgetfulness, and tearfully asked for prayers. Some unconverted young men were touched, and in the evening came to see their spiritual guide, till his little tent was crowded. In this regiment, a Wednesday evening prayer meeting is well sustained.

In another, the one service (there is but one) was in the morning. In the afternoon, at five o'clock, the chaplain holds a Bible-class, free to all to come or go. And in the week is one prayer meeting.

In another, the sermon is at ten o'clock in the morning; prayers accompany the dress parade every evening; and one prayer meeting a week is held.

In another, the sermon is at the hour just mentioned. One, or two, or three evenings a week, the ardent laborer preaches to a company, standing in the "Company Street" (for we have streets in the camps).

In another, the Sabbath service is at 4 P.M.; and a little morning prayer, meeting is held every day at the beating of "sick call" (which is the signal for men but slightly sick to go to the surgeon) – and a hundred attend.

In another, (I may as well say it is mine, and be minute,) the Sabbath service is held at half past four o'clock, P.M., under the lengthening shadows. The drum and fife play "church call;" the companies are formed as for parade. Each marches, to the sound of music, to its place, till the regiment forms three sides of a square, leaving perhaps fifteen feet each side of the preacher. Just within the square, are the field and staff officers, and the band, which plays a voluntary. At a word of command, the singers leave the ranks and stand near the band. In the service, the men stand until the time for sermon, when, at the word "Rest," all are seated, but still in order. The sermon closing, all instantly rise, uncovered, for prayer and benediction. These ended, -- "Attention Co. A, left face, march!" and, to the music of the band, the men march to their tents. There is no lack of attention, and never a disrespectful look. Sabbath evening, at half past seven o'clock, is our prayer meeting, lately established. It is held, now, on as open space near the tents of our band. Each time, it has been a dark evening. A few candles cast a dim light. The flame of near or distant camp-fires shines fitfully on the bronzed faces of hardy men, bringing into deeper shadow the somber blue of their uniform. They stand closely – a hundred of them. A familiar revival hymn, perhaps "Behold, behold, the Lamb of God," or "We're going home, to die not more," attracts others – for music is a great charm in camp. A prayer, reading of Scripture, a short address from the chaplain, singing, -- and then all are invited to speak or pray or sing. One comes forward quietly into the little vacant space, and in a low voice testifies to the grace of God. Then another; and one prays, or singing breaks forth; or one in whose heart the springs have been long choked up, bears witness that the fountain is once more gushing, and mourns over his sins. Here and there are visible tears rolling down some rough cheek, "it seems so like home," or "it makes us feel human," or "it reminds one of a praying father." The hour passes. Tired? No, though no cushioned seats have rested them; they – all, have been standing the whole period; but they have rested on the grace of God; and they look forward with yearning hearts to the Wednesday evening prayer meeting – Wednesday evening I chose for its beloved associations with the "Young People's Meeting" at home.

Now is the day ended. The drum will soon quiet this active camp, but one by one, some come to the chaplain's tent. Last Sabbath evening, some Christians came, to express their determination to withstand, more courageously, the awful tide of wickedness there is in this as in every camp; some are men whose old professions are again awakened; and one or two sons, followed by parents' prayers, who brush off the blessed tears. Parents, pray for your sons! Pray for the chaplains. The promise of God never fails. This is my comfort, as I visit the Hospital, and so often learn that the sick man, by whose low bed I bow, has, on earth or in Heaven, a praying father or mother; my comfort, when I see a treasured little volume carried by many a man in his hard day's march; my comfort even when the heart grows sick at wickedness, and cries "How long, O Lord, how long!"

The Second.

Clockwise from top left: Adjutant John A. Fox; Captain Daniel Oakey; Captain Francis W. Crowninshield; Captain William E. Perkins.

(Image courtesy of the United States Army Historical and Educational Center; Mollus Collection)

October 4, 1861

Correspondence from the Army
Pleasant Hill, near Darnestown, Md., Sept. 21, 1861

Three weeks have passed away since we encamped on this spot, -- how many of us I must not tell, though probably the enemy know with sufficient accuracy, from the traitors with which this section abounds. There is no harm in saying, however, that while Gen. McClellan is in command of this whole "Army of the Potomac," the immediate charge of the troops this side of Tunleytown [Tennallytown](a few miles out of Georgetown,) is divided between Gen. Banks – in whose Division we are – and Brigadier-General Stone, who is located further up the river.[28] Thus the north bank of the Potomac is lined with a fine army. As it becomes more evident that the enemy must cross, if cross at all, above Washington, our position becomes decidedly interesting. On the opposite bank are rebel troops in plenty, with whom our troops exchange various kind of courtesies, sometimes with good-natured greetings, sometimes with crashing shot and bursting shell, or with the Enfield Minnies,

---

28 Charles Pomeroy Stone (1824 – 1887) was a graduate of West Point (1845). He served in the artillery under Winfield Scott during the Mexican-American war and in 1861 General Scott made Stone the Inspector General of Washington, DC militia. After Bull Run, Stone was given command of a "corps of observation" along the North Potomac river, during which time one of his subordinates led a disastrous engagement at Ball's Bluff. Radical Republicans in Congress called for his cashiering, and Stone was arrested on February 8, 1862 in the middle of the night and imprisoned without charges for 189 days. Released without comment or exoneration, Stone served with General Nathaniel P. Banks in Louisiana, where he served with distinction. For 13 years, after the end of the war, Stone was General in Chief of the army of the Khedive of Egypt and was also engineer in charge of the pedestal for the Statue of Liberty.

which leap a mile or so at a jump. In such a neighborhood, we are by no means indifferent, when there comes, as it did last night at two o'clock, "Be ready for the field at a moment's notice." We were ready; the muskets of the Massachusetts Second are never out of order; their cartridge boxes are always full; their courage is always high; their order perfect; their bearing, stalwart, firm, and solid; in the midst of jealousies and occasional misrepresentations, the noble Second preserves the proud preeminence which qualified officers, intelligent and strong men, and fixed discipline, have given it; its material, active, hardy, and brave, -- embracing old soldiers of the Mexican or of the Florida war, of the English army, of the European Continent, of Sebastopol (both Russian and English), and of the noble Havelock in its march to Lucknow; its officers able and educated; its commander, a graduate of West Point, nine years in the army, a soldier in Kansas, in the Oregon wilds, and through the war which led our victorious troops to the city of Mexico, -- still bearing in his body the Mexican lead.[29] So far, the best Massachusetts Regiments are those which have followed the equipments of the Second. The regiment drills hours every day, waiting the hoped-for opportunity to show itself in action what a General officer told me it is, "the first regiment outside the regular army."

But the telegraph may have told you, long before this goes to print, of circumstances widely changed. The location of regiments may change at any moment. To-day, this division is here, working hard for discipline and drill. The time is not wasted while we wait; every day improves us, while delay does our enemy no good. Our regiment is still in the Second Brigade (Gen. Abercrombie's)[30],

---

29 George Henry Gordon (1824 - 1886) was a graduate of West Point (1846) and served as 2nd Lieutenant in the Mounted Rifles and sent to Mexico where he was wounded at the battles of Cerro Gordo and Vera Cruz. He left the army in 1853 and studied law at the Cambridge Law School and admitted to practice in 1857. Gordon was authorized to raise and commissioned Colonel of the 2nd Massachusetts Infantry. Gordon remained Colonel of the 2nd until June of 1862 when he was promoted to Brigadier General. Warner; *Generals in Blue; also,* Quint; *The Record of the Second Massachusetts Infantry.*

30 John Joseph Abercrombie (1798 – 1877) was one of the oldest officers in either army. Abercrombie graduated from West Point in the class of 1822. A career officer, Abercrombie saw service in the Black Hawk War, the Seminole War and the Mexican-American war. At the outbreak of the rebellion he was serving as Colonel of the 7th Infantry in Minnesota. Following the battle of Falling Waters, Abercrombie was assigned to command the 2nd Brigade of 1st Corps in the Army of the Potomac. Warner; *Generals in Blue*

with the 1ˢᵗ Pennsylvania Battery[31], the 12ᵗʰ and 16ᵗʰ Indiana[32], and the excellent 12ᵗʰ Massachusetts[33] – which last has just marched (by night) to a spot still nearer the river. Other brigades are around us. A system of signals is well organized. The telegraph is nearly established. And any attempt on the part of rebels, to cross the river, will precipitate upon them a vigilant and hardy army. Perfect confidence exists in our success.

The ordinary routine of campaigning of course goes on. We have few hardships; the food is good and abundant now; the climate is delightful; there is little sickness.

But this routine is sometimes changed. It was today. In the midst of active drill, the step ceased, the bugles were silent, the ranks took their iron position. It was when the band of another regiment passed by, pouring out their melancholy wailing for the dead. It was a soldiers funeral, and among the thousands in our camps, there was a reverent silence.

My thoughts went back to the first funeral at which I had officiated. It was at Harper's Ferry, while our regiment occupied that post. There had been brought into our Hospital, a soldier of the 15ᵗʰ Pennsylvania, then on its way home at the expiration of its three months' service, whom that regiment left with us one

---

31 1ˢᵗ Pennsylvania Battery was Battery F of the 43ʳᵈ Pennsylvania Volunteers (aka 1ˢᵗ Pennsylvania Light Artillery.) The battery was organized in Philadelphia, PA under Captain Ezra Matthews. While it served the entire war, the battery performed all of its service with the Army of the Potomac and the Army of the James. Hawks; "1ˢᵗ Pennsylvania Light Artillery, Battery F (43ʳᵈ Volunteers)."

32 The 12ᵗʰ Indiana was a one-year regiment raised at Indianapolis under Colonel John M. Wallace in May of 1861, although by October of 1861 the Lt. Colonel, William H. Link, had been promoted to Colonel of the Regiment. All of its service was in the Shenandoah Valley and along the Rappahannock. It lost a total of 24 men – all to disease. The 16ᵗʰ Indiana was also a one-year regiment raised under Colonel Pleasant A. Hackleman. They were marched to Edward's Ferry the evening of the Battle of Ball's Bluff and lost two soldiers to enemy fire. Hawks; "12ᵗʰ Indiana Infantry Regiment."

33 12ᵗʰ Massachusetts Infantry (The "Webster" Regiment) was raised in June of 1861 and organized at Fort Warren in Boston Harbor, this regiment took its nickname from its commander, Col. Fletcher Webster, son of the famous Daniel Webster. Colonel Webster was killed at the 2ⁿᵈ Bull Run in 1862 and his replacement, Major Elisha Burbank, was killed at Antietam. This regiment saw service until July of 1864 when it was mustered out of service by which time 18 of their officers would be killed in battle. Hawks; "12ᵗʰ Massachusetts Infantry Regiment;" and, Fox; *Regimental Losses*.

afternoon as they passed through that place. That evening, as I passed at a late hour through the Hospital, I noticed this new face, and on enquiry found the facts. He was sick with typhoid fever, very sick, -- little more than a boy in years. He was to me, then, nameless, not one of ours, but he was a suffering soldier – God bless every one of such. I did not press him to speak, but he recognized the name of our Saviour, and looked up as if waiting to hear. It was too late to reason, too late for human comfort. I dared say little, but I could not but think that some friends, father, mother, perhaps a yet closer one, whom I never saw and doubtless never shall see, whose very residence I know nothing of, might be glad to know that some of the blessed promises of our Lord were whispered in his ear, and that a few words of prayer asked for the soul of this dying man, whose hand I held, the favor of our Father and our Saviour. That night he died.

He was buried the next evening, in the way of soldiers, which, to one unaccustomed to the sight, is deeply interesting. A suitable escort (for a private eight rank and file, properly commanded,) is formed in two ranks opposite to the tent of the deceased, with shouldered arms and bayonets unfixed; on the appearance of the coffin, the soldiers present arms. The procession then forms, on each side of the coffin being three bearers, without arms; immediately preceding are the eight soldiers, with arms reversed (the musket under the left arm, barrel downward, and steadied by the right hand behind the back); in front is the music, than whose dirge no sadder sounds ever fell upon my ear, as they proceed to the place of burial. With slow and measured step, and muffled drum, they move. At the grave, the coffin is placed upon one side, the soldiers resting upon their arms, the muzzle upon the foot, the hands clasped upon the butt, and the head bowed upon the hands. The chaplain, who has walked in the rear of the coffin, conducts the burial service; "earth to earth, ashes to ashes, dust to dust." Three vollies are fired over the grave, and the last kindness to the comrade is over. The graveyard left, immediately the band strikes up a cheerful air, and take their way back to camp and to living duties.[34]

---

34 Harrisburg, Pennsylvania newspapers state that there were many sick soldiers in the 14th and 15th Pennsylvania Volunteers at this time. "The 14th and 15th Regiments;" The Harrisburg *Patriot*.

It was thus we buried the stranger soldier. He had no friend who knew him, there. No kindred wept by the side of the grave. His bed was made alone, in a deserted graveyard, on the bold cliff that overlooks the two rivers united in the mighty stream which pours its affluence into the Atlantic. But the soldiers subdued their roughness, and tenderly laid him down. The frequent oath was unheard. The solemn silence was scarcely broken by the low words of command. When the sharp vollies echoed up and down the vallies, the shadows were already fallen on the lordly rivers, the Potomac and Shenandoah, rolling by far below us; but the gorgeous evening sunlight was richly clothing the dark green forests of both Maryland and Virginia hights, towering over us. His grave was cut in a hard and rocky soil; but out of that soil the evergreen was thriving and the wild flowers perfumed the air. It was on the very day his regiment was mustered out of service, that we buried him; and turning backwards to our fragile homes, found the order already given, "Ready to march," and soon we struck our tents and forded the dark and foaming river which separated the rebel from the loyal, State. *He* had forded a darker and rougher river, which, we hoped as we left him, no longer kept him in a world of sin, and out of the land of perfect glory.

And so will throngs be buried, in this sad and mournful war. But out of the great clouds of private sorrow, will rise the triumph of our country's glory.

A. H. Q.

October 11, 1861

Letter from the Army
Near Darnestown, Md., Sept. 27, 1861

No movements have yet taken place here, beyond the occasional arrival and departure of regiments, and a now and then change of camp of some regiments. It is whispered that an advance may be made within a few weeks, but that silent man who wields the order of the army of the Potomac gives no sign. Intense activity prevails, however. Drill, drill, drill; and now the battalion drill is performed with knapsacks as if for march, by which the men are becoming prepared for the time when tents and wagons are left behind in camp, and they meet the foe face to face. Officers are hinted to with reference to the propriety of *their* having haversacks also, capacious enough for a few days' rations against the time when board will be scarce. All sorts of rumors fly round, and every new regiment expects to land directly into battle. But a little experience induces a cool distrust in everything, but absolute orders to march, especially in a regiment like ours, which is, I believe, the oldest in service here, having had the felicity to form part of "Patterson's Column," which, to new regiments seems antediluvian.

To-day is a rainy day. It drizzles awhile, it pours awhile, and then by way of variety, pours and drizzles and blows. All drill is suspended. Men stay in their tents, barring the luckless fellows who pace up and down in overcoats – with muskets reversed – relieved, however, every two hours, for another batch to get wet. Only the necessary duties of camp go on. In their tents, some men read; some write (often affectionate epistles – as their care to keep the sheet hidden shows, some mend trowsers and such things; some sing; some gamble (which is not made an offense by the articles of war,) and by which many of our men are stripped of every cent by experienced sharpers; poor moths, they will fly into the candle in spite of all remonstrance, -- though some have been saved. Some draw great enjoyment from tobacco smoke, their remedy for various ills. The sutler drives a brisk business in gingerbread, lemons, nuts, confectionery, and such like. And so the day wears on, not dismally to them, nor without opportunities of usefulness, to which the rain is no obstacle, when one has rubber coat, leggings, cap and cape – thanks to good friends at home.

The *ordinary* routine of the day in camp is this: at twenty minutes past sunrise the *dispatch* is beaten, drum echoing to drum, till regiment after regiment is again a hive of busy life. Roll call immediately follows, every man in company line. At seven o'clock the drum and file announce breakfast time, which cooks permanently detailed for each company, have been preparing. At half-past seven is sick call, when the surgeon meets all sick men not able to be out. At eight o'clock is guard mounting, which is quite on display. The band are in position at their ordinary place for dress parade. At their music, a detail numbering one lieutenant, one sergeant, four corporals, and seventy-two privates, from every company, marches to the parade. The line is formed, their arms are inspected, and their appearance noted. They are then marched to the post of each sentinel, where, after various useful, but to me mysterious conferences, the old sentinel is relieved, takes his place in the rear, and a new one stationed; and so on around the camp. The old guard discharge their pieces, and are dismissed, each one having been, for the twenty-four hours, two hours on guard and four off, in every six – a post of honor and of grave responsibility; for to sleep on his post may incur the penalty of death.

Then, in decent weather, at nine o'clock the music sounds for company drill, each company by itself, when all kinds of queer maneuvers are gone through for an hour and a half. At one o'clock is dinner. At three P.M. is battalion drill, when the regiment drills under a field officer, with a briskness and life probably pleasanter to see than to experience, although the men rather enjoy it. This lasts an hour and a half. At twenty minutes before five is the first call for evening parade; twenty minutes are devoted to the minute inspection of arms and equipments; and at five o'clock is the dress parade, the great show of the day. Six P.M. is supper. At half-past eight tattoo is beaten, and the roll called; at nine o'clock "taps" on the drum signalize "lights out!" And thereafter only the solitary step of pacing sentinels, with now and then a challenge and response, or perhaps the gallop of an orderly with some dispatch to the commander, breaks the stillness of the night. We have no locks on our doors, but one feels secure enough with eighty sentries around one's camp, and a thousand bayonets at hand; with yet other regiments and sentries still circling outside; and with mounted pickets scouring the land for miles in every direction.

The President's Fast Day, yesterday, received peculiar attention[35]. An order from Gen. Banks called attention to it, and directed its observance. It was a day of rest from drill, in fact from all work which could be dispensed with. The most noticeable feature of the day was the public service, held in a beautiful field near the little village of Darnestown, whither all the regiments in this immediate locality proceeded in full uniform, and with arms. It was a beautiful sight, when from other different camps the several regiments marched towards the field, some on the open road, some winding through the woods, all with their music. Each was assigned to its place in the most orderly way, until thousands upon thousands stood in a dense mass. a platform held the various chaplains, the commanding General and many of his officers of rank. The sight from this elevation was beautiful. The green wood skirted the field at a little distance on the right. The little village lay quietly in front. Directly before the platform were the solid ranks of infantry, reaching far right and left and in front, with dragoons on the one flank and artillery on the other – all ready for instant duty if needed. The multitude of banners, the motionless posture of men, the thousands standing in compact array, the glittering of the sunlight on a forest of bayonets, the firm and devout air – with the reflection that in a few days this mass of soldiery would be hurled upon the enemy – many, alas, in human probability, never more to return, could but inspire a beholder with mingled feelings of delight and sorrow.

---

35 Thursday, September 26, 1861 was set apart by Presidential proclamation to be a day of fasting, humiliation and prayer for the "fervent supplications to Almighty God for the safety and welfare of these States, his blessings on their arms, and a speedy restoration to peace;" "A National Fast;" *Salem Observer*.

The services were these. The President's proclamation was read by Chaplain Gaylord[36] of the 13th Massachusetts; Chaplain Reed of the 30th Pennsylvania,[37] offered the Prayer of Invocation; Chaplain of the 29th Pennsylvania,[38, 39] read selections of Scripture, and the hymn "My country, 'tis of thee," in which the united bands led the voices of the soldiers; Chaplain Phillips of the 9th New York[40] offered a prayer, and led in the Lord's prayer; the Chaplain of the 2d Massachusetts read the *Army Hymn*,[41] which was sung to "Old Hundred," in a majestic style – and made the address (or sermon it may be) for the day; and Chaplain Lasher of the 5th Connecticut,[42] offered

---

36 Noah Murray Gaylord (1823 - 1873) was a native of Ohio and a practicing attorney before going into the ministry. At the outbreak of the war Gaylord was appointed chaplain of the 13th Massachusetts Volunteers. After the war, he suffered various throat ailments and was forced to stop public speaking but served as chaplain of the Massachusetts General Court in 1868 and 1869. After his legislative service, Gaylord returned to practicing law, until accepting an appointment as Deputy Customs Collector of New York. Freemasons; *Proceedings of the Grand Lodge.*

37 The newspaper column says, "Thirtieth Regiment" while his "Potomac and Rapidan" books says "Thirteenth Regiment." According to a post-war report on Chaplains in the Army, Benjamin F. Reed was chaplain of the 30th Pennsylvania. Secretary of War; *Chaplains in the Army.*

38 Benjamin T. Sewell (1807 – 1885) was commissioned in July of 1861, Sewall was mustered out with the regiment in July of 1865. Before the war he ran the Bedford Street Mission (Methodist) in Philadelphia where he combatted poverty, crime, drunkenness and other societal ills. He is sometimes listed as "Benjamin F. Sewell." Secretary of War; *Chaplains in the Army*; and, Sewell; *Sorrow's Circuit.*

39 The 29th Pennsylvania Infantry was organized in July of 1861 under the command of Colonel John K. Murphy. They left their home state on August 3, 1861 for Harper's Ferry, WV. Their service record is almost identical to that of the 2nd Massachusetts with the exception of their being held in reserve at the Battle of Cedar Mountain and were guarding baggage trains at the Second Battle of Bull Run. They were mustered out of service in July of 1865. Hawks; "29th Pennsylvania Infantry Regiment."

40 Benjamin Thomas Phillips (1820 – 1892) was a graduate of Princeton Theological Seminary and a Presbyterian minister. Phillips was appointed chaplain of the 9th N.Y. Militia (served as the 83rd New York Vols.) by Col. Van Beuren. He resigned in 1863 due to ill health. During the war, he also served as a hospital chaplain and as an agent of the U.S. Sanitary Commission. Dulles; *Necrological Reports.*

41 The "Army Hymn" was written by Dr. Oliver Wendell Holmes and was widely published in newspapers prior to the war. The "Old Hundreth" is the tune to which is was set, was an old Protestant hymn in use in New England and beyond since the founding of the colonies. Holmes; *The Poems*

42 George William Lasher (1831 - 1920) was a graduate of Hamilton Literary Institute and the Hamilton Theological Seminary. He was first ordained minister of the First Baptist church of Norwalk Connecticut until he was mustered in as chaplain of the 5th Conn. Vols. in July of 1861. He resigned his post in December of 1861. Brinsfield; *Faith in the Fight*; and, Straub; "George William Lasher."

the concluding prayer, and after the doxology pronounced the benediction. The topic of the address, after an introduction alluding to our peculiar need of God's help, was "The cause in which we are enlisted is a cause on which we can hopefully ask God's blessing" – the cause of government against anarchy, of Government against an unprovoked rebellion, of a Government forbearing to the last moment, of a Government rebelled against because its instinctive principle is Liberty, by traitors whose sold moving principle is Slavery, and it closed with the augury of success:

> For right is right, since God is God;
> And right the day must win,
> To doubt would be disloyalty;
> To falter would be sin.

One could hardly realize the change from quiet home worship to the gathering in one service of a whole division of the army. But when the commanders had sprung to their saddles, the clashing of dragoon sabers had ceased, the rumbling of artillery wheels had passed out of hearing, the dancing banners had disappeared, -- then reveries of home came back, and faces of parishioners, and laughing eyes of children, and the mental photograph of tried and faithful friends, whom may God bless.

A. H. Q.

(We also have the following note of a letter date from the Chaplain of the Second Regiment, accompanied by an interesting letter on JOHN BROWN and the localities rendered memorable by his movements – which arrives at so late an hour that we are obliged to postpone its publication till next week.)

Camp Near Darnestown, MD., Oct. 5, 1861

No material changes have taken place here. The enemy, you are of course aware, are threatening several points on the river, and occasionally they waste shot and shell in a ridiculous manner. Your interest, as ours, concentrates of course, in Missouri and Kentucky. We are abundantly able to take care of the enemy opposite us, whenever the proper time comes. As to our own regiment, its men are excellently fed, are contented, are in good order, and still remain a model regiment. An order today has even detailed some of our sargeants to drill the men of other – Western – regiments. We have not much sickness, and all our sick are doing well, with the best and kindest care a regiment can furnish. Of our Hospital, I shall some time write; for I know the Second has many anxious friends watching for it and for their sons and husbands. Let them remember that not one of our soldiers but has *friends here*, and not one but has an Almighty Friends above.

    A.H.Q.

October 18, 1861

Letter from the Army.
Camp Near Darnestown, MD., Oct. 5, 1861

John Brown
In the absence of special news, why shall I not recall such rambling reminiscences as have outlasted our several later marches, regarding the places where John Brown acted and suffered? The movements of our regiment, it happened, led us to every spot memorable for his transactions; and there were few whose interests did not lead them to examine these localities. Why not? It is true that when one remembers the general disapproval with which the sober judgment of the North answered that startling raid, it seems strange that northern regiment should march through New York, with a thousand voices singing that particular song,

> "John Brown's gone to join the Army of the Lord,"
> With the gazing multitudes joining the wild chorus,
> "Glory, glory, Hallelujah!"

Nor am I now ready to approve of it; nor will many. But it was then evident that there existed a latent admiration for the stern, persistent, self-sacrificing man, periling and losing life for a cause he believed to be righteous. Nor is it possible to ignore the fact that now his enemies have made themselves our enemies; that the system whose outrages tasked, perhaps overpowered, the strength of his reason, has insanely raised its sacrilegious hand against our country; and that if John Brown deserved death, infinitely more does every rebel now in arms. His crime – if crime it was – is insignificant beside that of these perjured thieves and traitors. He was a *man*; what I think of the people here thus far, I will tell in some future letter.

We entered Charlestown, Va. (I shall take the places as we came to them), late in the evening, after a long and hard day's march. Our regiment had spent the preceding night in bivouac, where he had the pleasure of commencing an outdoor experience of not tents, with the ground for bed and, that night, a projecting root for pillow, -- than which no night's need have been better, barring a shower towards morning. At four o'clock in the morning our regiment was in column, and it had, during the day, an honorable position in the rear guard of an army of twenty-two thousand. It was evening when we approached Charlestown. The running of cars from Winchester – the rebel camp – to Charlestown, heard all the preceding night, had raised an expectation of active duty, but a few shell from a light battery had scattered the rebel cavalry, who left Charlestown as the head of our column entered. It was a beautiful evening. Light, fleecy clouds occasionally glided before the moon, only to bring out in silvery brilliancy the long column of dancing bayonets, visible in front or rear, as they rose and fell over the rolling ground. The tread of troops and the rumbling of wagons hardly broke the quiet. As we approached the town, the sentence was passed from one to another, "in this town John Brown was hung," and probably no thought was so predominant as that, when our tired men sank down upon the ground to sleep.

Late as it was, I had occasion to walk a mile or more, with one or two others, to the village, where our Assistant Surgeon had to provide accommodations for a sick officer.[43] It was past eleven when we entered the shabby town, and sought the hotel. On our road we met one of the guard, who showed us our way, and as we were crossing a stone bridge, he pointed to the right: "In that field, said he, "John Brown was hung."

---

43 The Assistant Surgeon of the regiment was Lincoln Ripley Stone (1832 – 1930) who received his MD from Harvard Medical School in 1854. Stone was promoted to Surgeon following the resignation of Surgeon Leland, and he himself would resign from the Surgeon's post early in 1863 to accept the commission as Surgeon of the 54th Massachusetts Regiment. Commissioned a "Surgeon of Volunteers" in December of 1863, Stone oversaw different General Hospitals until the end of the war. Quint; *The Record of the Second Massachusetts*; and, Adjutant General of Massachusetts; *Massachusetts Soldiers, Sailors and Marines in the Civil War*.

At the hotel he found the landlord somewhat impracticable. He was secession in feeling, and vexed – as all the Charlestown people were – at the entirely unexpected arrival of our army; and no better natured for the lateness of the hour. He was, in fact, somewhat sullen, until a thought entered my mind to try, at random, the effect of certain signs belonging to an institution which an absurdly humorous writer in your columns a year or two ago, called "the worship of demons," – to whom I owe thanks for many a hearty laugh those two or three weeks. The signs fortunately struck the right spot, and were responded to. Our sick were attended to, and a hot supper provided for ourselves; and we were speedily on terms of free chat with the landlord. Talking with him the crowds then in town – he replied: "We haven't had such a crowd since John Brown was hung." A little encouragement drew out his opinion, as well as a full account of the circumstances. The latter were in all the papers. The former showed the effect which John Brown's manliness had even on a Southern mind. He respected the old man. I particularly recollect the deep impression which John Brown's indignant refusal to avail himself of the plea of insanity urged by his council, had made. The very words were quoted, and it was the evident opinion that but for that, the life of the accused would have been saved. The quiet firmness of the death scene, and the apparent honesty throughout, were far from forgotten. The people evidently had felt that Brown was a hero, but in a bad cause.

The next day, I visited the jail and the room where he had been confined, and so did many others. It is upon the main street, and by no means repulsive. The kindness of the jailor was still commented upon. I visited also the court-room where the famous trial took place. I saw the spot where he had reposed. I sat down in the chair of the judge. The places where the counsel stood were pointed out; and I summoned up, as well as I could in fancy, the scenes which in that room had shaken half a continent. I saw also the field of execution, as did thousands upon thousands. The place of the gallows was ascertained – the timbers of which were preserved in town, -- and multitudes eagerly carried away memorials, even to the soil which pressed against the posts.

Our Regiment was, in a few days, sent forward to occupy Harper's Ferry, alone. It was an honorable post, and when has the Massachusetts 2d failed? We were welcomed with joy. To see tears rolling down many a cheek at the sight of the old flag, was a pleasant sight after the sullen hate of the other places where we had been. Here remaining for some weeks, with our own Colonel as commandant of the post, even after the bulk of the army had come, we had opportunities to visit every memorable spot. The famous Jefferson rock was there, but few visited it, while many curiously examined every place famous for John Brown's footsteps. The massive and beautiful bridge which he had held, over the Potomac, was in ruins. Southern vandals destroyed it. But the place of his guard was remembered. The spot where he had stopped, and then, not wisely, released the railway train; the arsenal held by him at first; the ruins of the very muskets once at his disposal, now lying in heaps where our own troops afterwards fired the building to keep them from rebel hands; the rock in the river where one of his men was barbarously shot in crossing; the mountain woods where another hid till driven out by hunger; all these, plenty of citizens were ready to show. But chief in interest was the engine-house where his final and useless defence took place. I recognized it from the pictures then published. It has two double doors, each wide enough for the entrance of a fire-engine, -- thick, massive doors. There still remain, unaltered, the several holes made through the brick walls, to enable the besiegers to fire on their assailants. Former spectators showed where the few United States soldiers unhesitatingly advanced to batter in the doors, and where companies of Virginia soldiers had wisely hid out of danger of the rifles, contenting themselves with preventing escape till men of some courage should dare a capture. All the arsenal buildings were worthy of inspection, but the long lines of noble shops were mainly in ghastly ruins; the very trees of that once beautiful spot, scorched to death, cast the shadows of their leafless limbs upon the blackened walls. One of them, still retaining a roof, I shall always remember as the place where our Northern regiment met to worship, while the roar of thunder and the flash of lightning were the accompaniments to the Psalms which rolled through the long structure. But, by some chance, the only building of that vast series, which still remains uninjured, is the engine-house which John Brown made his fortress; and over it still wave the green trees, unhurt. Is it a prophetic emblem?

Our Regiment, by and by, crossed the Potomac. It was by the same ford, unused for many years, till now reopened, by which the Virginia troops departed for Cambridge in 1775. On the Maryland Heights opposite, we bivouaced [sic] for weeks. Yet, by the providence which seemed to follow us, we were in the fields and snug to the house of the first man who met John Brown when, under an assumed name, he was looking for a farm to occupy, preparatory to his peculiar purpose. From him, whose heart was unlocked by the same key as the Charlestown landlord's I gathered full accounts of their conversation, and how a farm, mentioned by this man, as he and Brown stood at the gate before us, was taken. Brown had made a favorable impression, as well as his sons; "he never saw anything out of the way in him," though Brown could *never enter his house*. The farm was two or three miles off, and there is nothing peculiar there. The people were mystified by Brown's movements, he said. Some peculiar articles which he had they thought were some kind of *divining* implements; Brown laughed when he heard of it; they were *surveying* implements.

The last spot I saw in this connection, was the school-house where the arms were hid. One night, going out with our Adjutant,[44] who took particular care on that occasion in stationing our picket guard, about three-fourths of a mile from our guard we came to the building referred to. It is smaller than any of our country school-houses; like even dwelling houses here, it is of logs, with a layer of mud of equal thickness, alternating with each long, save at the corners. A respectable farmer in New England furnishes better accommodations for his pigs. The roof is now partly destroyed, it having been set on fire. The floor is nearly all gone. Under that floor the arms had been concealed, and there also was hidden one of the men while his enemies were searching the woods, and even entering the house. It was from this building that Brown dismissed the school one day, to take possession. It is a quiet place, half a mile from the Potomac, with nothing habitable near save the huts of boughs which rebel soldiers had since occupied and abandoned.

If I were asked the impression made upon my mind as to opinions in these localities, I should say that while John Brown was and is called a fanatic, he was and is respected. He was made, by the trial and execution, a hero. The daring exhibited in his attempt, the manliness he showed on his trial, the calmness with which he

---

44 Charles Wheaton, Jr. (1835 - 1914) was involved in mercantile business at the outbreak of the Civil War and was commissioned First Lieutenant in May of 1861 with the post of adjutant. In the summer of 1862, Wheaton was detailed to the staff of General Gordon as Commissary of Subsistence, and commissioned Captain. General Weitzel took Wheaton on as Chief-Commissary for Weitzel's commands, first the XVIII Corps and then the XXV Corps. Wheaton remained in the army and retired at Detroit, Michigan in June of 1913. Quint; *The Record of the Second Massachusetts*; and, Secretary of War; *Army Register*; and Henry; *Military Record*.

met death made a lasting and deep impression. The local effect was powerful. On our march to Charlestown, stopping for a few moments at a house by the way, I pointed out the path to the soldiers crowding in for water, that I might appease the needlessly frightened family. While waiting till all were satisfied, some conversation took place with some of the inmates, who were secessionists, in the course of which the mistress of the house said frankly, "We do not dare direct our servants as you spoke to those soldiers." I had merely and pleasantly kept them off the lawn, and I asked her "Why?" "We are afraid of them. We have not dared *order* them since old John Brown's affair. The servants have always said since, 'Well, somebody's coming like old Brown, yet.'" Such is the general feeling in that vicinity. Nor did the slaves hesitate to express their delight at our presence. Shame on the miserable business our army had, to send back fugitives!

Nor did residents there attach only a local importance to the transactions of that time. They felt, and I feel, with them, that thence dated this war. The South trembled on seeing that its pet system had no safe foundation. Its Enceladus was under the volcano, and the heavings were too perilous.[45] From that date it began to arm. All over the slave country military companies were formed. Its Wises began to plot. Its Floyds began to steal. And therefore, when the war began, the South was ready, while the unconscious North, which had disapproved the raid, and supposed it had thereby satisfied the slave power, was totally unprepared. Thank God, it is so no longer. The free North is pouring down its sons by hundreds of thousands – in no war to abolish slavery, it is true, but none the less to ensure its doom. Had the South remained loyal, slavery would still have been protected. It is now *too late*. And if our government be wise, beside its immense armies, in the fear of the Southern heart, John Brown's ghost is worth a hundred thousand men.

A. H. Q.

---

45 A reference to one of the Greek Gigantes, the children of Gaia, who was supposed to live beneath Mt. Etna. Earthquakes in ancient Greece were referred to "strikes of Enceladus." Mills; *Mythology: Myths, Legends, & Fantasies*.

November 1, 1861

Letter from the Army
Conrad's Ferry, Md, Thursday, Oct. 24, 1861
A Night March; A Sad Morning.

No longer at Darnestown, and no longer writing of a fixed camp and its routine of details.

It was on Monday evening last that orders came, suddenly, to cook two days rations for haversacks, and three days more for wagons; it was intended, however, that we should not leave till morning. A few minutes more and orders came to leave tents and wagons, and as speedily as possible to be upon the road. It was then eight o'clock; at *half past eight* our thorough and active men were in column, with knapsacks loaded, and on their backs, and their arms upon their shoulders; at half past three o'clock in the morning, the Second was at Conrad's Ferry, eighteen miles away; and in a few minutes our pickets lined a mile of the Potomac, in musket shot, across the river, opposite the scene of the mournful, stupid waste of life, which has carried on the wings of lightning, anguish to a multitude of Massachusetts homes.[46]

Our orders were based upon the passage of the river which had that day taken place here. It was at first supposed that the movement had been successful at Conrad's Ferry, as well as at Edwards' Ferry, four miles below; and Gen. Banks' Division was sent on to support the movement into Virginia. It was true that Gen.

---

46 A reference to the Battle of Ball's Bluff, October 21, 1861 in which Massachusetts regiments lost heavily.

Stone had succeeded in throwing over several thousand at the lower crossing. But how disastrous the result was at the upper, you too well know. It was this which hastened our march to the then entirely defenceless spot commanded by an exultant enemy.

Our men did not know whither they were bound, nor why – except that it was to the enemy's country. Never were they more happy. They took the road with songs – no instrumental music being now allowed on march. The weight of their heavy loads was unfelt. They needed but little pause for rest. The hope of meeting the foe was their life. Our admirable drill, our splendid equipments, our stalwart men and able officers – too long had it been felt that these were idle, while raw militia had been sent to spots they could never hold against the keen enemy we were to deal with. But our men were doomed to disappointment. Worse – they came only to meet the shattered remnants of broken regiments. Before we had been ordered to start, the battle had ended in defeat.

It was at Poolsville that the first news came of the defeat. There was the camp of our 15th, and there some of its sentries informed us of the result. All along the road from that point we met fugitives, straggling back to their camp. By the road were many men utterly worn down with fatigue, sleeping on the ground; and now and then were groups around a fire hastily built on the road-side, dejected, but still burning with a desire for a new struggle. We learned from them little more than that the river had been crossed, and that the 15th had been shattered almost to atoms. They did not know the circumstances nor extent of the loss.

The morning dawned, but the sun was invisible. With the grey of the early hours came down a steady, drizzling shower, deepening into a pouring rain which lasted for most of the day. Our Quartermaster had moved his train with wonderful ease and despatch, and at about 6 o'clock it arrived, enabling our men to secure a rude but substantial breakfast, and in the course of the morning we went into camp.[47]

---

47 Robert Morris Copeland (1830 - 1874) was responsible for obtaining Brook Farm for the regiment to use for the purposes of training. In August of 1861, Copeland served on the staff of General Banks until he was dismissed for violating "an important trust." This charge was investigated by Senator Charles Sumner and Copeland was exonerated. Despite his innocence, Copeland was unsuccessful in getting a further staff appointment. Quint; *The Record*

We found everything in mourning. There was *no* sunshine. Nearly opposite was plainly visible the spot where our gallant fellow soldiers had been led to slaughter. The howitzers which the enemy had captured, were mounted in sight. Between us and the opposite shore, was the island over which the advance had been made, and from it were coming the death and wounded – the results of the battle. In that island hospital strong and true men were dying, and many were suffering agonies. But the hardest feeling to bear was, that these lives had been wickedly thrown away on a useless, foolishly planned, foolishly executed expedition. In a house on the Maryland shore were others dying; and the dead were buried near, -- a house in which the holes still remained which, at a former day, the enemy's balls had plowed, and where their shells had exploded.

Of this affair, a multitude of reporters have already gathered probably every incident, and they are spread before you. Of its general character, perhaps I should give some account.

The expedition towards Leesburg was commanded by Col. Baker, a United States Senator from Oregon, as acting Brigadier.[48] He had at the ferry his own

---

of the Second Massachusetts; and, Adjutant General of Massachusetts; *Massachusetts Soldiers, Sailors and Marines in the Civil War.*

48 Edward Dickinson Baker (1811 – 1861) – A friend of President Lincoln's from Illinois, Baker had served in the Blackhawk war and the Mexican-American war as an officer in the Illinois militia. In an effort to procure a seat in Congress, Baker lived in several localities, and was finally encouraged by transplanted Illinoisans to run for the Senate in 1860, to which seat he was elected. Upon the outbreak of the war he raised the 1st California Volunteers regiment (mostly from the Philadelphia, Pa area) and was soon given a commission as a Major General. Baker was killed at the Battle of Ball's Bluff and was the only sitting Senator killed during the war. Warner; *Generals in Blue*

regiment (the 1st California),[49] the 15th,[50] 19th,[51] and 20th Massachusetts,[52] and the Tammany, (N.Y.) regiments.[53] The movement seems to have been intended rather

---

[49] The 1st California Infantry was raised in August of 1861 by Senator Edward Baker. The regiment was composed of 15 companies, was mostly composed of residents of Philadelphia and was uniformed in grey. After Ball's Bluff, with Baker being dead, the regiment was renamed the 71st Pennsylvania Volunteers. The regiment saw hard service, losing many of its men at Gettysburg, the Wilderness, Spotsylvania Court House and its last battle, Cold Harbor. It was mustered out of service in July of 1864. Hawks; "71st Pennsylvania Infantry Regiment."

[50] The Fifteenth Massachusetts infantry was mustered into service in July of 1861 and suffered the most of all the regiments at Ball's Bluff. At Antietam, the 15th would be flanked by Confederate forces and lose half of its fighting strength. It was engaged at Gettysburg and all other major battles of the Overland Campaign and by June 22, 1864 fielded only 75 officers and men outside of Petersburg. These men were captured on the Jerusalem Plank Road. Hawks; "15th Massachusetts Infantry Regiment;" and, Massachusetts, Adjutant General of; *Annual Report*.

[51] The Nineteenth Massachusetts was organized in August of 1861 and saw its first engagement at the battle of Ball's Bluff, where they covered the retreat of the forces which had crossed the river from Harrison's Island. It was heavily engaged in the battle of Fair Oaks during the Seven Days campaign, also at West Woods during the battle of Antietam. It was among the regiments that crossed the Rappahannock in boats at Fredericksburg in order to drive off sharpshooters so the engineers could finish the bridge. They also participated in the assault on Marye's Heights at Fredericksburg where they lost 104 officers and men, including 8 color bearers. At Gettysburg, the 19th captured 4 Confederate flags, losing fifty per cent of their available force in the process. Despite its dwindling numbers, the 19th managed to stave off amalgamation with other regiments, finally being mustered out in July of 1865. Hawks; "15th Massachusetts Infantry Regiment;" and, Massachusetts, Adjutant General of; *Annual Report*.

[52] The Twentieth Massachusetts is frequently referred to as "The Harvard Regiment" because of the preponderance of young Harvard men among its officer corps and private soldiers, though there are other regiments in the service of Massachusetts who had as many or more Havardians in their ranks. The 20th, however, took the Harvard crest and motto "Veritas" as their regimental symbol. Organized in September of 1861 by Colonel William R. Lee, the regiment remained in the field until July of 1865. According to some sources, the 20th Massachusetts suffered the greatest number of casualties of any other Massachusetts. Hawks; "20th Massachusetts Infantry Regiment;" and, Massachusetts, Adjutant General of; *Annual Report*. See also, Fox, *Regimental Losses*.

[53] The Tammany Regiment, or the 42nd New York Volunteer Infantry, was raised by Col. William D. Kennedy under the auspices of the Tammany Society of New York. At Ball's Bluff, they lost 133 officers and men, but their greatest loss was at Antietam where they lost 181 out of the 345 men fit for service. The regiment served throughout the Overland Campaign, and in July of 1864 the men who chose to reenlist were amalgamated into the 82nd New York and the remaining veterans of the 42nd were mustered out and the regiment disbanded. Hawks; "42nd New York Infantry Regiment;" and Fox, *Regimental Losses*.

as a reconnaissance. A scouting party of the 15th had been sent over the night before. Before daylight of Monday Col. Devens (in command),[54] with four companies of his regiment (the 15th) and one hundred men of the 20th Massachusetts, (Col. Lee accompanying) had reached the Virginia shore.[55] The crossing took place over the island, which had been occupied, and somewhat fortified at an earlier day, and which is about 125 yards from the Virginia shore, 450 from the Maryland. The only means of transportation to the hostile side of the river, consisted of a small boat, which would carry about twenty, and a scow, on which perhaps seventy men could be crowded, but old and leaky, as the final catastrophe most sadly proved. At one time in the afternoon, this boat was pulled across by a rope made up from pieces take from canal boats, but the service answered only a very brief time.

The Virginia shore is a bluff, said to be (and apparently correctly) about sixty feet high. Up this hight our men climbed, and advanced towards Leesburg, which is some four miles distant. They proceeded with care for perhaps half the distance, meeting some of the enemy, and driving them before them. But the force of the enemy, at first, doubtless, a full regiment, increased steadily. I think, also, that the statement made by several, of the existence of rifle pits, is correct. The enemy had sharpshooters in trees, also, to pick off officers. Our men fought nobly, but eventually the superior numbers of the enemy drove them back, until by gradual steps, always fighting, they had returned to the brink of the river. It had been a constant fight of skirmishes, till half past two p.m.

At about 12 o'clock, Col. Baker, the acting Brigadier in command, began to send over reinforcements, and soon crossed himself. The 1st California went over

---

54 Charles Devens (1820 – 1891) was a graduate of Boston Latin School, Harvard College and Harvard Law School. Devens practiced law in Worcester, Massachusetts from which place he raised and was commissioned Colonel of the 15th Massachusetts. Wounded at the Battle of Ball's Bluff, Deven's was later promoted to Brigadier General in April of 1862. Devens would be wounded twice more, once at Fair Oaks and once at Chancellorsville. Following the war, Devens served in the Massachusetts Supreme Judicial Court and was Attorney General of the United States under Rutherford B. Hayes. Warner; *Generals in Blue*
55 William Raymond Lee (1807 – 1891) attended West Point in the class of 1829 with Robert E. Lee, although he would not graduate. At the outbreak of the war Colonel Lee was commissioned by Governor Andrew to be Colonel of the 20th Massachusetts. Lee was captured at the Battle of Ball's Bluff. Released in April of 1862, Lee remained in command of his regiment until after the battle of Fredericksburg, following which he resigned. Ellis; *Norwich University.*

entire, as rapidly as the poor means of transportation allowed. Three companies of the Tammany (N.Y.) Regiment, with Col. Cogswell,[56] and more of the 20th Massachusetts also crossed.

As the reinforcements reached the gallant 15th, they found them little beyond the river. I have said already that the bank was over sixty feet high. Climbing to the summit, they found a track about seventy feet in width, exceedingly broken, and curved, with rocks, bushes, and bogs, impassable, indeed, for a horse. Beyond this was an open place, almost a lawn, about 300 feet wide by 450 yards long, -- the length being towards Leesburg. Here the battle was resumed with great energy. AT 3 P.M. the firing was very brisk, and for the next hour it was exceedingly furious on both sides. An order for artillery had been sent immediately after the first reinforcements arrived, -- the enemy all the time rapidly increasing. Two howitzers (regulars) were sent over with great difficulty, and about a quarter past four, Lieut. Bramhall, of a Battery attached to the New York Ninth, with a rifled cannon, a six pounder to throw 13 pound shell.[57] Those guns had to be carried to the Southward of the high bluff and rugged track, to reach the open scene. As the forces were then placed, our troops were on that side of the open field which was nearest the river, the right and left wing a little advanced, so as to form a concave front towards the enemy, but in a corner of the bushes; a howitzer was at each extremity, and Lieut. Bramhall's gun a little in advance of the center, on slightly elevated ground. The enemy were also under cover of the woods, their sharpshooters in trees for

---

56 Milton Cogswell (1825 - 1885) was a career army officer who graduated from West Point in the class of 1849. He served with the 8th U.S. Infantry through July of 1861 when he transferred to 42nd New York Volunteer Infantry. Colonel Cogswell was captured at the Battle of Ball's Bluff. Cogswell would later transfer to the 2nd New York Volunteer Infantry and back to the 8th U.S. Infantry before the end of the Civil War. Colonel Cogswell served briefly as mayor of Charleston at the end of the Rebellion. Cogswell retired from the army in 1871 and is buried in Arlington National Cemetery. Patterson; "Milton Cogswell."

57 Walter Morrell Bramhall (1839 - 1913) a Lieutenant of Battery K attached to the 9th New York Militia, Bramhall was ordered to assume command over a section of Battery B, 1st Rhode Island Light Artillery when its commander wasn't present to supervise the battery's crossing of the Potomac and its subsequent engagement at Ball's Bluff. Bramhall was wounded about the time of the first discharge of the gun and received three wounds that day, before being helped off the field by two members of the 15th Massachusetts. Bramhall would go on to become Captain of the 6th New York Independent Battery. Rhodes; *The History of Battery B*; and, Says; "Walter M. Bramhall."

more deadly aim, and rarely coming into sight for a large part of the fight. Our men had skirmishers on both flanks, in the woods, where much fighting took place. For several hours the fighting was severe. The enemy fired in heavy vollies, as if a regiment were shooting at once. "The bullets fell like hail," says an officer, who, though fighting with the greatest bravery, strangely escaped uninjured. The enemy had no cannon, but their force was not less, it now appears, than five or six thousand, to which our forces had but about sixteen hundred in opposition.

Our men fought with the utmost bravery, but they were gradually overpowered by numbers. About 3 o'clock, Col. Baker was killed. "Had I two more Massachusetts regiments," said he, a few minutes before he was shot, "I could beat them yet." Col. Cogswell of the Tammany, took command. The fight still continued, but in vain. It was at last determined to attempt a movement towards Edwards' Ferry. The formation of the troops was commenced with that view, and partially executed, when a dash of the Tammany companies into the open space was met by such a murderous fire, as to throw everything into confusion. Our troops then descended the bluff, and formed on the plateau below. Resistance was still made, but in vain. Our men took to the water. Many were drowned. Many were shot in the water. The boats had both been sunk entire, with their loads, and no transportation remained. Half of our troops are killed, wounded or missing.[58]

The policy of the enemy was skilful. It was to worry our men for the day, and then to throw a heavy body of reserve upon our exhausted soldiers, and it succeeded perfectly. The sadness of the results are equalled only by the stupidity of the plan, which *never emanated* from responsible leaders. The crossing at this bluff – while half a mile distant was an open and level shore; the criminal neglect to provide proper transportation over, and to secure a possible retreat; and the uselessness of the enterprise deserve rigid examination. No Massachusetts men flinched. They fought with the utmost coolness and daring. It was a terrible defeat, but it shows the spirit of our men; and our officers acted nobly.

The next day, Gen. McClellan came. The troops across the Edward's Ferry were ordered back. But what plans that General has, nobody knows. If not interfered with by ambitious and foolish men, he will succeed.

---

[58] According to final reports, of the 2,000 Union troops engaged, there were 921 casualties. Ballard; *Battle of Ball's Bluff*.

One lesson taught here, is, to *keep politicians* at home. Give our army suitable officers, and they will beat the world. Suffer no more Senators to plan campaigns; no more men desirous of making a figure, to sacrifice the noble sons of our State.

Last evening we had an order to move to Edward's Ferry. "The enemy threaten us in force," was the order; "Send two of your regiments, especially the second Massachusetts." We marched six miles, and then, were sent back, the emergency having passed. And we are still in camp.

A.H.Q

Harper's Ferry during the Civil War. (Courtesy of the Library of Congress)

November 15, 1861

Letter from the Army
Muddy Branch Camp, MD., Oct. 31, 1861

Change of Location – Glimpses of Home – In an Enemy's Country – Little Union Sentiment – Harper's Ferry – The "Irrepressible Conflict" – Scorn for Yankees – the Rebels Must be "Conquered" – A General Cinfiscation Act – A Mistaken Policy – The Army Loathe to Return Slaves – Renovation of the South

No more "near Darnestown." No more of that hard-trodden field, where our camp lay; nor that road by its side, with multitude of pedlers. We have been to "Harrison Island," and in sight of "Ball's Bluff," which rested as quiet and silent, as though the blood had not dyed its soil. We have countermarched, and our division is near the river, below Gen. Stone's command, and near Darnestown as a fact, but not as a *date*. We now are in a quiet, pleasant field, away from the road, which itself is away from the main road. The "field and staff" have pitched their tents in the edge of the wood, and as I sit at the "door of my tent," the shade of oak and walnut are pleasant, this beautiful "fall" day. A little fire is burning a few feet before me, and the smoke curls up lazily in the sunshine. The air has the lovely, dreamy haze of Autumn. The trees are gently shaking off the ripe leaves. The hum of insects is not yet ended. Near, are the strokes of our woodcutters' axes. Farther off, is the murmur of a rapid and steep waterfall. The season is

"Like an Emperor triumphing,
With gorgeous robes of Tyrian dyes,

> Full flush of fragrant blossoming,
> And glowing purple canopies."[59]

A few hours hence, and some of ours will see the broad Potomac, where our men do duty; where

> "The wide, clear waters sleeping lie
> Beneath the evening's wings of gold;
> And on their glassy breast of sky,
> And banks, their mingled hues unfold."

It is a "muster day," and drill is omitted, and music silent. It is a day to dream of home! Home! Thanks for a home, whither the needle points steadily. And prayers for one sad man to whom yesterday's letter said his home was broken; his wife had left this world, and so left her four now motherless children, with no relative this side the Atlantic save their father, and he bound by his oath to his country.

I have had a glimpse or two of home. One was when the Norfolk Conference, your paper said, did not forget one of their number with the army. Another, when Rev. Mr. Alvord[60] came, in his great plan of systematic distribution of religious reading, to oversee which he ought to be kept in this vicinity this winter, without a moment's hesitation. He occupied for a day and night half of the chaplain's tent. The third was the sight of Rev. Mr. Cushing of North Brookfield,[61] whose full heart sent him to see the sons of his church in the 15th, or to hear of the prisoners.

---

59 This and the next poetic fragment are from a poem on Autumn authored by Fanny Kemble in October 1832. Butler; *Journal of a Residence.*

60 John Watson Alvord (1807 – 1880) was a principal participant in the American Tract Society's branch office in Boston. Commissioned a Christian Commission agent, he aided regiments in procuring tents to be used for religious services and prayer meetings, in the distribution of religious reading material and following the war he was an active agent for the Freedmen's Bureau. Moss; *Annals of the United States Christian Commission.*

61 Christopher Cushing (1820 - 1881) was a graduate of Yale (1844) and Andover Theological Seminary (1847). Cushing was ordained as pastor of the Edwards Church in Boston before accepting a post in North Brookfield. He was an active and energetic member of the American Congregational Union. Cushing was involved in editing the Congregational Quarterly with Alonzo Quint. Andover Theological Seminary; *General Catalogue.*

But to another topic.

Dear *Congregationalist*, I know that my handwriting is usually blind. My parents, still spared in mercy, insist that it is undoubtedly an imitation of Greek. They are almost like the father of Dr. Chalmers, (was it not?) who saved his sons letters for the Dr. to read at his semi-annual visit.[62] I have suffered maledictions from your compositers, I know; and perhaps you remember how I once determined to prove that I could write legibly; and how I wrote an article in the old-fashioned, round, Boston hand, which was a marvel of clearness and beauty. Alas! It was like the century plant; one bloom exhausted my powers, and I have never written a decent hand since.

It is not strange, therefore, that you made me say "we have been in *no* enemy's country," when I really said, "we have been in *an* enemy's country." Small errors I pass by; this I correct, because of its involving a mournful truth.

We have been in *an* enemy's country. Sent into central Virginia, a continuation of the beautiful Cumberland valley, -- the central of the three parts into which mountain ranges divide Virginia, -- a medium as to slave population, between the Eastern and Western portions, -- midway between a loyal and a rebellious section, -- we found it as alien from the Government as any foreign power, and as hostile as the bitterest war could render it. I see much in Northern papers about freeing Union sentiment, awakening loyalty, and the like. But I did not see it in Central Virginia, where it ought, above all places on rebel soil, to have been exhibited. Nor do I see much of it in Maryland, where it ought to be predominant.

Confining myself to Central Virginia, I do not believe we met, outside of Harper's Ferry, half a dozen reliable Union men. The people were willing to buy and sell, and they could teach Yankees lessons in sharpness. But as to any open ingenuous loyalty to the Constitution, it was almost unknown. At best they were sullenly quiet, but by no means hearty. Sometimes they were outspoken. One good lady expressed to me the hope that every Northern soldier would be killed. At Middleway, the stars and stripes were greeted with the ugliest of expressions, and "The Star Spangled Banner" and "Hail Columbia," with which our Band endeavored to edify them, met with disgust. At Charlestown, every shop was closed as we entered, save one, and

---

62 Thomas Chalmers (1780 – 1847) was a noted Scottish minister and social reformer in the early 19th century.

the occupant of that, though displaying a Union flag, proved the meanest rebel of all. Nor has there been a single place where a little stay did not enable us to learn that the bulk of the inhabitants were in favor of the Southern Confederacy, except Harper's Ferry, which, from its industrial pursuits, had a population entirely different from that of slaveholding places generally. There was a large mechanical population once employed in government workshops. They had earned some money by hard labor and good wages. They had bought, of Government, neat homes, at a low price, paying by installments for the last four years. They had helped build good churches, and had established common and Sabbath schools. In front of most houses is a little piece of ground, and formerly there were a few flowers, a rare sight in this part of the country. Such a population, though not particularly, Anti-slavery, was, and principally is, for the Union. Now the churches are mainly shut up. The schools are abandoned. The sidewalks and streets are rough and ragged. Many homes are deserted. Property often their little all, is valueless. Their incomes are destroyed, with the destruction of the government shops. Some of the workmen were persuaded to carry their knowledge and experience to Richmond or to North Carolina, and most of the true men are left totally destitute. Government will probably never restore the ruined buildings, and Harper's Ferry is ruined. Still, many men there are faithful to their country, in spite of all inducements to treason.

There is no mistaking the general feelings of a people. This people regarded us as invaders. Most of them have no loyalty to be awakened. I write this with a little doubt as to the propriety of uprooting this convenient stepping-stone, one which I myself traveled into a clearer path. But that it is the fact, I am persuaded by an observation of nearly four months in localities which must be far in advance of Southern States in loyalty; and I except only occasional places.

That there will be *apparent* loyalty as our armies advance, is doubtless true, but it will be self-interest, not love, nor to be trusted as anything else tan a convenient instrument. This state of things arises from two facts:

First, there *is* an "irrepressible conflict" between freedom and slavery. Free labor and slave *cannot* flourish together. Where industry is considered menial, it loses its vitality. Whites despise it, and become, if poor, meaner than the meanest of negroes; "poor white trash" is their legitimate title. Between, therefore, the two kinds of labor, the sympathy of those who have the power is entirely with the South. Not because slave labor here is profitable; it is not profitable; there are not slaves enough, nor the kind of work, to make it pay, while there are just enough to make their masters lazy. And in the latter fact is their liking for Southern institutions. While, further, there is the deeper feeling that the North despises and dislikes slavery, on conscientious principles, which principles the owner of one slave feels the burden of, as well as the owner of a thousand – a small slaveholder in Virginia, as well as the plantation owner in South Carolina. Out of such companionship as that of freedom-loving Northerner, these people are anxious to get.

The second fact is, that the Southern feeling is, and always has been, that of scorn for "Yankees," as they call all Northerners. Most Southerners have carried with them the manners of the plantation, and have always looked down upon the industrious North. They are afraid of Northern thrift and enterprise, while they assume to be a superior race. They dislike its democracy, and prefer the aristocracy of the South – to be tyrannical, if of the favored class, to favor, if they are inferiors. All really slaveholding States must gravitate towards the South.

That the rebels must be "conquered," "subjugated," or whatever you please to call it, admits no question. Our country's coasts, its rivers, its mines, its roads, its telegraphs, demand that it be *one*. The success of self-government requires it. But how to succeed is the question. That our armies will eventually triumph, is sure, in the fact that Southerners never dare meet an equal force of Northerners in the field. When we have *officers*, we shall conquer. But what to do then? Is any compromise possible to satisfy them? *None.* To restore the South to its old status, would only restore the old conflicts, more embittered than ever. The old braggarts; the old liars and thieves; far more haughty boasting, more impudent lies, more successful thefts. Nothing is settled till it is settled right.

But when the South is conquered, it must be held. And that will require a social revolution at the South. Not a mere emancipation of slaves, but a change in the ownership of property. The property holders will always be the dominant class in reality. Introduce a loyal race of property holders, and loyal men of industry, and the problem is worked out. While you are discussing the Fremont proclamation, you forget that the simplest way of proceeding is for the Congress soon to assemble, to pass a general confiscation act, by which every man committing an overt act of rebellion, shall forfeit *all* his property. For this the army arches. They see rebels protected, their houses guarded, their property sentineled. They see disloyal men "conciliated," even though soldiers should suffer. What think you of taking particular pains to restore slaves claimed specially on the ground that as the whites of the family were all absent, the blacks were indispensable for gathering the crops, while those very whites were officers in the rebel army at Manassas? Or, of restoring houses taken for public use, and receipted for, on the same plea of crops, while the proceeds of those crops were to help support Southern soldiers? What think you of Union men being left without work, while notorious secessionists were hired in rebuilding bridges and the like work? Where the policy originated, I do not know; but such things happened in the column of the famous General now returned to private life, until the spirit seemed to be that of the "reward and forgetfulness" act of Charles II., which he carried out by forgetting his friends, and rewarding his enemies.

Such a policy will never succeed. It conciliates no rebels; it disgusts friends. But if "general emancipation" were now made the object of this war, I fully believe that two-thirds of our armies would melt away. Our men are fighting for the FLAG, not for the abolition of slavery. So far as the army goes, slavery is not a prominent theme or thought. The supremacy of law, and the honor of the stars and stripes – these are the soldier's principles. General emancipation would add untold horrors as the nobility of a true and gallant soldier, has no desire to witness; and would violate constitutional principles, beyond which our armies would be palsied. At the same time, if there is any work which our soldiers loathe, it is the returning of fugitive slaves. They despise it, and they are despised for it by the chuckling scoundrels who claim the "guaranties" of the Constitution which they have deliberately thrown off. But they are not fighting for "abolition," and you must remember that the army is now a POWER.

But if you confiscate the property of the rebels, you have the means to pour in a new population. At the end of this war there will be hundreds of thousands of young men ready to take and hold, with an arm used to the rifle, such properties. There are plenty of stalwart mechanics who could and would redeem this Southern soil from the blight with which Southern shiftlessness has cursed it. Of its Harper's Ferries, with magnificent water powers, with their vicinity to the land of cotton, with all needed avenues to the sea, Northern skill would make new Lowells and Lawrences. These houses of half log, half mud, would give place to New England villages. The church and the school house would renovate the character of the population, and the iron hand of Northern power would rule with a strength against which Southern impetuousness would struggle in vain, as Southerners have always been powerless, the world over, against Northern steel. Slavery itself would vanish before such a resistless power as free labor, enlightened by a free conscience, and the blacks, thus freed, would become supporters to a system of national industry. The now dominant class, once poor, would lose their pride with their power, and a new race of men would come into being.

Strike, then, for a General Confiscation Act; and do not divide the North, and weaken our armies by impracticable propositions of unconstitutional measures.[63]

A.H.Q.

---

[63] A Confiscation Act had already been passed in August of 1861 which President Lincoln signed into law. This allowed for the confiscation of all property (including slaves) being used to support the Confederate cause, with a particular focus on military hardware. A 2nd Confiscation act was passed in July of 1862 which specifically stated that any Confederate civilian or military officer who did not surrender in 60 days would have their slaves freed by a court proceeding and have their personal property seized by the Union Army. "Explanation of the Confiscation Act;" *Wisconsin Daily Patriot;* and, "The Federal Confiscation Act;" *Times-Picayune.*

November 29, 1861

Letter from the Army.
Near Seneca, Md., Nov. 15, 1861

Newspapers Precious – Resumé of War News in the Congregationalist – Mistakes of the Pictorials – A New Camp – The Matter of Health – Hygienic Arrangements – The Hospital – The Inmates well Cared for.

The news which delights our minds, is doubtless the same as with you, -- the successful attack at Port Royal.[64] We are far more tranquil than you are in regard to news; less excitable, less worried. We are away from the sensation despatches appearing hour after hour on the bulletin-boards, where one statement is contradicted by the next. A newspaper, with us, is a precious article. A Baltimore daily, which I succeeded in picking up yesterday, passed through a multitude of hands, until pretty thoroughly used up. It rejoiced our hearts with the official account of the success on South Carolina soil.

One advantage *your* readers have over those who gather their news out of the dailies, is in the excellent *resumé* you give, once a week, of the war items. I have been surprised and pleased, with the careful, comprehensive, and accurate summary you furnish; while the undigested mass of items in the dailies, excite a good deal of ridicule in the quarters of which they profess to speak. The errors which a

---

[64] This attack occurred on November 7, 1861 and featured about 12,000 Union troops under General Thomas W. Sherman and 77 Union vessels under Commodore Samuel F. Dupont seizing Port Royal and the Confederate forts. They were opposed by about 3,000 Confederate troops under the Command of Brig. General Thomas F. Drayton.

mere lack of care allows, are sometimes inexcusable. Thus *Harper's Weekly* points a moral from the defeat at "Edwards Ferry," whereas at that place there was no battle. "Right wing" and "Left wing" are huddled up in inextricable confusion, until it is noted that Col. Baker's force was the "right wing" of the entire movement, covering the ends of three miles; while Col. Baker's force had itself a right and left, covering but a few hundred feet. One Boston daily takes somebody to task for calling Gen. McClellan "Commander-in-Chief," and then gravely announces that his true title is "Lieutenant-General, -- a grade created by special act of Congress, for Gen. Scott, and, by that very act, to cease to exist when Gen. Scott ceases to bear the title. But some of the pictorials are the richest in ability. The places they portray are frequently beyond recognition. A picture of the burning of the arsenals at Harper's Ferry, which I chanced to take up a few days ago, amused me somewhat, from the fact that the only two buildings which it represents as burning, are the only two there which bear no mark of fire!

There have been no marked changes in this vicinity since the Ball's Bluff affair, and the consequent immediate movement of troops. Between Washington and Muddy Branch there are few troops this side of the river, but the Virginia side is occupied. Gen. Banks Division lies at Muddy Branch and Seneca. Gen. Stone is next above, covering the river nearly to a point opposite Leesburgh; and various parts of these Divisions are stationed at the Point of Rocks, Sandy Hook, and Williamsport.

Our own Regiment has moved its camp a fourth of a mile, to secure a healthier location. The former site was a clayey soil, hard to dry after a rain. In fact, the ground was never really dry after the first day or two of our camping, and the result has been in the poorer condition of a generally healthy regiment. The few days which have elapsed since our change, show already a marked improvement. Our present camp is on high ground, and overlooks the Potomac, visible less than half a mile distant. The health of most of the Regiments in this Division is good, but reports of visitors to some Regiments on the Alexandria side of the Potomac, represent an unfortunate state of things. It is impossible to keep health good on low ground near this beautiful but deadly river. The miasma is terrible. Old residents shun it as much as possible, and those who cannot do so, are a lank, sickly, cadaverous race; and, so far as I can judge, the character of most of them answers to their looks.

The matter of health has always been attended to in this Regiment. In reading an article in the *Atlantic* for November, I noticed that every valuable suggestion therein made, has always been observed in the Second Massachusetts. The "Sanitary Commission"[65] was an organization of supererogation for us – a proof of the value of having experienced army officers in charge of affairs. Nor can too much attention be devoted to the health of soldiers. A sickly army cannot fight well; nor is it fair to men who have left their homes for their country's welfare, that they should be needlessly exposed to disease.

The measures taken against disease, are of two kinds, namely – the hygienic arrangements of camp, and the medical means of cure of sickness. The first are of the greatest importance. In selecting a site for a camp, one is sought for which is dry in its character, -- elevated, but not too bleak, -- gently sloping, to prevent stagnant water from rains, -- open to the sun, and airy, but shielded somewhat from winds and storms, if possible. The first work, after the places for our tents is selected, is to sweep and otherwise clean the ground thoroughly. The whole camp ground is carefully swept every day by a force specially detailed, till not even a chip remains. No impurities are allowed near the camp. At the kitchen fires, in front of the company tents, deep holes are dug, in which the offal from cooking is thrown, and every day a layer of earth is thrown in. The tents themselves are struck not infrequently in warm, sunny days, (if the camping remains long in one spot,) and the sites dried. If there is straw in the tents, it is required to be thoroughly dried at frequent intervals. The Sibley tents, which our men use, are well ventilated at the top, by a hole coverable at pleasure.[66] Unwholsome food, the Regulations allow to

---

65 The Sanitary Commission was founded by a group of New York philanthropists who took to heart the lessons learned by the British during the Crimean War. The Commission they founded had branches in every state in the Union and went everywhere the army did and was responsible for providing millions of dollars' worth of "luxuries" to sick and wounded soldiers. They also provided transportation, nursing and medical care, and additional clothing for soldiers. Quint begins as a lukewarm fan of the Commission, but his appreciation of them grows as he interacts with them over the course of the war. Stillé; History *of the United States Sanitary Commission*.

66 The Sibley tent was patented in 1856 by career army officer Henry Hopkins Sibley who took his idea from the teepee shelters used by the Plains Indians. The tent was conical and featured a telescoping center pole. The sides were pegged to the ground and did not require guy ropes for stabilization. The tent could be fitted with a stove and a cowl fit over the central opening (through which the tent pole ran) allowing for ventilation. While more than 40,000

be condemned, and new and good demanded. To ensure the care of the camp in regard to order and cleanliness, an "officer of police" is daily appointed.

The arrangements for the sick are under the direction of the Surgeon, who has also an Assistant, both regularly educated physicians. Every morning, any man taken sick, reports to the First Sergeant of his company, who enrolls his name in a company book kept for the purpose. Shortly after breakfast, the drum and fife give the "sick call," when those of the enrolled who are able, go to the Surgeon, who prescribes as needed. If but little indisposed, the sick man returns to his tent, excused from duty, -- the medicine allowed being furnished in the course of the morning by the "Hospital Steward," who attends to the preparation of prescriptions. If too ill to render it prudent for the patient to remain "in quarters," he is sent, by the Surgeon, to the Hospital of the Regiment. If one newly reported sick is not able to attend the "sick call," the Surgeon or Assistant visits him at his tent, and directs his removal if necessary. Our Hospital consists of two tents of thick canvas, about twenty-five by fourteen feet in size. Each will accommodate easily ten patients, and is supplied with bedsteads, straw beds, &c. The "Hospital Steward" has general charge of the hospital, and specially secures the administering of medicines, &c. A "Ward Master" has charge of beds, bedding, cleanliness, food, &c., and has several "nurses," – of which the allowance (exceeded in our Regiment,) is one to ten patients. Two cooks prepare the necessary food; and other assistants attend to transportation and the like. If a man is likely to be long sick, as when a broken leg is to be healed, or there is some chronic disease, he is sent to a "General Hospital," – ours being at Baltimore, in the old "National House;" as the necessity of movements by a Regiment, render it undesirable to have men in its local Hospital, to whom movement might be disastrous. When men shall be discharged from Hospital is under control of the Surgeon, -- as indeed are all matters relative to disease. There is but one head, -- which makes the excellence of army discipline. Medicines and instruments are furnished by Government, freely and according to the experience of years.

The above are the arrangements in camp. For the sad effects of battle fields, litters are ready, and attendants detailed, -- that none of our brave men shall suffer more than indispensable.

---

of his tents were in use during the war by the Union army, Sibley himself went on to serve in the Confederate army. Volo; *Daily Life.*

I write of this topic, because so many hearts are anxious at home, and such details may interest them; and to assure them that, while nothing is a substitute for *home*, with its warm hearts and gentle hands, yet everything is done which can be done, to lighten the burden of disease. Our Surgeons[67] spare no labor, night nor day; and our Colonel is a frequent visitor among the sick; our Hospital Steward[68] is a most skillful worker in medicine; our Ward Master is kind-hearted and unwearied; our Hospital cooks are experienced. Yet, in spite of all human skill and care, death cannot be excluded here, but will enter our canvas doors, as he glides into the houses of wood and stone at home – at will, or rather, at Our Father's will, before which who of us has not been made to weep? Two of our number here, have lately died; both stricken with disease in great severity; and both delirious from the hour of their entrance into the Hospital; so delirious, that neither could converse. What preparation they had made for the future *must* have been made before they lay on a sick bed. We committed them to God, who is rich in mercy, for the great love wherewith He loved us.

A.H.Q.

---

67 Lucius Manlius Sargent (1826 - 1864) of Milford, Mass., was the Surgeon of the 2nd Massachusetts from the outbreak of the war. A graduate of Harvard (1847) and Harvard Medical School (1858), Sargent was a practicing physician and surgeon at the Massachusetts General Hospital. However, about the time of this letter, Sargent resigned his medical commission to accept one as a Captain in the 1st Massachusetts Cavalry. He would later be killed during a cavalry charge outside of Petersburg in 1864. Following the resignation of Sargent in October of 1861, Francis Leland (1818 - 1867) became the regimental surgeon. Leland was a graduate of Brown University(1838) and Harvard Medical School (1842). In May of 1862, following the Battle of Winchester, Leland was captured with the wounded he was caring for in a house in Kernstown, VA. He was released on parole about a week later. He remained surgeon until October of 1862, when he resigned due to ill health stemming from a wound to the head he had received at the Battle of Cedar Mountain. The Assistant Surgeon from the formation of the regiment was Lincoln Ripley Stone (1832 – 1930) received his MD from Harvard Medical School in 1854. Stone was promoted to Surgeon following the resignation of Surgeon Leland, though he himself would resign from the Surgeon's post early in 1863 to accept the commission as Surgeon of the 54th Massachusetts Regiment. Commissioned a "Surgeon of Volunteers" in December of 1863, Stone oversaw different General Hospitals until the end of the war. Quint; *The Record of the Second Massachusetts*; and, Adjutant General of Massachusetts; *Massachusetts Soldiers, Sailors and Marines in the Civil War.*

68 Joseph Warren Nutting (1832 – 1863) was born in Danvers, was an apothecary in Boston prior to the war and died in 1863 in Quincy, Mass., while on furlough. *The Record of the Second Massachusetts*; and, Adjutant General of Massachusetts; *Massachusetts Soldiers, Sailors and Marines in the Civil War.*

November 29, 1861

Our Thanksgiving Day.
By. Rev. A. H. Quint

It was not a day of striking incidents. It was only a quiet, cheerful, happy, day. Some other regiments from Massachusetts did not celebrate it; and some made great preparations. But our way did us good.

We feared, on Wednesday evening, that the next day would be rainy. For a day or two the air had had that peculiar mildness which forebodes a storm. The skies were covered with somber clouds, when the sun went down beyond the hills, and the wind was moving, not harshly, but threateningly. And we went to sleep with the words, "it will be wet to-morrow." We? All but the guard, who, one third at a time, pace round over camp all the night, as well as all the day. But as the night settled down, the clouds dissolved; so early that the evening star appeared in all its glory. And when the *reveille* was beating on the morning of Thanksgiving day, the sun was shining cheerfully through the autumn haze, and melting the white frost which carpeted the ground; and the river mists were sullenly creeping away, frightened at the sunshine, and revealing the dark woods of the Virginia shore which our pickets watch night and day.

Thanksgiving day is one thing at home. You gather around the family table, three generations – grave parents, stalwart sons and daughters, and happy children. If not all there, the merry children are forgetful of the departed who are still in your memory, and *they* make it happy. Thanksgiving day is another thing, when you are away from home, alone perhaps, and thinking of the dear gathering you cannot see. I have tried both ways. But it is still another thing, when a thousand

Massachusetts men form a home to themselves; a wandering, shifting home; a home of canvas shelter; a home of sword, and rifle, and bayonet; in sight of a river, on whose other bank are nightly camp fires of an enemy.

But our men made themselves happy. Our Major[69] commanding determined it should be a pleasant festival, and what *he* undertakes, you may be sure is done. Our officers did all in their power to help. Our men were in the best of spirits. They were relieved from drill, or course. The company which would have lined the river's bank on a cold and dismal duty, was replaced, through our Major's efforts, by an Indiana company, who poor fellows, had no Thanksgiving day to keep. The usual guard duty could not, of course, be omitted, but each sentry was relieved in order, and all were in sight, and none failed of his dinner.

At ten o'clock we had public service. Our companies marched to a spot cleared off for the occasion. The "minister's" pulpit was the ground beneath an old oak tree, on a level with his congregation. The band played an anthem. The Governor's Proclamation was read – the Massachusetts Governor's – and it sounded strangely to hear, on Maryland soil, the time honored closing, "God save the Commonwealth of Massachusetts!" It was a good proclamation, and many a heart responded to the final aspiration. A prayer followed. And then singing the hymn, familiar to you:

"Praise to God, the great Creator,"

The chaplain took as text, the words, "What shall I render unto the Lord for all his benefits towards me?" *Home* was on every mind. Such a question at home, if we were suddenly transported thither, would be natural. Had we reason to remember "benefits" in our present position – away from home – often enduring hardships – in the approach of danger? Most truly. Not merely for common personal blessings, but for reasons none but soldiers could have. The glorious position of a *soldier* in defence of our flag, while so many remained in irksome quiet at home. The noble

---

69 Wilder Dwight (1833 – 1862) was a graduate of Phillips – Exeter Academy and Harvard College (1853). Commissioned Major in May of 1861, Dwight rose to the rank of Lieutenant Colonel before being killed at the battle of Antietam. *The Record of the Second Massachusetts*; and, Adjutant General of Massachusetts; *Massachusetts Soldiers, Sailors and Marines in the Civil War*.

privilege of enduring hardships, and perhaps death itself, in so holy a cause as love of country. The tide of sympathies, and love, and prayers, in so many households; and the crown of honor which every faithful soldier will wear, when the cause shall have triumphed – till, when he shall die, it will be said as his choicest epitaph, "He was a soldier from Massachusetts."

Our men are patriotic. They showed it in their faces. They are brave men, too. And why such regiments, with months of drill, and in splendid discipline, should be kept in Maryland, while raw recruits are sent on distant service, surpasses explanation.

I doubt if many congregations in Massachusetts were as orderly as ours. But then we have a peculiar way of our own. I have repeatedly thought that I should like to see a Massachusetts congregation arrayed in the same style. First, let the whole society go to worship without attention to mere feelings. Let them stand during the whole service, and stand in order, and stand "attention," or at best, "parade rest." It would cure divers people of sleepiness, and would secure, at least, outward respect to the public worship of God. Our commander deems public worship worthy of respect from his regiment as a whole; it pays proper honors to a commander; why not to God?

It was not long after service, before various amusements were under weigh. Bat and ball engrossed a good many. Others were singing, and others were trying their skill with pistols, and other groups with the rifle. The utmost freedom of proper remark prevailed, and sometimes very free shots. The cheers at success were inspiring, and the laughter at failures was taken in good part. The prizes were turkeys, borne off in great delight – three out of four taken by the shots of officers from my own village.

The dinner was a New England dinner. Turkeys, geese, chickens and plum puddings. Turkeys done to a turn, with just the nicest brown outside, and such stuffing! Puddings, with heaps of raisins as thick as pebbles of Roxbury pudding stone![70] Around every company kitchen it was pleasant to see the groups watching

---

70 Now the official rock of Massachusetts, the Roxbury Puddingstone is a conglomerate bed-rock that underlies most of the Greater Boston area. It was named for its outcropping in Roxbury, Massachusetts and from the fact that it looked like an old-fashioned boiled pudding. McPherson; *GeoSymbols*

proceedings, as turkeys and geese were cut up, and just the right amount of gravy dispensed. Hands off till dinner call! Then, such appetites. Not that they cared so much for turkeys; but we had turkeys "at home." Some companies built tables and long seats, and planted rows of evergreens, and *sat down* to dinner, and invited your correspondent, -- which he could not accept, because *one* dinner does for a day, and because a twenty-pound turkey availed the Field and Staff, and an invited guest, the beloved Chaplain of the 12th,[71] was coming to help eat it. For the edification of the friends of our soldiers, I made a "statistical table" of the various amounts of provisions, and here is the "Summary." Ninety-four turkeys, weighing nine hundred and seventy-three pounds; seventy-six geese, weighing six hundred and sixty-six pounds; seventy-three chickens, weighing on hundred and seventy-six pounds; and ninety-five plum-puddings, weighing eleven hundred and seventy-nine pounds; besides apples, nuts, figs, raisins, &c. Do you ask where our turkeys were cooked? In ovens, of course; huge stone ovens, built by our men, and a great deal better than stoves and ranges at home. I have no doubt but that our Regiment would decide by an overwhelming vote, in which I fully coincide, that no cookery ever yet excelled that of yesterday's turkeys. So fond of their dinner were the men, that a multitude secured *bones*, out of which to manufacture some souvenir of their Thanksgiving. Who *paid* for the turkeys? Company funds, which are constantly accumulating out of the savings of rations.

After dinner, there were faint attempts to renew games – very faint. Most preferred to rest. But after supper, the band came out, -- an excellent band. I must confess that their music was rather lively. I also record that it seemed to excite the feet of nearly the whole Regiment. Nor did their manœuvers appear to be patterned after Hardee or Scott.[72] With perfect order, but infinite humor, the extem-

---

71   Edward Lord Clark (1838 – 1910) was commissioned Chaplain of the 12th Massachusetts in June of 1861. A graduate of Brown University (1858) and Andover Theological Seminary (1863), Clark would resign his commission after a year to accept a post at the First Congregational Church of North Bridgewater. Following the war, he was Chaplain of the Massachusetts Order of the Loyal Legion of the United States. Andover Theological Seminary; *General Catalogue*.
72   Hardee and Scott refer to the prevailing manual of arms for the civil war soldier. Winfield Scott wrote his "Infantry Tactics" book in 1835 to provide a cohesive manual of arms to be used by the standing army and militia alike. Scott's manual remained the standard until 1855, although some state militias were still using it well after. Major William Hardee set out to bring the manual of arms up to date, based on the new French model, and wrote his "Rifle

pore dance on the hard ground proceeded, -- with a total destitution of female partners, and without the dress considered strictly appropriate to such affairs at home. It was decidedly better than "knapsack drill," and no more harmful, -- especially as good hours were kept. In fact, our regularity sometimes reminds me of a good lady in New Hampshire, near whom I used to live, whose son was sent to a State Prison. A neighbor being about to go to Concord, the mother asked him to visit her son. He did so. "Well, how is Johnny?" said she. "Oh very well, indeed." "Is he regular in his habits?" asked she. "Oh, *perfectly* regular." "But does he go out evenings?" she enquired, anxiously. "No," said he, "I don't think he has been out a single evening since he went to Concord." "Well, I am *real* glad," said the relieved mother; "going out evenings was the ruin of him."

But it did not need "tattoo" to stop the dance. *Mail* came in, and when that happened, the rush was all for letters. Tidings from home! When you want to find a soldier's heart, touch the home-chord. In the hardest and rudest, there is one sacred spot. No soldier every speaks slightingly of his mother, nor his wife, nor his child. Many a man with rough outside, has taken occasion, when nobody was near, to pull out of some inside pocket a little picture for me to look at; I unclasp it, and find some delicate woman's face, or some chubby boy or girl, or a matron's aged features; and the hardy man looks at me to see what I think, and a word of enquiry finds the heart and sometimes the tear. Mail came in. It was a fitting close to a day when everybody had talked of home. A good, large mail, too. I counted the letters. Six hundred and two. And the papers. Nearly five hundred. And the daguerreotypes and the pocket handkerchiefs, and the mittens, and the neck-ties – all come by mail. And many a man's heart was made glad that night. And *I* had *six* letters. One – first of all to me – from *my* treasures. And one troubled by "Enquirer's" annihilation of an unlucky sentence of your demolished correspondent. And then, one to know if rumors of misconduct and drunkenness were true of a certain person – to which I can say "No." And one to beg my help in regard to a brother here, who needed special help; but I knew the case before. And one from an anxious mother, to know about her son, from whom she had not heard for six weeks; yes, he *is* well.

---

and Light Infantry" tactics in 1855. This remained the standard, although during the Civil War the book was issued by the U.S. Government without the author's name on the title page because he was in the Confederate army at the time. Griffith; *Battle Tactics*.

And one, with regard to the body of a deceased soldier – which his parents wish may rest beside another son, gone long ago.

Tattoo beats. The day is ended. No strife, no drunkenness, no disorder, that day, -- though the hand of discipline was unfelt. They were men – Massachusetts men. Then the camp sank to quiet. Then the stars came out. Then the sentinels paced forward and back, as ever. Then the waterfall near by, stoutly murmured its monotone, and the rapids of the river mingled their lighter and varying music; and the frost soon covered the ground again, while our men lay dreaming of home.

Camp near Seneca, Md., Nov. 22, 1861.

December 20, 1861

Letter from the Army.
Camp Hicks, near Frederick, Md., Dec. 13, 1861

Change of Location – Only Twenty-four Hours from Home – Christening of a Jackknife – Making Tea for the Sick – One Poor Fellow Left – Scenes among the Sick – March of the Brigade – Camping at Night – Hunting the "Branch" – Fifteen Miles in Four Hours and a Quarter – the Orders Concerning Chaplains.

The change in our situation, since I wrote last, is delightful. Moving hither from "Seneca Creek," or "Muddy Branch," or "Near Darnestown," we came out of the malaria of the Potomac, into pure country air; out of a shelterless, dismal field, into a pleasant grove, gently sloping to the south, where the warm sun lies beautifully down; and out of barbarism into civilization. We hear, by night, the hours struck. We hear the whistle of the locomotive near us, and think how, though five hundred miles from home, that power would take us there in twenty-four hours. We hear, on the Sabbath, the church-going bell," and how pleasantly its music rolls over the intervening three miles and a half, -- after our nearly six months' deprival of such a sound.

We had had rumors of removal for several weeks. But nobody paid any regard to them until orders came to send away the sick men of the Division by canal. This was as certain a precursor of marching as though the orders were published.

It was on Saturday that the first departure of the sick took place, near two weeks ago. They were to go to hospital at Washington, some twenty-five miles off. So our own sick men were sent down to the canal-lock, about a mile from us, there to join with those of other regiments. Special duty led me there, and we were at the lock about half an hour after noon. We had sent over twenty men, and from all the regiments there were between thirty and forty ambulance loads, carrying nearly two hundred.

While awaiting the boat, we built a rousing good fire under the shelter of an abutment. When I was a boy I always was particular about the first use of a new *knife*, and I had frequent occasions to try new ones, inasmuch as I lost so many that my indulgent father used to joke me with the statement that if knives would sprout, our yard would be full of jack-knife trees. Well, I shall always entertain great regard for *this* knife (a capital one just sent me by that same good father,) from the fact that its christening took place in whittling shavings to kindle the fire. For one side of that fire was a rock; on the other we drove a crotched stick; and across we put another stick, on which we hung a borrowed kettle, and in that kettle we boiled water, of which our hospital attendants made tea for the sick men, followed by good beef tea as food. Two things are to be noted about the fire, for the benefit of future laborers; first, it took one man extra with a dipper, to put out the fire; and, secondly, I thought it discreet not to ask where the wood came from, the men's sickness overruling my – curiosity.

We tried to keep up the men's spirits, and they did act nobly. The boat came, and was loaded. I was the last out, and found the advantage of a pair of stout arms with which to pull myself up six or seven feet. The boat started with its precious freight, and many hand-pressures and "God bless you's."

There was not room for all, and quite a number remained for another day or so. Of those left behind, several were placed in the two houses snug by. Our surgeon and assistant surgeon took care of our own men and some others; found beds for them; appointed nurses; secured sentries; provided food, and furnished necessaries. One poor fellow of another regiment excited my pity. He was sitting alone, on a bench in a kind of entry, and leaning in the corner of the room. I spoke with him. He told me his regiment. He had been brought down there, placed in a corner, and, by some accident, left. The boat had gone without him. His knapsack had gone aboard. The persons in charge of him had gone back to camp. He had no food. He was convalescent from typhoid fever, but was entirely helpless form difficulty in the hip. Our assistant surgeon needed only the sight of him to provide for him, and the warm-hearted men of the Second were ready to take care of him.

So they did of others, one of whom was too sick – a cavalry man – to be moved further.

On Monday the remainder were to go – by canal up to the Point of Rocks on the Baltimore and Ohio Railroad, and thence to Frederick. So, Sunday evening, I accompanied the Assistant Surgeon and Ward Master to the houses occupied by the sick. It was dark, and we picked our way by the light of a lantern, down through the plowed fields, and over little brooks. At one house, a sutler's establishment was open for trade, but we were not in that line. Our sick men were doing well. In one room lay several of them, comfortably provided for, -- a low – in a mean locality – and with beds upon the floor, but still very comfortable, thanks to our medical and hospital men. And poor as was the place, and dim as its one candle left it, it was a spot where our Lord stood with us, and where the hearts of the sick soldiers were refreshed. Even there were words of praise from spirits which had "peace and joy in believing." But the sick cavalry man was without his senses.

On Monday the second party from the Division went. This time *our* Assistant Surgeon had charge. The boat was ready at the time. The ambulance drivers reported to him, and he saw to the embarkation. He saw that nurses did their duty. It was by night they went, but when morning came, he roused up the attendants, and had warm, relishing food provided. He drove away the whiskey dealers at Point-of-Rocks, and though they had to wait there awhile, the train came at last, and carried them safely to a good hospital in Frederick. But, one of our men, a mere boy rather, taken out of a hospital at Darnestown, died the next day, and Wisconsin men fired the vollies over his grave, as we buried him. All the sick, save a few to go with the Regiments, thus were carried away. Not *all* thus. When the last party started, the cavalry soldier was dead.

On Tuesday our Brigade started. The march was like all others, save that both days were very cold. The first day we went to Barnesville, a Maryland village of the genuine kind. Feeling *figurative*, I counted the number of houses; twenty-six. I mistook barns for houses, or houses for barns in several intricate cases. We camped in a beautiful wood. It is strange how dreary a wood or field looks in a cold day, as your Regiment enters it; and how cheerful it becomes as tough arms raise the city of tents, and build huge roaring fires. So it was here. The next morning reveille beat at a quarter past four. It was cold work to toss aside our blankets and leave our heaps of straw, in the raw air. Great fires again thawed out the chill. Hunger vanished soon. You never appreciate coffee till you try it before daylight, in camps, of a cold morning, -- after having attended to a moderate toilet by the light of a candle for which a two-bladed knife furnishes a candlestick, -- one blade horizontal in a tree, and a smaller pointing up at right angles with the candle stuck upon it. Probably you never yet have learned how good a dish is made of hard biscuit fried with salt pork; though the flavor depends somewhat upon a hard march the day before, a raw morning, and before sunrise.

Between six and seven we were moving again. Down came the tents as the final roll of the "general" beat; into wagons went tents and baggage. The line is formed among the trees. "Forward!" And just as dawn was disclosing "Old Sugar Loaf," – the Kearsarge or Ascutney of this region, the Regiment plunged down into the valley mists which wrapped its base.[73]

The road was beautiful; only with cold fingers and feet, it is hard to appreciate scenery. In summer it must be delightful – winding around the base of Sugar Loaf, over a spur of it, along by tossing brooks, fording shallow streams, -- it reminded one of New England Mountain Scenery. The reminder was not in customs nor idioms. Calling at a small house whose joint proprietors were doing a brisk business in coffee and pies, and where I made acquaintance with four or five broad-faced, good-natured children, I was amused to hear the father tell one to "go hunt the brank." I ventured to inquire the meaning, and learned that "the branch" was the *brook*, and "hunting" it, meant to wash his face in it. I was equally interested in learning that the title of "Koot," which one little girl bore, was intended as "the short" for "Margaret Adelaide," as the mother informed me, after asking the father what the child's name was. But the poor family – none of whose children go to school – is the first family on any road in Maryland – rich or poor – which I have known to decline receiving pay for a cup of coffee or other little luxury. Of course I felt obliged to leave a little token with "Koot."

That day brought us to "near Frederick." That day? Four hours and a quarter took our Regiment *fifteen miles*, the Field officers marching on foot with their men, the whole distance. Then, in a bleak field, and in a cold wind, we stood three hours

---

73 Mt. Kearsarge is a mountain in Wilmot, NH, near Lake Sunapee, while Ascutney is in Weathersfield, VT. Both are prominent peaks in their region.

and a half, waiting for orders where to camp. We were then sent to a spot near the Monocacy bridge, and pitched our tents, and spread our straw, and built our fires.

Next morning we were sent to this beautiful camp ground. Our camp is always famous for its neatness. And here, underbrush has been cut up by the roots, every leaf swept off, and trees trimmed of low branches. We have the right of the line, the 16th Indiana is next to us, the 30th Pennsylvania[74] a little in the rear, and the 12th Massachusetts on the left.

Our regiment acted admirably in this moving. They never marched better. They behaved well. There was little drinking, and no disorder. Nor can it be said of many regiments anywhere that one marched fifteen miles in four hours and half, with forty pounds of load per man, and came in entire, and in marching order. It could not be said of us, as one officer said of another regiment, (his own) on the road, "The – had a gay old drunk last night, officers and men." Our officers did not, as did multitudes, rush into Frederick for comfortable beds and coal fires at hotels; for our commander is too old a soldier to leave his men under canvas in cold weather, and take to luxurious shelter himself; and he has too good officers to expect worse to them. In fact, if his chaplain had asked for leave to join a small swarm of chaplains (none Massachusetts) at hotels in Frederick, he would have found something else on his Colonel's face than the kind look he is in the habit of seeing.

Though I have perhaps taken too much room already, you must let me say a word on the recent orders as to chaplains, concerning dress, &c. It is said, in some papers, that many chaplains are dissatisfied. This may be true at Washington, but it is not so in this division. It is perhaps pleasing to me that the simple dress now prescribed is the precise one stated to me as proper by our commander, when I was leaving home, and which, of course, I adopted. The shoulder straps, gilt buttons,

---

74 The history of this brief regiment is every bit equivalent to the chaos and disorganization that doomed its existence. Raised in the Philadelphia area on the authority of the Secretary of War and not State authorities, the regiment was sent to Darnestown as the "30th Pennsylvania" with a battalion of only 600 men and not part of the State quota. Shortly after arriving in Darnestown, it was added to the Pennsylvania Line and re-named the 66th Pennsylvania. Because of its disorganization and lack of numbers, the Governor of Pennsylvania ordered it broken up and the men amalgamated with the 73rd and 99th Pennsylvania Infantry. Hawks; "66th Pennsylvania Infantry." And, Bates; *History of Pennsylvania Volunteers.*

and swords, on some chaplains, have always excited the ridicule of army officers. The less a chaplain assumes to be a military man, the better. His influence is that of a *Christian minister*. Men expect that, but they do not expect a mere preaching officer. As to rank, due respect, &c., a chaplain needs no military ranks, nor exacted salutations. As General Scott informed a Committee, a chaplain will secure that position his qualities entitle him to occupy; that is, when *officers* are *gentlemen*. Some regiments – many – have officers not what they should be, and there the best of chaplains find trouble. But the reverse is sometimes true. In this division, we are glad of a new regulation. We believe that a chaplain's position is too noble for him to need gilt and tinsel. General Jackson once told a minister applying for an office, "ye have a higher office than is in my power to bestow." So has a chaplain, but it is not a military office; it is that of friend, spiritual adviser, and helper, to both officer and private alike. With such material as our noble Second has, God bless it, a chaplain feels no lack of rank or show.

    A. H. Q.

December 27, 1861

The Two Months "Near Darnestown."
By Rev. A. H. Quint

I wrote you of our march from Seneca, or "near Darnestown." But I cannot leave that place without a parting salutation. There, our Regiment spent more than two months, varied only by a location in three different places, and of a hasty march to the mournful Conrad's Ferry. There, we made acquaintances, and, what interested me more, I had some clerical duties to perform not usually falling to the lot of chaplains in marching Regiments, viz: I married one couple, and I baptized two children. The bridegroom was one of our own men. The children were in two families at Seneca. Both kinds of service were performed with great satisfaction – especially the latter. The latter, especially, not only because my confidence in God's covenant with Christian parents had long ago forgotten early doubts; but also from the lesser motive – call it not selfish – that it was a luxury to see a helpless little babe. To hear one *cry*, even, is a comfort to one deprived of the privilege he had at home. I wonder I was ever impatient at it. I mourn over former hard-heartedness. I warn every father against recklessness in this particular. I beg my ministerial brethren, especially, to guard against any possible fretfulness on this account, even though it be Saturday evening, and to-morrow's sermon yet remains a "skeleton." Do not say to faithful mother or careful nurse, "why don't your hush that baby?" Soberly now. Thank God there is one to hush. Take it in your arms, and let its head rest trustingly on your shoulder, O strong man, and so learn yourself, how to rest as confidingly on God's strong arm and loving heart. "For as a father pitieth his children, so the Lord pitieth them that put their trust in Him." For, if that little one leave you,

you will be sad for many a year, believe me, over every impatient and stern word, though those words were only the ripples on the surface of your tide of love.

But about leaving Darnestown.

First of all, spell it with an *e*. Mr. Darne, whose father's name and residence gave title to the place, spells it with an *e*. In ingenuity of nomenclature, they seldom rise, in these parts, above attaching some termination to the name of a prominent resident. Thus came Harper's Ferry, Clarks-burg, Hyattstown, Pools-ville, Buckey-town. Darnestown itself is a little village on the road from Washington to Poolsville, which runs almost as parallel with the Potomac as the crooked character of that river allows, and about twenty-five miles from Washington. Most of its houses are of the log-and-mud style. It boasts no hotel, though some hospitable people would afford entertainment for man and beast. It had three "country" stores, where hard ware, dry goods, groceries, boots and shoes, quack medicines, and whiskey were sold in rather small quantities – barring the whiskey as to the *small*. There was a blacksmith shop, but no shoemaker's. A Post Office was in one of the stores, and before our advent, a stage-coach passed up through one day and down through the next. The few houses of more than usual pretension, would hardly pass muster in a New England village, and the poorer ones were sadly dilapidated. "These build-ings seem out of repair," it was said one day to a native. "Wal, yes," was the reply. "Why don't the people repair them?" "Wal, we kinder take things easy, and when they tumble down, we build up new ones," – a work which several gave indications of soon needing. Two or three houses were enclosed with fences, and had a few flowers in front; but as a whole, the village of one street was of the Rip Van Winkle order, where you would and sill see, black women cutting fire wood before the door, while a white man sat on the door step lazily smoking his pipe, and the pigs enjoying the free use of the road, too lazy to move out of the way of the infrequent traveler.

But Darnestown woke up one day. A division of the army grouped itself on either side. The pigs and the wood-cutting went on the same, but sentries at the doors of the shops interfered sadly with the sale of whiskey. Along the street was run a telegraph office. Coaches ran every day. Soldiers lounged about. Regiments moved up and down. Dragoon orderlies cantered up and down at all hours. Trade inflated. The at first bewildered traders increased their stock of goods. Peddlers came. Daguerreotype artists extemporized small buildings. From a gimlet to a pair of boots, (marked Claflin, Boston,) whatever you wanted was of Yankee make, save the execrable pies which flooded the country, unmistakably Darnestown. Darnestown went to making money with more than Yankee shrewdness, and Darnestown – was Union – when the army came.

Of schools – there was one little building, but the frightened school ma'am vanished, and the schoolhouse became a peddler's shop. The principal school was at Rockville, ten miles off. I asked one man, a magistrate a mile away, what a little building in his yard was erected for. "The front room for a store, the back for a school room." Then he and a neighbor discussed the several teachers. One in particular, they agree upon as an excellent teacher, a thorough teacher. They paid him three dollars and a half per quarter for each scholar. "But we had to give him up," said the owner, "he got the children along as far as he could go, but he had never learned the *higher* branches, such as grammar and geography, and we had to let him go." In one house of a family of pretension, I was told that only four books were discernible, a Bible, a Prayer-Book, a catalogue of some school, and some work of fiction, whose name I now forget.

There are two churches at Darnestown, at opposite extremities of the village; or rather, each is a little out of the village. One is Old School Presbyterian; the other, Baptist. The meeting-house of the latter is log-and-mud, and open to the roof. It has, of course, a negro gallery, entirely separating the black from the white Christians, and reached by a staircase built outside. It is very comforting to know that by this arrangement, there is no possible danger of contamination. The Presbyterian church is quite a handsome building, framed, boarded, and painted a neutral tint. *Its* gallery is reached by a staircase *inside*; and the basement, has, I think been sometimes used as a school-room. Neither church had preaching every Sabbath. The Baptist was open about once a month; the Presbyterian, once in two weeks. Neither of the preachers was a resident, I believe; and they divided their time between this place and Rockville, which is a much larger town. The Baptist church became a station for pickets, and on Mondays, for a chaplain's meeting; and subsequently was turned into a hospital. When I saw it last a battery was exercising by its side. The Presbyterians, with an attendance largely increased by soldiers, came to have public worship every Sabbath.

As our services were then in the afternoon, I have had occasional opportunity to worship mornings with other congregations. I did so there, at a distance from camp of several miles each way, in the saddle. The first time I attended the Presbyterian church, at the hour appointed for public worship, a prayer-meeting was in progress. Some resident brother conducted the services, and "deaconed off" the hymns, which, though an old New England custom, was new to me. The same brother led the singing, which I should have enjoyed, had he not invariably pronounced the first syllable of each line as "nah." Chaplains were the principal supporters of the meeting. This meeting ended, the minister entered the pulpit, and, assisted by a Presbyterian chaplain, held divine service. The text of his sermon was, "Israel doth not know, my people doth not consider," which he applied to the impenitent. Barring the misapplication of the text, he made a forcible and truthful exhibition of the heedlessness of sinners. The sermon was well written, and thoroughly Calvinistic. His tone was severe, Presbyterianly severe, in which he evidently did injustice to his nature. From his general style, I judged him to be liberally educated, but not remarkably patriotic. His whole sermon was directed by eye and gesture to a small boy in a far corner of the church.

The soldiers listened with attention and respect. Here officers and men met on a level. Here all arms of the service were blended. The sober army blue of our Massachusetts men contrasted with the gayer trappings of New York. The light blue stripe of infantry sat by the scarlet of artillery, and the yellow stripe and spurs of cavalry. Here the plain dress of private mingled with the chevrons of the corporal and sergeant, nor was repelled by the epaulettes or shoulder straps of captains or colonels. And occasionally might be seen the buff sash, and the two stars glistening in silence on the shoulder of the firmly knit, keen-eyed, resolute Major General. The rank was outside. Beneath, were men, each under the same law, invited by the same gospel. Beneath, too, were Christians. In witnessing a division review, I have thought how infantry, artillery, cavalry, engineers, though distinct in dress, and arms, and drill, are yet animated by one principle; the infantry may have the Enfield rifle, or the Springfield, the smooth bore, or the altered lock, and yet do service in harmony; even every regiment has its two flags, one its State banner, with its own name thereon, the other, loftier, the stars and stripes; and yet all form one army, whose great center of fealty is the flag; so all Christians, though equipped differently, mayhap, and marching to a special flag of its own, yet bear above that the banner of the cross, and form a great unit, acknowledging allegiance to its one great captain, Jesus Christ. How paltry are all quarrelings among Christians, as to what arm of the service one belongs, or what dress he wears. The Banner, the Great Banner! The Captain, the Great Captain!

In the rear of this church is a burial ground, the one most used. Not many graves were there till we came, but there used to grown larger every week, a row of single graves placed side by side. They are the graves of soldiers. And here, on many a day, the village people used to stroll along as the muffled drum passed by, and curiously, yet sympathizingly, see the burial, and hear the three vollies over the open grave, and wonder where his home had been, and whether he had a mother. And they were often kind to our poor sick soldiers, for which, the blessing of our Lord be upon them!

There were good Christians there, too. I made some friendships, though they were not with any of the high in their own estimation, but with the more humble. Those of self-importance were generally Secessionists. In some families were many religious books, and I respect one good man, who came to our Regiment with tracts, only to find more there than he probably ever saw at once before. The family were I baptized the one child was Union. I hope to see yet, in future years, that little one, who knew or seemed to know, when my hand held her, and always smiled when I took her. That family was sorry that we must leave. They said that with other regiments near them before, they had been in constant fear, and constantly suffering loss. But the SECOND MASSACHUSETTS had been orderly, courteous and kind, and had been a protection. The reason was, we have Men, and we have Officers. Many other Regiments have *one*, but not *both*.

> "The other child I shall never see on earth. He has already gone;
> "And we know, for God hath told us this,
> That he is now at rest.
> Whither other blessed children are,
> On the Saviour's loving breast."

Camp Hicks, near Frederick, MD.,
Dec. 19, 1861

1862

The 2nd Massachusetts Volunteer Infantry in 1862

Beginning in February of 1862 the 2nd Massachusetts left Harper's Ferry and took up an occupation of Charlestown, WV moving down into Winchester following General Thomas J. "Stonewall" Jackson's evacuation of that town. The 2nd took the advance of the column and was responsible for sending out skirmishers and flankers as a precaution. A section of Cothran's battery provided artillery support and counter battery fire when the Confederate artillery set up to slow the pursuit of Banks' army. It was in this way that the 2nd had their first man, Private Wallace Bonney of Company I, wounded by enemy fire.

Here, just outside Edinburg, the column spent two weeks resting and resupplying. They resumed their march southward, marching all the way to Harrisonburg, Virginia when orders from the War Department ordered General Banks to retire back to Strasburg. Strasburg, Virginia was, says Quint, the "dirtiest, meanest town of all the dirty, shiftless villages of the valley."[75] Here they were ordered by the War Department to spend the summer of 1862.

Since Strasburg sits at the top of the Shenandoah Valley bottlenecking any advance up the valley towards Snickers Gap or Harpers Ferry, General Banks sent a small force under the command of Colonel Kenley of the First Maryland Infantry to Front Royal to guard his eastern flank, the only other approach to Strasburg. It was at Front Royal that Jackson chose to strike first, sending Ewell's Corps up the eastern side of the Massanutten Range to attack the small force at Front Royal.

---

75 Quint; *Record of the Second Massachusetts Infantry*; p. 78

General Banks was uncertain what to make of the attack on Front Royal, and only too late did he realize that his left flank was being captured or killed by a superior Confederate force. On the 24th of May, Banks ordered a withdrawal of his forces to Winchester, just thirteen miles away. From Front Royal the Confederate forces took the road to Middletown, which bisected the turnpike from Strasburg to Winchester.

Despite a few attempts by Confederate cavalry to harass the head of the Union column, Banks and the first brigade of men made it through to Winchester with some ease. The second brigade, commanded by Colonel Gordon and containing the 2nd Massachusetts made it as far as Bartonville before being turned back to act as a rear guard when the Union cavalry was cut off by Confederate forces.

Reaching Newtown (present day Stephens City), Gordon found the 27th Indiana holding a position just north of the town and utilizing their artillery to fire upon Confederate forces holding the town. Gordon sent the 2nd Massachusetts into Newtown supported by the 27th Indiana and two sections of artillery to take the town, which they did, driving the Confederates back to a height just south of Newtown. While they held back the Confederate tide the 2nd Massachusetts used their national colors to signal Brigadier General Hatch and his cavalry that Newtown was still in Union hands if he could safely reach their lines, which he did with significant losses.

At nightfall, Colonel Gordon ordered his small command to retire to Winchester, with the 2nd Massachusetts acting as rearguard for the withdrawal. From that position in the column, the 2nd Massachusetts fought a rearguard action against General Jackson's cavalry pulling out an old Napoleonic tactic of "forming square" against cavalry. As the resistance to his cavalry stiffened, Jackson called up a regiment of Virginia infantry to drive off the 2nd Massachusetts which they did, receiving and inflicting heavy losses. Lacking ambulances to carry his wounded, they were instead transported on the gun carriages.

Upon reaching Kernstown, just a mile and a half outside of Winchester the 2nd Massachusetts stopped to wait for ambulances and conveyed their wounded into a brick house where they could be better seen to by the surgical staff. The Confederate army came upon them again and despite determined resistance on the part of the 2nd Massachusetts the regiment was forced to continue their march leaving their wounded and medical staff to be captured by the Confederate forces. The 2nd Massachusetts arrived in Winchester at 2 A.M. on May 25th having marched and fought all day. The loss of the Regiment was 3 killed and 17 wounded.[76]

The 2nd Massachusetts barely had time to sit down among the relative safety of their comrades at Winchester when Jackson and his army appeared in force. General Banks brought his army into line and the 2nd Massachusetts took their place in the center of the right wing on the edge of Bower's Hill. The regiment successfully defended their position even after the two regiments on their right broke, leaving the 2nd Massachusetts to suffer a flanking fire from the Confederate forces.

As Jackson poured more and more troops onto Bank's right flank, the decision was made to retire to the relative safety of Williamsport, Maryland. Banks withdrew his army through Winchester, and up the Martinsburg Pike to the Potomac River just opposite Williamsport. The 2nd Massachusetts with other members of their brigade held the southern approaches to the river while the rest of Banks' force and the remaining baggage trains crossed over, when they joined them. In the engagement at Winchester the 2nd Massachusetts lost 17 men killed, 47 wounded, including Capt. Mudge and Lt. Crowninshield, and 84, notably Major Dwight, were listed as missing.[77]

On the 10th of June, the regiment was again on the move back south, Jackson having evacuated down the valley because of the threat arising from General Fremont's movement from Western Virginia into the middle part of the Shenandoah Valley, threatening to cut off the communication and supply lines of General Jackson. The 2nd reached Bartonsville, just south of Winchester, on the 12th. From this point, they were sent east to Warrenton, which they reached on the 11th of July and then back west to Little Washington on the 17th of July where they joined the army of Major General John Pope.

---

76 Adjutant General of Massachusetts; *Annual Report of the Adjutant General of the Commonwealth of Massachusetts.... for the year ending December 31, 1862*; p. 97

77 Adjutant General of Massachusetts; *Annual Report of the Adjutant General of the Commonwealth of Massachusetts.... for the year ending December 31, 1862*; p. 98

The 6th of August the regiment and General Gordon's brigade was sent to Culpepper Court House in support of General Crawford's Brigade there.

The march to Cedar Mountain was a very hot day, recorded as 98 degrees at 2:00 P.M. and the fighting didn't begin for another hour and a half. Many men fell out due to the heat, one of which, Private Carey of Co. F died from heat exhaustion. Once they reached Crawford's Brigade, Gordon formed his men up on the right side, remaining north of Cedar Creek. From Here, Banks' force of about 8,000 men attacked the Jackson's Confederate army of 16,000 men, though the Confederate forces were not all initially engaged.

Crawford's brigade suffered greatly during the opening artillery duel between the Union and Confederate forces, and an ill-advised, un-supported advance against the rebel lines further decimated his numbers and his forces retired. Gordon's brigade filled the space and renewed the attack against four Confederate brigades though Gordon's own forces were in great danger of being overlapped on their right. His regiments suffered heavily, particularly among the officer corps. Eventually Gordon was ordered to bring his men back to their original starting position and they were put in the center of a new line of battle established by General Pope.

Almost thirty per cent of the mortal casualties suffered by the 2nd Massachusetts during the entire war occurred at Cedar Mountain. They had 34 killed outright and another 12 died of wounds received during the battle. 108 were wounded and recovered and 31 were listed as missing. Over fifty of the wounded were left in Chaplain Quint's care in a hospital that was soon in enemy territory, but were safely evacuated during the night to the Union lines. Only 8 of 22 officers remained unhurt after the battle and the regiment lost half of their non-commissioned officers and nearly one-third of their privates fit for duty.[78]

From Culpepper, the regiment moved with the rest of General Pope's Army towards Manassas, though the 2nd Massachusetts spent more than a week on the north bank of the Rappahannock River where they bivouacked nightly without tents or other baggage and often reduced to eating the corn

---

78 Adjutant General of Massachusetts; *Annual Report of the Adjutant General of the Commonwealth of Massachusetts.... for the year ending December 31, 1862*; p. 100

growing in the fields nearby. It was here that they received a shipment of 90 new recruits and the regiment that was left after the action at Cedar Mountain was grateful for the reinforcement.

On the 26th of August, they were ordered to march north where Banks' corps were kept in reserve during the Second Battle of Bull Run. Fearing that Banks' Corps was cut off from the rest of the army they were ordered to burn their baggage and by stealth cross the Occaquan Creek to the security of the defenses of Washington. Gordon elected to keep his baggage intact and safely brought his regiments to the desired rallying point on the 2nd of September. Give a few days to resupply and having a new Army Commander, Gen. McClellan, as well as a new Corps Commander in General Mansfield, the 2nd Massachusetts was ordered back into Maryland and it marched North towards the community of Sharpsburg, which it reached the outskirts of on the 16th of September at Antietam Creek.

During the Battle of Antietam, General Gordon's brigade idled on the edge of the conflict for much of the morning, being sent in about 8:30 in support of Hooker's attack on the cornfield. About 9:30 A.M., the 2nd Regiment with the rest of Gordon's brigade was repositioned around to the East Woods, facing west and when General Sedgwick's troops were routed in the West Woods, the 2nd Mass and 13th New Jersey marched forward across the fields to the Hagerstown Turnpike to stop the Confederate advance. This movement was where the regiment took most of its casualties, including their popular Major Wilder Dwight. Forced to retire, the 2nd Massachusetts spent the rest of the day and night in support of the Union artillery. The 2nd Massachusetts had 15 men killed that day and about 50 wounded.

After the Battle of Antietam, the 2nd and the rest of Gordon's Brigade were sent to Maryland Heights, opposite Harper's Ferry where they remained for about six weeks. At the end of October 1862, the regiment moved to Blackford's Ford opposite Shepardstown, Virginia. Here the regiment was kept in constant watch on the Ford, as well as operations against suspected Virginia guerrillas, such as the infamous Captain Burke that Quint describes in his letter of November 1862. Fortunately for the regiment, their assignment to guard the Potomac crossing spared them from the fatal fight at Fredericksburg in December of 1862.

ALONZO H. QUINT
TO THE
CONGREGATIONALIST

January 10, 1862

Letter from the Army Cantonment Hicks, near Frederick, Md., Jan. 6, 1862

Log Houses – Marching Orders Countermanded – the Men Disappointed – Have Patience – Officers and Discipline – the Great Wants of the Army – Winter – Mrs. Banks – the Women of Frederick.

    Cantonment, not camp, by order of Brigadier General. "Camp," says the army Regulations, "is the place where troops are established in tents, in huts, or in bivouac. Cantonments are the inhabited places which troops occupy when not put in barracks." Then the Brigade is in 'inhabited places?' Not at all, but several regiments have built log houses and so wanted a better sounding name than "camp." As the Brigade order says "Cantonment," "Cantonment" it is. It reminds one of the mince-pies a boy was calling for sale. "Hot mince pies! Hot mince pies!" shouted the boy. "But why do you call them *hot*?" said a disappointed purchaser; "they are as cold as a stone!" "O, that's the *name* of them," replied the boy.

    Several regiments have erected excellent log houses. The 12th, in particular, has built a small city, in manner and quality very creditable. Our own regiment having Sibling tents, with floors and stoves and straw beds, as yet find no difficulty in keeping comfortable. The General-in-chief at Washington says that Sibley tents are sufficient for this climate. *Ergo*, this Division is not in winter quarters.

    It is a little interesting, that the very day when the order went into operation, re-christening our temporary home, whereby some idea of permanence was intended, -- there came a sudden order to the whole division to cook two days' rations and be ready to march at moment's notice. That was yesterday. Rumor said that somebody had been attacked by some rebel somebody, with a force of 17,000 men at Hancock, where is an advanced portion of the Western Virginian force, a place a little west of north from Martinsburg, and on the Potomac; and that the whole Division would go there. But we had had so many orders to cook two days' rations, &c., that we pretty generally believed it would result only in an accumulation of cold victuals. And so it seems. It would have been a smart business, to march sixty miles without tents or baggage, and we indulged in pleasant reflections as to the sleeping of nights. We have apparently been deprived of the pleasure, but it may come any time. In fact, I am satisfied that the chances are against our remaining here a great while. There is no great obstacle to winter campaigning in this section, when the ground is frozen as it now is. When the plan of the proper leader is developed in the several directions which look plausible, Gen. Banks will not be condemned to inaction. Raw troops are sent off in the various expeditions; why are the drilled and disciplined regiments left, except to see hard service? The men were delighted yesterday at the prospect of marching and fighting. They were merry as larks, and packed knapsacks with songs and jollity. But *impatience* is the great danger again, at home. Do let the General's plans work. If anybody wants to urge an immediate advance on Manassas, let him expect, if he were gratified, such a mourning over the slaughtered, as would fill the North with dismay. Do people reflect what it is to make a direct attack on an able enemy, on his own ground, in a place admirably arranged by nature to be defended, where months have been used to fortify every point, where engineers have selected sites for every battery, where a multitude of the heaviest guns command every avenue, where the range of every piece has been calculated, and where an immense and well disciplined army covers the ground? Ought not people to reflect that they *cannot* understand the art of war like Generals, who have made it the study of a life-time? They would not interfere with the blacksmith who shoes their horses; shall they teach an experienced General how to fight?

It is curious to see the queer notions which prevail in some minds. In the matter of promotions, for instance. I saw a few days ago, the recommendation of a particular person for the rank of Brigadier-General; it had four points, and not one of them said, "he has the requisite qualifications!" A member of Congress was urging the appointment of another person. "But he does not know how to manage a Brigade," it was said, "Well, he can learn, can't he?" was the wise reply; as, if you were going to have your watch cleaned, you would take it to a man who "could learn," would you? And you would commit the lives and honor of four thousand men to a man who "could learn," instead of appointing experienced soldiers! And there are multitudes of officers who received commissions because they raised companies, or from the exertions of political friends. Many of them are now shaking over, and in, the examinations which Boards are making, from whose doings you may look out for vacancies. The great want of our army still, is *officers*. And the next is discipline. It is very pretty to tell what a patriotic militia can do, but even the superficial reader of history knows better. In our revolutionary war – often alluded to – it is forgotten that the early troops of multitudes of "old French war" soldiers; and that as the war progressed, the constant entreaties of Washington were asking for a regular army, and time for drill and discipline. It was not until such troops were made, that our country became successful on a regular field of battle. Nor, from our peaceful habits, is there that previous experience which can extemporize an army. Our country will never attain its true power, until it has an army; a large standing army; nor, until every man is obliged, as in some European countries, to serve from one to three years; nor until vastly more young men have a military education, which, from considerable observation, I am satisfied is the best that *any* young man can have, as preparatory to *any* profession.

We are having, just now, a little touch of winter. The snow is two whole inches deep. The cold is by no means troublesome, and our men are sweeping the camp ground clean. It has a New England look, and makes the men from Massachusetts contented. Wood-cutters, too, resume their occupation, and things are quite lively. In Frederick it is *quite* a lively season. A quiet old place, rather Dutchy from its origin – the entrance of such a number of soldiers is a comfort to many. Epaulettes, sashes, and swords are as attractive to a certain class of a delicate and tender age, as they have been the world over. Visiting, driving, and party-ing are rife. On New Years, many families kept open house, and dispensed hospitalities. Mrs. Banks' reception was particularly thronged, of course, to a great extent by military but with sprinklings of both sexes.[79] It is not indelicate, I hope, to say that this lady is very popular and deserves it. As an instance of kindness – the mother of one of our

---

79 Mary Theodosia Palmer (1819 – 1901) was a former mill girl who met Nathaniel Banks in 1836 but did not marry him until 1848. They would have four children together. As a former first lady

sick soldiers, was on her way from Massachusetts to her son's bedside. She chanced to be in the same car with the wife of the General, and in some manner Mrs. B. became possessed of her story, and, on arriving at Frederick, at a late hour, she took the mother directly to her own home, at Head-Quarters, where she was welcomed to the tea-table; and, as the son was at some private house, she knew not where, the General immediately despatched a mounted orderly, to learn, who returned with the requisite knowledge. The mother reached her son that night, some distance in the country; and two or three days after, the thoughtful General and his wife appeared, to visit the sick, and sympathize with the mother. This considerate kindness to a stranger, and regard to the sick (who was not an officer) tempers the severities of such a wandering life. And I have myself heard at the General Hospital, the praises of this lady's kindness.

Nor ought I, while on this topic, to neglect the mention the Christian kindness of many women of Frederick to the sick. If I mistake not, there is the nucleus of an organization which acts systematically. And, in that, and it addition thereto, the women here are earnest and faithful in their kindness. Many a little comfort finds its way to the Hospital; many a delicate article of food is carried there. And the very presence of these ladies, as they daily pass through the wards, with a kind smile and word, is often equal at least, to all other means of recovery. It makes the heavy walls look home-like. And yet, there are those here in Frederick who discourage such attentions to the sick. They are rebel sympathizers, of course; and it illustrates what I have so often observed that I believe it to be nearly universal, and the rebels have lost, in their act of rebellion, almost all Christian virtues, as well as the sense of honor. It is a strange phenomenon, but it is true, that from an active rebel, you need not expect, in general, honor, truth, or principle. The public stealings which

---

of Massachusetts, Mrs. Banks was experienced in hosting large holiday levees. Hollandsworth; *Pretense of Glory*.

characterized the Floyds,[80] the Rhetts,[81] and the Benjamins,[82] were in the indications of rebel character. Southern chivalry is a myth. Southern honor is a theory of the past. Throwing off their allegiance, forswearing their oaths, plotting and conspiring, they are corrupted through and through. I have sometimes thought it is like the case of a crotchety, insubordinate, self-exalted church-member. When he begins by ignoring due authority, he is apt to lose the Christian graces, and, if not mercifully brought back by Divine Grace, loses all ground of a personal Christian hope.

A.H.Q.

P.S. The 3d Brigade, Gen. Williams, has actually gone.[83]

---

80 John Buchanan Floyd (1806 – 1863) was a graduate of South Carolina College (1826) who rose to become Governor of Virginia from 1849 – 1852. James Buchanan chose him for the post of Secretary of War, at which Floyd was discovered to be inept, and Buchanan was forced to ask for his resignation. With the formation of the Confederacy, Floyd accepted a commission as a Brigadier General, but his poor performance in defense of Fort Donelson found him relieved of his command. Warner; *Generals in Gray*.

81 Robert Barnwell Rhett, Sr. (1800 – 1876) was editor of the Charleston Mercury who had also represented South Carolina in the U.S. House of Representatives and the U. S. Senate. Rhett was a member of South Carolina's Secession Convention and was elected a representative to the Confederate Congress. *South Carolina Biographical Dictionary*.

82 Judah Philip Benjamin (1811 – 1884) was elected Senator from the State of Louisiana in 1852. Following the formation of the Confederate States of America, Benjamin served as Attorney General, Secretary of War and Secretary of State for Jefferson Davis' government. Benjamin was the only high-ranking Confederate government official to escape being captured. He lives most of the rest of his life in London and Paris. Ritter and Wakelyn; *Leaders of the American Civil War*.

83 Alpheus Starkey Williams (1810 – 1878) was a resident of Detroit, Michigan, in which place he settled after taking a law degree from Yale in 1831. Active in politics, law and journalism, Williams also was an active officer in the Michigan militia. Williams was commissioned Brigadier General in May of 1861 and assigned as a brigade commander to Gen. Bank's Division. William's command briefly joined John Pope's "Army of Virginia" but came back to the Army of the Potomac after the Second Battle of Bull Run. William's was put in command of 1st Division, XII Corps. It is with XII corps that Williams would remain associated for the rest of the war, eventually arising to command the amalgamation of XI and XII corps, called XX corps for the period between the Battle of Atlanta and the Battle of Bentonville, NC. After the war, he accepted a post as U.S. Minister to San Salvador, and was elected to Congress in 1875, dying in the Capitol Building of a stroke in 1875. Warner; *Generals in Blue*

January 31, 1862

Letter from the Army.
Cantonment Hicks, near Frederick, Md., Jan. 20, 1862

The brush at Hancock amounted to little. Of course, the rebels destroyed with impunity a part of the line of the Baltimore and Ohio Railroad, as we had but a small force guarding it. A piece of road of this length it would take fifty thousand men to guard, as each part must be secure against any sudden and concentrated attack of the enemy who occupy the country on the other side of it. The faint attempt to guard such part of the road as is now in our possession, and the entire neglect to open the whole, indicate that the General-in-Chief regards the avenue as of slight consequence in his whole comprehensive plan. A general success would open the road of itself. With a broad scheme in mind, such incidental matters can well be postponed.

Last night there came orders to the Division to be ready to move "at a moment's notice." This old stereotyped phrase has rather lost its force; but this time we think a little more of it, as it came from the General-in-Chief. There were also sent orders to grant no leaves of absence, which looks as if something was meant. It somewhat disappoints the longing looks of some towards a day or two at home, but nobody would care to be absent if there is anything to be done beyond taking scrupulous care of the secessionists wood-lot where we are in camp. And that matters are rapidly ripening to a crisis, nobody doubts. IF Congress will provide "ways and means," and leave the conducting of armies to soldiers, success seems certain. Many persons seem forcibly to think that victory can be legislated, or that legislation or popular preference can make a General. It takes *six months* to make a good infantry private; how much more to understand, not only particulars, but the art of war?

The soldier's life here has been varied a little by a vicinity to a city. Not that *our* officers have been on "sprees" in Frederick, or that discipline has been loose. But a certain number of men daily, have been granted permits to visit the city, and have seen the sights – one of the chief of which is a grogshop every few doors on various streets, where sentries seem almost useless. Frederick is a great place for liquor. And some soldiers will drink to excess. The summary method of dealing with these places would be best; such as our commanding officer took when, a few days ago, it was discovered that some loose literature had got into camp among a class that way affected; he instantly seized all to be found, and had it committed to the flames, when it speedily became *very* "light" literature indeed. The evil was not general, as we have many sterling men in this Regiment; and it was summarily disposed of. The morals of camp, will, I believe, compare favorably with communities at home.

There have been various "parties," and the like, at Frederick. One musical entertainment has also been given, a military concert by our band. The house was crowded; Generals, Brigadiers, Colonels, were there, with plenty of citizens. The music was superb, and received the warmest applause; while the really gentlemanly look of the musicians was pleasantly noticed.

My own work, the past week, has been in different direction – to the General Hospital. It was found, some weeks, that while Regimental Chaplains, visited to some extent, their own men there, yet there was no adequate religious care as a system. There is, as yet, no law authorizing the appointment of Chaplains to hospitals, but, on representation to Gen. Banks, he heartily approved a plan to have the Chaplains of the Regiments officiate there in turn, visit the sick, and bury the dead. The past week was my turn.

The General Hospital is one, established in some convenient place, to which the regimental surgeons send men likely to be sick for some length of time, or to have a severe sickness. It is established in buildings, and well systematized. The Division Hospital is in the "Barracks," so called, two buildings of stone, erected in the time of Gen. Braddock, and in that war, used for army quarters.[84] You will remember that

---

84 The "Hessian Barracks" remain, in part, still in Frederick. What remains is a two-story, stone structure with an upper gallery porch. Two of the original buildings were demolished

Braddock's army passed through Frederick, on its disastrous advance; and, personally, I have felt an interest in the fact that my own great grandfather was in that army, and once encamped by a spring near here; and that no member of the family has been here since, until Providence attached me to this Division in a holier war. There the buildings have stood for more than a hundred years, still strong and firm. The original plan was to build a quadrangle, but only one side, and a little turning of the two angles were ever erected. Nor is the one side continuous; there is a break, and in that is now a low building, used for kitchen and dining room. On the inner side of the building, east of the two stories is attached a covered walk, from which you gain entrance into the dozen rooms or "wards," into which each building is divided. Old fashioned chimnies offer great hearths for roaring fires, cheerful, and capital for ventilation. Hideous, destructive stoves are unknown. (Ought not stove dealers to be classed next to grog sellers?) One room is kept for office, one for surgery, and one for the soldier's knapsacks.

A "medical Director" has the entire oversight. The present one is Dr. Stone, our own excellent assistant surgeon, whose administration warrants the important confidence placed in him. He has three assistant surgeons, a general steward, and a nurse to each room, besides two female nurses, who exercise a general and beneficial care of the neatness and comfort of the wards – and whose kind hands often arrange the pillow, or smooth the hair of the poor fellows with a humanizing touch of home. Of course, there are clerks, cooks, in plenty. And there are good beds, and excellent bedding.

Here there were, the day I went semi-officially, (I knew the place before, for we had men there,) one hundred and fifty-five patients. Most of them were able to sit up, but some were low. One was very sick, an Indiana man. I saw him that day, but he was almost steadily delirious. He was thinking of other scenes; "mother," and "sister," – such were his often repeated calls. He seemed to think he saw them; poor fellow, never more in this world. They will wait in vain. A little change in the lines:

> "For men must fight, though women may weep,
> And the sooner 'tis o'er, the sooner we sleep."

---

in 1871. Modern scholarship casts doubt on the buildings being built by Braddock's army.

He died that night. And next day, we buried him, far from home, mother, sister, -- with only six bearers, the eight muskets, and the three vollies at his grave, but with Christian service and reverence.

In one room, a small one, with four beds, I said to the nurse, "When I was in this room last, there were four very sick men from an Indiana Regiment." "Yes," said he, "and they are all dead." They were all nearly hopeless cases when brought there. And I remembered that all four were delirious. Many, however, very severely sick, are recovered; as many, perhaps, as at home in the same number. The care is good, the medical advice excellent. But it is a solemn thought that almost every one I have had to visit in a fatal sickness, has not had his senses in his last days.

It is sad, too, to see a few cases of consumption. It was easy to know that no skill could save them. And yet, every one "had only a cough," and perhaps "a pain in his side." That flattering disease had here its usual characteristics, "soon to be better." Army life had developed the seeds of the disease brought from home; while on the other hand, it is often the case that apparent tendency to lung disease has disappeared in this open way of living. Some, indeed, who were delicately sheltered, and who sought a warm climate in winters, are now hardened into robust health by this exposure.

But it was not all sad. I will forbear "anecdote." But never have I seen men more open to religious friendship. Many are Christians, and all seemed ready and eager to listen. They know the feeling of a warm hand-shake, and believe in any manly sympathy extended to them. They had some reading, religious and secular, left them by kind visitors, but there were few, very few Bibles, and such were well worn. This latter want is already attended to, and speedily every room will be amply supplied. It would have done you good to see how happy some of our own men were when I took from my pockets their letters, which I had brought from camp. Be sick away from home, in a soldier's hospital, and you would learn the comfort of words from home. And none the less would it have excited your Christian sympathy, to see how quiet the groups around the fires would become, when the Bible was read, and how reverently they would listen; and how many of them kneeled in prayer, and how hearty was their "amen" at its close. In my ministry I have seen many sick. I have witnessed the supporting power of Christian faith in its most favorable aspects at home; in fact I can look back on no departed one of my congregation to whom our Lord had not given a firm hope in Him. But the experience of a sick man among strangers, or at best, fellow soldiers, is peculiar. And Christ is sufficient for them. These men, whether Christians or not, were not afraid to speak of religion – not merely very sick men, but those nearly restored to health. They "hunger and thirst;" and the sooner Congress can find time to provide chaplains for hospitals, the sooner it will be doing some good.

A. H. Q.

February 21, 1862

Letter from the Army.
Cantonment Hicks, near Frederick, MD., Feb. 10, 1862.
Home and Back Again.

My application for leave of absence, after passing through the hands of various military dignitaries for ten days, was granted, and so, receiving it in the evening, I was next morning on my way home. Home, so remote, and yet so near; nigh five hundred miles in distance, less than twenty-four hours in time. The sixth State off, territorially, but snug in the heart always.

First, the camp disappeared. Then the soldier-lined streets of Frederick were left behind. And from Havre-de-Grace, picket and patrol were things of the past. The cars never, I thought, went so slowly before on civilized railroad; but Baltimore, Philadelphia, New York, Boston, all came in season. It was with strange sensations I entered home, after five months of absence. To sleep in a real house; to sit at one's family table; to be partially choked every morning by the *reveille* of a three year old's chubby fingers; to be slowly recognized in the street; to shake hands with the whole congregation; to preach in one's own pulpit; to feel refreshed now and then at seeing a blue uniform of some soldier on furlough; to pass one night under the roof of father and mother; altogether it took several days to get over the "bewilderment." But when a "realizing sense" of the behavior needed in Massachusetts was obtained, the change was decidedly comfortable. I am free to confess that notwithstanding the great advantages of tents as places of residence, there is much to be said in support of the popular prejudice in favor of houses. I detest furnaces, however, and stoves, as much as ever.

If you think such a visit is rest, I wish you could try it. Such a quantity of errands to be fulfilled; such numbers of mothers, sisters, wives and sweethearts to be talked with about our soldiers; such a multitude of enquiries to be answered; such a variety of "letters or *very* small parcels," which I innocently told the public I would take back, and for which I had to buy a trunk! Besides four sermons, all new; but what are four, or forty sermons, when one has got something to say? Indeed, I am satisfied that the principal difficulty in preaching (*don't* say "sermonizing" any more), is in having something to say! When I had the honor of being a high officer in an "engine company," we found no trouble in keeping up a steady stream, even with a "blunderbuss," on the leading hose, if there was water enough in the cistern; when she "drew mud" was the trouble, brother minister!

I am glad I went home, besides the reason that it was home. I did not know how many friends I had, nor how glad they would be to seem me. I did not know how intense was the interest in our soldiery, both as to their bodily and spiritual welfare. I did not conceive of the generosity which said so many times, "what can we do or give to help the men of the Second?" Thanks, friends; the jealousies which have scattered the meanest slanders about the Second, have had no effect; it is still your favorite, as it nobly deserves to be. Our men shall know your warmth of love better, and their hearts will be stouter and happier for your care. And we will never dishonor your trust, nor the same of the good old State, when the time shall come for fiery bullets and cold steel. "The soldiers are always called "boys," are they not?" I was asked. "Not in the SECOND," said I; "our soldiers are *men*." They are; many of them sturdy, noble *men*;; they know they are on a manly errand, and they mean to do it in a manly way.

It seems dream-like, now, that visit. I knew I had to leave, being a man "*under* authority" literally. There was the new parting from the tender but brave heart which bears hard separation and unusual responsibility, for her country's sake; the unloosing of the little arms which plead so earnestly, "please, papa, *don't* go to the war again;" from the church which waits so patiently and so generously for a pastor absent in their and his country's cause. When at the Boston station, I remember seeing a woman parting from a soldier just leaving by the same train, and weeping so bitterly – both were strangers to me – while he was trying to comfort her, and her friends were saying, "Never mind, he will come back again." *Will* he? Never did I so realize the sacrifices this war exacts. Truly, not the hardships of a soldier's life, nor even his peril, nor the taxes to be paid, are the cost of this contest. That is in the tears of many a wife and child, the anxieties of many a father and mother, told to God in the daily prayers of many a thousand households. Never did I so feel sympathy with our brave men, separated from their homes, perhaps forever. It will be over by-an-bye. Many will return. But many? But last evening – it was the Sabbath – as I was sitting in my tent, I heard from many lips a volume of sound which overpowered all hum of camp,

> "O that will be joyful, joyful, joyful;
> O, that will be joyful,
> When we meet to part no more.
> 'Tis there we meet at Jesus' feet,
> When we meet to part no more."
> "Even so, Lord Jesus."[85]

And soon after I heard old "Coronation," it's last two lines rolling upward seemingly from a multitude of voices,

> "Bring forth the royal diadem,
> And crown him Lord of all!"[86]

That shall we do. "We give thee thanks, O Lord God Almighty, which art, and wast, and art to come; because thous has taken to Thee Thy great power, and hast reigned."

    A night and a day brought me back. Need I say I was somewhat restless to see our officers and men? That I used to wonder how our sick men were? The dead body of one of our faithful soldiers had gone home with me; would there be any dead in my absence? Yes, one had died. Delirious, yet the day before I left, when

---

85 This hymn appeared about 1830 and is classified as a "Revival Hymn."
86 The hymn "Coronation," was composed by Oliver Holden (1765 – 1844) in 1793 to fit Edward Perronet's words "All Hail the Power of Jesus' Name." It remains the standard version of this hymn today. Music and Richardson; *"I Will Sing a Wondrous Story."*

I saw him at Frederick, he knew me readily; and my brother[87] of the Wisconsin Third[88] had promised to see him often. And two others were near death, and have since gone. Of the one who died in my absence, his comrades had, with soldierly generosity, sent home the body, and in addition thereto, had added a liberal, very liberal sum from their hard earnings, to help his family. Our Lord will surely bless them. No others are dangerously, or even severely sick. And some had recovered, and have left the hospital.

Are there any signs of movement? I can see none. One look at the mud would satisfy anybody. Everywhere is mud, mud, mud. It is not like New England mud. It is more like mortar, and deep beyond young imagination. Off from the turnpike roads, it is almost impassable for any respectable load. It rains often, and that deepens the mud. It snows an inch or two, and that becomes mud. The comic picture of a wagoner sitting on a fence and gazing intently downwards in search of his wagon and horses which have settled there, is rather an exaggeration, it is true; but it *suggests* a solemn truth. In fact, the embargo on legislation in Congress is hardly more fixed than that on the army of the Potomac. In the meantime, rejoice at the successes in Kentucky and Tennessee. Rejoice at the recent shelling of Harper's Ferry, whereby a lot of mean old buildings which we knew mainly as grog-shops, were burned together with the Hotel of as pestilent a secessionist as ever trod. I shall not shed tears if Charlestown, in Virginia, where they threw water on our soldiers, shares the same fate. In fact, many a Southern town would be improved by a share of the same course of discipline. The rascality of the rebel soldiers at Harper's Ferry, in concealing themselves while a flag of truce was displayed, and firing on the flag coming in return, is Southern chivalry. The running of the gallant Mississippians at

---

87 William Loomis Mather (1806 - 1868) was a graduate of Hamilton College (1828) and Andover Theological Seminary (1831) and was for a time minister of the Congregational Church in Concord, Massachusetts, Mattapoisett, MA, Fond du Lac, WI, Green Bay, WI, and Geneva, WI. He resigned from the 3rd Wisconsin in 1862 and became a hospital chaplain at Louisville, KY, New Albany, IN and Willett's Point, NY until 1865. Andover Theological Seminary; *General Catalogue*.

88 The 3rd Wisconsin was organized in Fond du Lac in June of 1861 and joined Banks' army in July of 1861. The 2nd Mass. and the 3rd Wisconsin would spend the entire war in the same brigade and both had long and unique terms of service. Hawks. "Wisconsin: Infantry:3rd Regiment."

Mill Spring before a bayonet charge, is Southern valor. Two to one is their ratio of equal forces.

But while I found, on returning, an embargo on movement, I found none on the liquor business. I wrote you before of the briskness of that trade in Frederick. On the day of my return, I found the road spotted with drunken men. It seems as though liquor dealers held carnival. It is hard to believe that it could not be stopped. Some Maryland law protects the dealers, I believe; but the power which sends men to Fort Lafayette by mere executive warrant, one would think need not hesitate to pour into the street the stock which, in defiance of orders, is sold to soldiers, and to turn out of doors the fellows who are getting men intoxicated by hundreds. As it is, our own regiment is kept from it as much as possible. It is not good for a trader to be found near our lines in such an occupation. "Your officer," complained a liquor-selling Dutchman, "come to my house and did speel all my leetel peer." "Served your right," was his comfort. If any of our men get drunk, it is not through the remissness of our Colonel. He is not afraid to take the responsibility, wherever he conceives duty to lie.

A. H. Q.

February 28, 1862

Letter from the Army.
Cantonment Hicks, near Frederick, MD.
Feb. 21, 1862

"Why should I write," I have asked myself. Who will want to hear from the army whose share in the news column has for so long a time, been "all quiet on the Potomac," while a series of splendid victories at Roanoke, in Tennessee, in Missouri, have crowned their armies with glory? But, I think to myself, our turn will come soon. Armies on either side, of five times the size of either Western force, will yet have something to do and to tell. And in the mean time multitudes of families are still as earnest as ever in love for their sons in this section of the broad field, by whom a letter will yet be read.

It is true we are still quiet. A skirmish above us, by Gen. Lander's force, is the only noticeable incident.[89] You saw, of course, the order of thanks to that General, and he deserves it. But the implied comparisons in that order are strange. He is complimented for "showing how much may be done in the worst weather, and

---

89 Frederick William Lander (1821 – 1862) was a native of Salem, Massachusetts. He attended Phillips Academy in Andover and the Norwich Military Academy (now Norwich University) and accepted a commission in the U.S. Army as an engineer. Lander explored possible routes for a Transcontinental Railroad. Lander commanded a brigade in General Stone's division and was wounded in a small skirmish the day after the Battle of Ball's Bluff. Lander successfully defended Hancock, Maryland against a bombardment from Stonewall Jackson's forces. He caught a chill while encamped at Camp Chase, Paw Paw, VA, and shortly died. On February 14, 1862, a portion of Lander's force attacked and routed the Confederates at Bloomery Gap. Warner; *Generals in Blue*

worst roads by a spirited officer at the head of a small force of brave men, unwilling to waste life in camp when the enemies of their country are in reach." Who would suppose from this that the other Divisions, though chafing with impatience to meet the enemy, are kept in their present places by positive orders from the central authority? But such is the fact. And if anybody supposes that any General or Division hereabouts *is* "willing to waste life in camp when the enemies of their country are within reach," just let him get leave from proper authority to move, instead of keeping us tied to a telegraph wire.

We have been reading of the enthusiasm with which Boston was alive at the tidings of victory. There was no less joy here. When the information came from Head-Quarters (reliable accounts are regularly telegraphed to the General, and thence communicated through the Brigadiers to the Colonels,) our commander instantly informed the captains, and they their companies. Such an uproar of enthusiasm! Out poured the men from their tents and cheered by companies right lustily. Out came the band, with Star-Spangled Banner and Yankee Doodle, amidst the cheers of the whole regiment gathered round them. You would have thought the staid and sober Second had gone wild. Then the next regiment in line had caught the news, and their music joined in, almost drowned by the shouts of the stout Indianians; and so the next and the next, until the whole Brigade seemed crazy. But who would not shout at such victories over the haughty, lying, thieving, rebels? Certainly they would who saw as ours did, the wounded and dead at Ball's Bluff – for which our Massachusetts men owe yet, and mean to pay, a terrible retribution.

A few days since a few of our men had opportunity for service offered. Orders came to select men from the New England Regiments to go West immediately to man the gunboats for the descent of the Mississippi. Only fifteen men were wanted, but scores and scores volunteered. Our fifteen, mainly old sailors, were joined to those from other Regiments, and left, with a short and stirring address from our Colonel, who has the "art of putting things," and amidst the cheers of the men. The whole form this Division are now far on their way, under charge of Capt. Cary, of our regiment.[90]

---

90 Richard Cary (1835 – 1862) was educated at Boston Latin School after which he went to Mobile, AL where he found training as a commission agent. In 1860, he moved to New

While thus waiting, and impatient at it, our men have gained much in bodily condition, and so far, inaction is a benefit. Few regiments did as much hard duty as ours on the Potomac, for weeks without the use of their tents, and it told sadly in our general strength. The rest was needed. Men cannot be transformed in a day into hardy soldiers, and the exposures and toil of a soldier's life are hard to bear at first. Of all our deaths, the proportion was excessive in a body of recruits who came out in the autumn and entered at once on a service to which the bulk of the regiment had got seasoned. We had a large sick list at Seneca; but now, only one man of our whole number is sick enough to be in bed, and he not dangerously ill. A few days ago there was not one. There are a few, however, in the Hospital, whom it is not thought best to hurry back to their quarters, but all are out of doors at pleasure. It would be hard to find now a healthier regiment than ours. This will save many a man's life in the coming campaign.

Nor do I find that this inaction demoralizes the regiment. I see that some New York paper, to sustain its unscrupulous dislike of Gen. McClellan, speaks of the troops as in worse spirits than two months ago. It is not so here. Our men are in the finest spirits, and eager for work. Discipline was never better, nor more kindly submitted to. Arms and equipments are in the best order. The usual routine of camp duties is not at all relaxed. Comparative idleness, of course, has some evil results. There is, and always will be, more or less vice in a camp of a thousand men; but there is no marked increase. In fact, I am more and more impressed with the fact that in addition to the excellence of our officers, we have a great proportion of upright men, who came into the service from motives of the heartiest patriotism.

Among other devices for this vacation period, we have a small Regimental Library. While at home, I found that such a help was easily procurable, and soon after my return, a good heavy box of standard and readable books came on. I owe public thanks for this, especially to your neighbor down stairs, M. H.

Orleans but returned North with his family in March of 1861. He joined the 2nd as Captain of Co. G as soon as they announced recruiting plans, and he served with them until Cedar Mountain where he was mortally wounded. Obviously Capt. Cary delivered the men to the recruiting point and returned to be with the 2nd Mass. before Cedar Mountain. Quint; *The Record of the Second Massachusetts*; and, Adjutant General of Massachusetts; *Massachusetts Soldiers, Sailors and Marines in the Civil War.*

Sargeant,[91] who interested himself most generously and heartily in obtaining and forwarding the books, -- the nest-egg of which was a kind donation from Rev. Mr. Tolman's church, at Wilmington.[92] (A few more donations in money, left with Bro. Sargeant, would suit me exactly.) If Bro. Sargeant could see, and all other donors, the eagerness with which the books are read, they would feel happier in doing good. Although none but private notice was given to the men, the demand for good and profitable books was and is great. Among those most read, (I take from the book where I charge the volumes, to show the taste,) are the charming life of Dea. Safford, Winthrop's John Brent, Dickens' Christmas Stories, Abbott's Practical Christianity, Dexter's Street Thoughts, the lives of Washington, Jackson, Freemont, Franklin, and Boone, Palissy the Potter, Annals of the Poor, and all the stories of the Massachusetts Sabbath School Society which were sent. I wish I had a hundred more good books immediately.[93]

But I suppose before many weeks our library will be packed up and deposited in the Government storehouse to await a further quiet. That is, when we start for Virginia. People must not think, in their present enthusiasm, that the war is over. Great successes have been ours, but greater toils await us. The rebels still have formidable armies, able Generals, large amounts of the munitions of war, an immense territory, and the desperation of leaders who fight in sight of the gallows. There is much fighting yet necessary; much blood to be shed; much suffering to be endured. There is no less need of patience, persistence, and energy. The spring campaign will

---

91 Moses Hale Sargent (1825 – 1897) was from the Newburyport, MA area and began his career as a bookseller's clerk, along with John B. Gough, the noted temperance lecturer. At the age of 27 he became the agent and Treasurer of the Massachusetts Sabbath School Society. He travelled and lectured widely and continued in the book publishing business until his death. "Moses H. Sargent;" *Boston Journal*.

92 Samuel Howe Tolman (1826 – 1873) was a graduate of Andover Theological Seminary (1852) and ordained minister at Wilmington, MA which post he held from 1856 – 1870 when he accepted a post at Lenox, MA. Andover Theological Seminary; *General Catalogue*.

93 The more obscure volumes listed here are <u>A Memoir of Daniel Safford by His Wife</u>, published by the American Tract Society, 1861; <u>John Brent, a novel</u>, by Theodore Winthrop, published by Ticknor & Fields, 1862; <u>Practical Chritisianity, a Treatise Specially Designed for Young Men</u>, by John S. C. Abbott, published by Harper & Bros., 1862; <u>Street Thoughts</u> by Henry M. Dexter, published by Crosby, Nichols, & Co., 1859; <u>The Life of Bernard Palissy, of Saintes</u>, by Henry Morley, published by Ticknor & Fields, 1853; <u>Annals of the Poor</u>, by Rev. Leigh Raymond, published by the American Sunday School Union, 1862.

be no holiday. Nor can we hope for uninterrupted successes everywhere. Do not call me a prophet of evil; I am only warning against too great security, though without the slightest doubt of the final result. I am cautioning against alternations of exultation and depression. The Southern scoundrels who deify stealing and lying have too much at stake to submit yet, careless though they ruin their whole territory. Moreover slavery still exists. Slaveholding has trained them to be despots, and despots they will be to the end. It makes men thieves, and they will steal as long as they can. It makes them braggarts, and they will brag on the very brink of destruction. When the South is overwhelmed, there will be only an apparent peace; for I have learned even so far North as Virginia and Maryland, mingling with all classes, that as society is now constituted, we are two peoples. Men may cry "peace," but until the removal of slavery is plainly, quietly, constitutionally provided for, whether instant or remote is a small question, there is no peace. Slavery is the root of our troubles, because slavery makes men tyrants, and tyrants thwarted are rebels. On such a question I have no ability to show the method. I only fear two things; one, that in the desire for peace, the Government will let traitors go finally unhung, and the cause of their treason guaranteed a new life; the other, lest in trying to remove the evil, we should, as in Hawthorne's exquisite story of the Birth-mark, destroy the life in rash reform.[94]

In our idleness we read the papers. Heaps of Baltimore and New York dailies are sold in camp, at the moderate profit of two hundred and fifty per cent. We read with great interest of the doings in Congress, for, though temporary absentees, we are still constituents, and will cast a heavy vote when we get home again. If members of Congress could serve a moderate apprenticeship in the army, it might give them light on a few topics. One is, sutlerships. Senator Wilson[95] deserves credit

---

94 Nathaniel Hawthorne's short story "The Birth Mark" appeared in the 3rd (and last) edition of *The Pioneer* literary magazine edited by James Russell Lowell. Lowell's attempt at a literary magazine utilized authors out of the main stream in ante-bellum America, but now acknowledged masters of literary craft such as Edgar Allen Poe, Nathaniel Hawthorne, and Elizabeth Barrett Browning. The story of "The Birth Mark" features a man who becomes obsessed with the removal of his wife's birth mark on her cheek, the removal of which ultimately causes her death. The story has been seen as both a commentary on human obsession with perfection as well as a rebuke on hasty social reform.

95 Henry Wilson (1812 – 1875) was born Jeremiah Jones Colbath and was a leading "Radical" Republican during the American Civil War. He served three terms as Senator

for his attacks on this monstrous monopoly. A sutler has the exclusive right to sell in camp. A council of administration may fix prices, but it is of little avail. Vast amounts of trash are disposed of at exorbitant rates. One great evil is, that many purchasing unhealthy eatables, lose relish for the wholesome food which government provides. While we were at Seneca, and many men were sick of dysenteries, and similar diseases, I knew of the sale in one regiment of *six hundred and fifty* full size, unhealthy, New York pies, in *one forenoon*.

Another matter where Congress would do well to pause, is the discharge of regimental bands. Those who advocate this, cannot have an idea of their value among soldiers. I do not know anything particular of the science or practice of music; (in fact, I leave that to an amply qualified partner at home, who attends admirably to that department, with the assistance of a small specimen, whom I found on a recent visit thoroughly communicative on the fact that "John Brown's body lies a-mouldering in the grave;") but I see the effects of a good band, like ours, continually. It scatters the dismal part of camp-life; gives new spirit to men jaded by or on a march; wakes up their enthusiasm. Could you see our men, when, of an evening, our band comes out, and plays its sweet stirring music, you would say, if retrenchment must come, let it be somewhere else. Let Congress lay an income tax of ten per cent., if it will, on officers, while men at home pay but one – as a reward for patriotic sacrifices; but let the men have their music.[96]

Then you have read, with us, the account of a magnificent party, whose refreshments cost "many thousands." I can tell you an expenditure far greater. There are many sick soldiers in hospitals. They are provided with none of the delicacies of home. In one town, there is a poor woman, who supports herself by hard labor;

---

and one term as the 18th Vice President of the United States under President Grant. In 1861, Wilson helped to raise the 22nd Massachusetts Volunteer Infantry and remained its Colonel for about a month before he resigned to return to Congress. Ritter and Wakelyn; *Leaders of the American Civil War.*

96 A wide-ranging Act, no. 165, passed 17 July 1862, this act required that all regimental bands allowed by legislation passed in 1861 be disbanded. If the twenty-four members of the band were sworn in as private soldiers to make up a band, they were returned to their ranks. If the members of the band were recruited and sworn in as musicians, they could apply for one of 16 positions in a brigade band. Otherwise they were discharged. Some regiments opted to pay for the bands out of regimental funds. "Public Acts, Passed May Session, 1862;" *Connecticut Courant*

very poor, and very hard working; so much so that she has to weigh *every cent* carefully before spending it. But his poor woman deprives herself of comforts, to buy milk and eggs, that she may make some delicacies for the stranger-soldiers in their illness and their exile. That woman, carrying her few custards to the sick men, is, to men, a noble being. It recalls another scene, where "Jesus sat over against the treasury.....and there came a certain poor widow, and she threw in two mites."[97]

The public prints do not chronicle this poor woman's deed; but there is One who says, "Inasmuch as ye did it unto one of the least of these, ye did it unto Me."[98]

A.H.Q.

---

97 Mark 12:42
98 Matthew 25:40

March 14, 1862

Letter from the Army.
Charlestown, Va., March 3, 1862

I will never prophesy again. A little time since, I told you that any movement was impossible; while, suddenly here we are, thirty odd miles off form my last place of date, in the midst of the enemy's country, and quartered, so far as *our* field and staff are concerned, in the hotel of a certain landlord, by an unlucky allusion to whom, in one of my letters, I came near being involved in a controversy from which your good sense saved me. A very sensible paper is the *Congregationalist*, and our men, of all denominations, say its spirit is admirable. The landlord's rooms are unfortunately bare of furniture, as he had sold off.

How came we here? Well, soon after celebrating Washington's birthday, we saw symptoms of movement. On that birthday, by the way, our whole Brigade marched into Frederick, and there met the Michigan Cavalry[99] and the Maryland 2d,[100] and listened to the Farewell Address, read from the balcony. We also took

---

99 1st Michigan Cavalry was organized at Detroit and mustered into U.S. service in September of 1861 under the command of Thornton F. Brodhead. The regiment stayed in the valley until June 1862 when it joined General Pope's army. It lost heavily at 2nd Bull Run, including their colonel being mortally wounded. It would eventually join up with other Michigan Cavalry units to form the Michigan Cavalry Brigade under the command of General George A. Custer. Hawks; "1st Michigan Cavalry Unit;" and, Fox; *Regimental Losses*.
100 The 2nd Maryland Infantry was formed in Baltimore in October of 1861 under the command of Col. John Summer, a Mexican-American war veteran. It participated in the assault on New Bern with General Burnside, as well as the Peninsula Campaign with General McClellan. They suffered heavily at 2nd Bull Run and Antietam (where they captured

off our caps as a mark of respect to the Being invoked in prayer, but not with any respect for the sleek individual who read the prayer. That officiating clergyman was known early in these troubles as a sympathizer with the South. He it was whom I told you of as omitting prayer for the President from his liturgy, and restoring it on a gentle hint that he had better do so. His prayer, so far as I could see was a tame generalization, recognizing no treason, no war, no army; an insult to his country, to Washington, to the soldiers, and to God; it excited the profoundest disgust. Why could not he have been a *man*, and if he could not pray outright for his country, say so to those inviting him? Some other ministers in Frederick are plainly Union; the Rev. Dr. Zacharias will be, when the tide sets that way strong enough to make it pay.[101]

A week ago yesterday we had hints to pack up. On Monday, orders to cook. Then we heard that Gen. McClellan himself was at Harper's Ferry. Then we waited impatiently, until, on Thursday morning, reveille beat at four o'clock, and before daylight we began our march in the mud and mist. At Frederick we took the cars; at evening reached Sandy Hook; crossed on the pontoon bridge, and occupied the empty houses in that desolated place. We did not sleep on feather beds that night; our wagons were in Maryland, and in our "mess" you would have laughed at the scanty supply of crockery, the unmatchable cups, the broken knives, and the solitary fork and single spoon, which we took turns in using; *we* laughed.

Early Friday morning, our Second, the Wisconsin 3d, five squadrons of the Michigan cavalry, and two sections of artillery, were chosen to make a reconnaissance towards or to Charlestown, as might seem best, under command of our own

---

"Burnside's Bridge) following which only 25% of the regiment remained. Many of these were captured at the siege of Knoxville in November 1863. After the Knoxville Campaign the regiment returned home on furlough, a majority of the remaining regiment having reenlisted. They served in the Army of the Potomac until Lee's surrender at Appomattox. Wilmer, Jarrett, and Vernon; *History and Roster of Maryland Volunteers, War of 1861-5*

101 Daniel Zacharias (1805 – 1873) was the minister of the German Reformed Church in Frederick, Maryland from 1835 to 1875. He had attended Hagerstown Academy, Jefferson College (until his junior year) and the Theological Seminary at Carlisle, PA. Licensed to preach in 1828 he first ministered at Creutz Creek in York county and Harrisburg, PA. He was active in the hierarchy of the Reformed Church and a prominent member of the Christian community in the Frederick, Maryland area. He counted Barbara Frietchie among his parishioners. Scharf; *History of Western Maryland*.

Col. Gordon. Speedily we were on the road, the skirmishers in advance, flankers on either side, and pressed forward. The cavalry, with Col. Gordon at the head, drove on the rebel cavalry pickets, and as the former dashed into and though Charlestown, at full speed, the rebels barely made their escape, leaving arms in their hurried flight. Artillery had been posted, and infantry stationed with the batteries, just outside of Charlestown, when Gen. McClellan himself came, and after hasty examination, turned our reconnaissance into occupation. It was the first time I had seen the General, and all I could notice in the brief moments was, that his pictures fail to show what he is, and that he has an eagle glance, sees everything at once, and has the air of one born to command, and able to do it. The next day on came other troops, of whose numbers I will tell you (privately); there are a good many infantry, quite a number of cavalry, and considerable artillery.

So here we are in Charlestown again. Most of the men are away to the war, on the rebel side. What are left look as sour as they did last July. They were very anxious, as they had been told we were going to burn the town. The negroes had been informed by the masters that we were going to sell them off to Cuba, or elsewhere. And leaders had urged the people to burn the houses and retire. But they were considerate. Like the discarded suitor who did not throw himself out of a three-story window, because he reflected that

> "A lover forsaken,
> A new love may get;
> But a neck that's once broken,
> Can never be set,"[102]

So they thought that their property once burned up it was gone. This twaddle about their burning their towns is supremely silly. Suppose they do; *we* don't want to live in their shabby villages. The few traders left have little stock, but that little they are perfectly ready to sell to us, as we give them what is a rare sight here, silver! Their eyes glisten at it. Ridiculous shin-plasters, of five cents, ten, twelve and a half, twenty-five, and fifty, are their currency, and dirty stuff it is, too. Salt is thirty dollars a sack; shoes, ten to fifteen dollars a pair; coffee, none; and everything but

---

102 From *The Despairing Lover* by William Walsh (1663 – 1708).

wheat scarce and high. Supplies will now come in, and trade revive. Our soldiers had not been Harper's Ferry twenty hours, before new signs were out, "military equipments," "salt-fish, groceries, rum and whiskey." And in a few days, the bogus currency here will not be worth two cents a peck.

John Brown's memory is still the center of attraction. Our men came in singing the "Glory, Hallelujah," and our soldier's sing it everywhere. Strange as that medley is, "his soul's marching on," does have a marvelous fascination to our army. The daring and manliness of that old man eclipses his fault, and he has become a hero. Again the soldiers visit the room in the jail where he was confined, the court house, and the place of his execution. The room where Cook was imprisoned, is now tenanted by secessionists, and the court house by the Second Massachusetts.[103] The papers relating to his trial are here, guarded with the other public records, and they excite great interest. Various handbills, ballots, and such like papers, are obtainable, and are treasured as mementoes. A few of them, which citizens have, I shall send the Historical Society.

Yesterday we had public service. It was a great comfort, after quite a long deprivation. The men were attentive and reverent, and the singing capital. But the place made it memorable. It was the court room where John Brown was tried, convicted and sentenced. There seven companies of Massachusetts soldiers filled the room. There was the spot where John Brown had lain upon his litter. There, in front of the judges' platform, were the jurors' seats. The chair which the judge had occupied was tenanted by a Massachusetts chaplain, and Massachusetts sentinels were on guard at the door and gate. There, the first time for many a month, in this town, did prayer go up for the President of the United States, the restoration of peace, the supremacy of law, and the freedom of our country of its sins. Such are time's changes. I did not feel it manly to take such an occasion to trample on Southern feeling, and I preached as I thought our soldiers needed. But who could forget the events of the spot? Let us hope that, as Massachusetts men occupied that place, so

---

103 John Edwin Cook (1830 – 1859) was one of John Brown's co-conspirators in the raid on the Harper's Ferry arsenal. Cook was from Connecticut but met Brown in Kansas in 1856 and became one of his raiders. Cook escaped that night from Harper's Ferry, but an injudicious stop at a house for food led to his arrest. He was tried in November of 1859 in Charlestown WV (then Virginia) and hanged on December 16, 1859. Because of his "confession" written while he was in jail, he was called the "Judas" of the raid. Hinton; *John Brown and His Men*.

Massachusetts honor, freedom and chivalry may yet imbue this whole section with principles which will recognize public morality and the rights of a now oppressed race.

Whether we go immediately to Winchester, no man knows, but one who keeps his own secrets. I have perfect confidence that we shall, if it is for the best. Our present position opens that valuable artery – the Baltimore and Ohio Railway; our communications are easy; and we are in position to do service. The whole army of the Potomac has, indeed done its part. It has not fought but military men say it has done as much. The line of our armies reaches from Monroe to Kansas. The army of the Potomac is the left wing. It, having the most disciplined soldiers, has held as "in a vice" the rebel army of the Potomac, with *their* best soldiers, and thus enabled the right wing to win its victories in the West. Their line is now turned. They dare not throw troops towards Tennessee in very great numbers, as they would thereby render Manassas an easy prey. And now their Virginia stronghold is isolated. If it be of any value, I can say from most reliable authority, that the general plan of operations as now carried out in the West, was made known to some entitled to receive it, as long ago as November – the plan of the senior General. He will yet have the credit for plans which others in their proper place have so brilliantly executed.

Our troops have captured large supplies of food. The rebels have evidently kept this fertile section as a late resort, and have collected and stored large quantities of provisions, which are falling into our hands. But there is more yet to be done than this. It will be strange, I am satisfied, if this section is not the base of most important operations.

For the use of the office, editor, I enclose a shin-plaster – illegally issued, it is true, but good as a specimen; also a rebel postage stamp. Please credit them to my account for that excellent paper, the *Congregationalist*.

A.H.Q.

P.S. *March 8.* – There are no changes since I wrote, at least of any consequence. The rebels are now cleaned out of the territory above Winchester, but that town is strongly fortified – or rather the hills two miles South of the town – and a brisk fight is expected there.

Workmen are as busy as bees on the Baltimore and Ohio Railway, which will soon be open. Large quantities of the iron rails stolen from that road are piled up on the Winchester road, and have fallen into our hands.

March 21, 1862

Letter from the Army.
Winchester, Va., March 13, 1862.

Yes, Winchester at last. We started for this place on the eighth day of July, 1861, from Boston, and have just arrived, contemporaneously with the occupation of Manassas by the center of the army of the Potomac.

Two weeks ago to-day, we left Frederick. That evening, we were in Harper's Ferry. The next morning, Col. Gordon led a reconnaissance to Charlestown, and we remained there, and Gen. Banks, with most of the division, came on the next day, as I wrote before. On Saturday last, Gen. Sedgewick (successor to Gen. Stone) brought up his several Brigades.[104]

Little happened at Charlestown, except what I wrote, -- and one other expedition of our regiment. We had left our quarters in the town, and gone into camp just outside, on Wednesday, March 5th. Our camp was located in the extensive grounds of somebody's residence, -- that is, a wooded field; but the family purporting to be Union, and not wanting Union soldiers very near, our stay there was limited to one night, and we had to move in the morning, to a new field.

---

104 John Sedgwick (1813 – 1864) was a graduate of West Point (1837) and served in the Seminole and Mexican-American War, as well as the Indian Wars on the Plains. Sedgwick was in Washington at the outbreak of the war recovering from cholera. Promoted to Brigadier General in August of 1861, eventually rising to command the 2nd Division of II Corps. He was wounded at the Battle of Glendale in June of 1862, Antietam, and was finally killed at the Battle of Spotsylvania in May of 1864. Warner; *Generals in Blue*.

It was really novel to go into mere tents again. We had become attached to our board floors and few feet of side protection, though I did not part with mine with such feelings as I left Seneca; for there I venerated my stone fire-place as being built of the exact material of the Smithsonian Institute. We questioned a little whether we should feel the cold; but we find no trouble. Again we gather, of an evening, about the brilliant camp-fires, and enjoy the simplicity of camp-life.

I mentioned the fact that we had one expedition. It was on Thursday night, a week ago. News came suddenly to Gen. Banks that the enemy had attacked Col. Maulsby's Maryland regiment, in force, and that the said regiment was "cut to pieces."[105] So the General ordered Col. Gordon to hasten with his regiment thitherward, adding to his command some other infantry and plenty of artillery. It was half past two o'clock, but the Second was soon on the road, and in due time the force had traversed the six miles to Kabletown. Of course Col. Maulsby's regiment was in safety; the whole trouble had arisen from the blunder of somebody, by which a cavalry patrol and Col. Maulsby's pickets had fired into each other. Nothing was left but to kindle huge bivouac fires, and wait till morn. The supposed exigency shows the estimation in which our commander and our regiment is held, -- in their selection for this delicate night service.

Our forces threatened Winchester by four roads. The most eastern was by way of Berryville, in which our regiment was placed. Next at Smithfield was a Brigade. Next, from Bunker Hill; and still further west, Gen. Shields' Division (late under the lamented Lander.)[106] And still nearer to Washington was Col. Geary,[107]

---

105 William P. Maulsby (1815 – 1894) was a graduate of Union College (1832) and practiced law in Frederick. Maulsby served in various public offices in Maryland and also as President of the Chesapeake Canal. He raised the First Regiment of the Potomac Home Brigade raised in Frederick Maryland for three years. They saw service at Harper's Ferry, in the Shenandoah Valley, Gettysburg, New Market and Monocacy. Wilmer, Jarrett, and Vernon; *History and Roster of Maryland Volunteers, War of 1861-5*.

106 James Shields (1810 – 1879) was a native of County Tyrone in Ireland and is the only person to serve as Senator for three different U.S. States (Illinois, Minnesota & Missouri). Shields is also unique for having once challenged Abraham Lincoln to a duel. He commanded a brigade of Volunteers in the Mexican-American war. Shield's was wounded at the Battle of Kernstown in March of 1862. His poor performance in the Shenandoah Valley led to his resignation from the army. Warner; *Generals in Blue*.

107 John White Geary (1819 – 1873) was born in Pennsylvania and studied at Jefferson College, eventually taking a degree in 1841. He served as Lt. Colonel in the 2nd Pennsylvania

who had occupied Leesburg, and could easily advance through gaps in the Blue Ridge towards Winchester. Towards and into Berryville Gen. Gorman moved, last Monday, with one Brigade, but before reaching that place sent back for additional forces.[108] Our own Brigade, Gen. Abercrombie's hastened onward, and reached Berryville towards sundown. I have heard of but one exploit of the Brigade first moving. Seeing a body of rebels on a hill, a couple of shells dispersed them with ease. Possibly the apparent danger of the enterprize may be modified by the fact that the rebel *force* subsequently appeared to have been a farmer on horseback superintending a few laborers at work with a *threshing machine*.

Moving in haste, we left tents standing; nor did our wagons reach us until the next day. So we tried our old habit of bivouac. For the definition of that work look in the Dictionary, being sure to "Get the Best!" Then imagine the place of bivouac of a rough piece of land, sparsely wooded; huge piles of straw accumulated; great fires along company and officers' lines; here and there a half-shelter hastily planned and built of the rails no longer in fences; groups eating the rations from their haversacks, and merrily drinking coffee made in kettles brought on, each by two men; -- and then smoking their pipes, humble clay, and more elegant briar-wood, or

---

Infantry during the Mexican-American War and was wounded five times at Chapultepec. After the war, Geary became postmaster and then Alcalde of San Francisco. Following Statehood, Geary became the first elected mayor of San Francisco. Geary became Territorial Governor of Kansas in 1856, but the violence between Pro-slavery and Anti-slavery forces led to Geary to fear for his life. President Buchanan fired Gear in March of 1857. At the outbreak of the Civil War, Geary raised the 28th Pennsylvania infantry. In March of 1862, Geary was wounded and captured at Leesburg, VA. Promoted to Brigadier General, Geary was wounded again leading his brigade at the Battle of Cedar Mountain in August of 1862. Geary commanded one of the brigades in XII corps and followed the brigade through its whole service in the East and with Sherman's army as they marched through Georgia. He briefly served as military governor of Savannah and at the end of the war Geary served two terms of his native Pennsylvania. Warner; *Generals in Blue*

108 Willis Arnold Gorman (1816 – 1876) also served in the Mexican-American war and was wounded at the Battle of Buena Vista. After the war, he returned to Indiana and served as is representative to Congress from 1849 – 1853. He became the second Territorial governor of Minnesota, appointed by President Pierce. Appointed Colonel of the 1st Minnesota they made the journey to Washington in time for the First Battle of Bull Run. In September of 1861, Gorman was made Brigadier General. His brigade suffered greatly in the West Woods at Antietam, and shortly thereafter Gorman was assigned to command the District of Eastern Arkansas. Warner; *Generals in Blue*

pretentious meerschaum; and by and by, as the tattoo was about to beat, I saw here and there one kneeling alone, reverently, undisturbed, both Protestant and Catholic, and I knew why. And then the deepening clouds grew blacker. Then the wet drops pattered on the ground. Then the rain poured down, and the wind whirled the dead leaves about, and the men lay stretched on the straw-piles, buried under blanket and rubber blanket. Then, after a few hours, the clouds cleared away, but a cold, hard wind blew until many roused themselves and guilt up the decaying fires, and sat in their warm circle till daylight. The sun rose warm, and the birds went to singing, and the trouble of the wet and cold bivouac night was forgotten.

Our wagons came one. But after one night in tents we moved again. Tidings came that Winchester was occupied. Then, at "retreat," came hasty orders to move immediately, the messenger saying that the rebel Gen. Jackson had skillfully marched to the rear of our force at Winchester, captured Gen. Shields and seven thousand men, and that Gen. Hamilton was still engaged.[109] It was a ridiculous falsehood, for which no explanation is made, but it was believed. Our men received orders with a universal cheer. In twenty-five minutes, our regiment, with packed knapsacks and partly filled haversacks, were in column, on the road. As regiment after regiment received orders, ad with shouts joined the line, the scene was intensely interesting. You would have thought it was a gigantic pleasure party. Day was shading into night as we moved on. We passed regiments and whole Brigades, ready formed, and waiting the word, "forward." "What regiment is that?" was the regular salutation. Cheers followed, and when Massachusetts troops thus met, the shouts were tremendous. Mile after mile was passed over. "I wish I was in Dixie," or, "I'm bound for the land of Canaan," or, "John Brown's body," enlivened the march. But as hours wore away, all sank into comparative silence. The foolish tale which

---

109 Charles Smith Hamilton (1822 – 1891) was a graduate of West Point (1843) and served with the 2nd US Infantry in the Mexican-American war. He received a brevet to the rank of the Captain for his valor at the battles of Contreras and Churubusco, and was later wounded at Molino del Rey. After the Mexican adventure, he resigned from the army and settled in Wisconsin. At the outbreak of war, he raised and was appointed Colonel of the 3rd Wisconsin Infantry. General Banks had him promoted to Brigadier General and during the Peninsula Campaign he commanded 3rd Division, III Corps. Differences with McClellan led to his being relieved of command by McClellan, but Lincoln and Halleck had him transferred (and promoted) to the Army of the Mississippi. A disagreement with General Grant led Hamilton to resign from the army in April of 1863. Warner; *Generals in Blue*

called us on being contradicted, at midnight the Brigadier ordered a halt, a few miles from Winchester. We turned into a grove tangled and rough. Again, in every direction were roaring fires. Pine branches made beautiful beds, and the regiments went to sleep in the still and calm moonlight.

When morning came we waited impatiently for orders. It was noon before they came – a tantalizing delay. It began to rain before we were bid to camp only a few rods off. Our wagons were on hand, and we were a city again.

Jackson had evacuated Winchester. He had done it with as great deliberation as he pleased; removed all his stores, guns, and munitions of war; carried off such private property as he fancied; and left naked the small defences, in which, with five thousand men, he had deluded a whole division. "Strategy" is a great thing; but driving rebels at the point of the bayonet is the only lesson the South will ever appreciate.

Of course, if the fact of our position is not public, you will suppress this. But it is a curious truth that while our papers could not publish the movement of Gen. Banks, it had been known at Richmond, on the first of the three days occupied in crossing. Our advance seemed sudden by the Boston papers, but only because you were allowed no intelligence. Really, it has taken a fortnight to get here from Frederick, while no enemy has been met except their retreating pickets.

A.H.Q.

March 28, 1862

Letter from the Army.
Winchester, Va., March 22, 1862

Our regiment remains located as when I last wrote you, though transferred to another Brigade. In the new arrangements of corps, Brig.-Gen. Hamilton is transferred to the late command of Gen. Heintzelman.[110] Our regiment has been removed to Gen. Hamilton's late Brigade, (two others being taken out of that) that Col. Gordon, as senior officer, might hold temporary command. So admirably fitted as he is for the permanent position of Brigadier, it is the country's loss that incompetent men have been bolstered into such places by political maneuvers, while petty local spite has operated against a man who has been repeatedly the resource of our Major-General in dangerous and delicate operations.

Winchester is in "the Valley." Everywhere you see the cognomen. There is the "Bank of the Valley" – just now removed; the "Valley Agricultural Society," – office closed at present; "Valley" this, and "Valley" that. Advertisers have the most complete assortment of whatever goods they deal in, "to be found in the Valley." The Valley is rich, agriculturally. The scenery of the Valley is beautiful. But the town of the Valley, Winchester, is dirty and shiftless. Laid out, they tell me, by Lord Fairfax,

---

110 Samuel Peter Heintzelman (1805 – 1880) was a graduate of West Point (1826) and served with distinction in the Seminole Wars, the Mexican-American War and the Yuma uprising in California. Heinztelman commanded a division at the First Battle of Bull Run, during which he was wounded, but he recovered in time to participate in the Peninsula Campaign and the Second Battle of Bull Run. Late in 1862, Heintzelman was assigned to the defense of Washington DC and he remained there for the rest of the war. Warner; *Generals in Blue*

its streets are straight, and paved with rough rocks. There are exceptional houses of good appearance, but the bulk of the town is mean. It has a medical school, or had; a young ladies' institute, price $200 a year; several hotels, at the principal one of which, Taylor's, a dark and gloomy affair, you can get as mean board as you wish at $2.50 per day; five or six churches, -- Methodist, Lutheran, Episcopal, Presbyterian, &c. Winchester's population is mixed. It has much of what I have seen so often that I think it must be genuine "Valley Virginian," – rather undersized, slight built, thin face, black hair, dark eyes, quick-motioned, regular features, rather sullen in look, passionate, easily prejudiced, without marks of mental vigor, and sharp in trade as Yankees are reputed to be. Then there is the "colored" population in great numbers, -- thick as grasshoppers in hay time. And it is wonderful to see the effect of *climate* on complexion. There are very few blacks here. But from mulatto to Virginia white, there is abundance. A very large number of these unfortunates would pass, but for certain traces of African features, for white persons; showing that, in the course of several generations, the climate of Virginia has nearly bleached the African race. Indeed, among hundreds of this people, I have seen but *one* negro of the genuine color.

Winchester is further remarkable as the residence – when the individual is at home – of Ex-Senator Mason.[111] His house stands a little out of town, westerly, -- a large, square, old-fashioned, white, house, -- on a sharp knoll, -- with moderate grounds in front, -- a sharp flight of steps ascending to the door, over which door is a portico, and over which portico now floats the American Flag. The family, library, &c., left town about ten days ago; the contents of his law-office departed also. Our friend is not popular in his own town. I was told by an old and trustworthy citizen, that Mason could not secure an election as Delegate from Winchester, and that he was considered as not more than a second or third-rate lawyer. "Beef and liquor is

---

111 James Murray Mason (1798 – 1871) was a graduate of the University of Pennsylvania (1818) and received his law degree from the College of William and Mary (1820). He served one term as Congressman and was elected three times as Senator from Virginia. His greatest legislative contribution was the second Fugitive Slave Law of 1850 that was part of the compromise legislation of that year. Mason is perhaps most famous for his arrest while onboard the British Mail steamer *Trent* by the *USS San Jacinto*. Mason spent almost two months in prison at Fort Warren in Boston Harbor before being allowed to continue on his mission to represent the Confederacy in London. Ritter and Wakelyn; Leaders *of the American Civil War.*

all he is fit for," said the citizen. Doubtless his slave-driving manners, intensified in Congress, have some effect on his popularity.

Quite a number of northern persons are also living in Winchester. Some years ago a joint-stock boot and shoe manufactory was established here, and workmen were imported from New England. Some came from Milford in our State. Quite a number of northern-born people also reside in Berryville, about ten miles easterly, where they have been these twenty years. These latter are bitter secessionists, and the former consider it prudent, even the best of them, to be very quiet at least. When the outrageous oppression exercised towards Union men is considered, I do not wonder that real Union men keep still. Of course it is a mean loyalty which succumbs to threats; but few persons have the manliness to do right against public sentiment, or when it requires real sacrifices. The "conciliating" policy also has its effect. "If you don't take the Southern side," says the rebel Government to a man, "we'll confiscate your property and imprison you." "If you *do* take the Southern side," our Government practically says, "we will not harm you."

Yet, no doubt, as soon as our Government shows that it can and will hold the country, the majority will swing around. Virginia is a mean State, at the best. You remember is double-dealing last year, when it pretended to be neutral, only to gain time to plunder fortresses and arsenals; and how, after it had passed the ordinance of secession, it kept the fact secret, and continued to delude our Government. Capt. Baylor is a fair specimen of Virginia chivalry.[112] At Harper's Ferry a few weeks ago, to get into his reach a Mr. Rohr, a loyal Virginian ferryman, he made his servant hoist a white flag.[113] Rohr started to come on, as before, with another flag. As he approached the shore, Baylor, with some of his men, hidden in an archway, deliberately shot Rohr dead. When at the Ferry, I inquired into the facts, and learned that

---

112 Robert William Baylor (1813 – 1883) commanded a detachment of cavalry known as Co. B of the 12th Virginia Cavalry, also called "Baylor's Light Horse." Wounded at McGaheysville in April of 1862, Baylor was discovered while recuperating in a home nearby, tried on the charges of violating a flag of truce and murder in the Rohr case. Baylor was sentenced to be executed but his sentence was set aside by General Kelley and he was taken to Fort McHenry for imprisonment. War Department; *The War of the Rebellion.*

113 George Rohr (1830 – 1862) and his brother were wagon and carriage makers in Harper's Ferry prior to the war. As a loyal unionist, his property was destroyed by Confederate forces. Because of Rohr's murder, Union forces under Colonel Geary burned a whole block of buildings, many of which belonged to the Baltimore & Ohio Railroad.

Baylor had publicly declared his intention of killing Rohr in this way, and that the black who raised the flag was forced to it by threats. And yet this scoundrel was a Union man up to the latest moment! If this villain should be caught, would he be hung? No. "Conciliate." "Conciliate." And this Baylor is a fair specimen of Virginians. South Carolina was bold and open; Virginia mean and sneaking. I respect the former; I despise the latter.

You see accounts of Southern brutality, occasionally. I have never believed much of that – knowing some noble Southerners. But I am satisfied. A clergyman of this county, I will not give his name, a man who only from compulsion became silent, as to the guilt of secession, assures me on his honor, that "Yankee skulls" were hawked about his town after the Bull Run battle, at ten dollars a piece. Spurs, also, were made of jaw-bones, to his personal knowledge. A member of his own church, who was at Bull Run, told him that hundreds of bodies were left headless, for such purposes. But I am not at all surprised. I have ceased to feel any wonder at the brutalities of a slaveholding people.

Notwithstanding the occupation of Winchester by the "Northern vandals," shops are open as usual, and last Sabbath the churches were occupied. I took the opportunity to attend service with the Methodists. The minister of that church was known as a Union man; indeed, a printed sermon of his before the "Young Men's Christian Association" of Winchester, attacked secession without gloves, and it forced him subsequently to hide.[114] I chose his church, because, although the Presbyterian would have hit my doctrinal notes a little better, *that* is rank "secesh," and I will have nothing to do with "secesh" religion, not even in those eminently Christian evangelicals of England who have so meanly leant their influence against us in our time of trial. So I went to the Methodist church. The building is a very substantial and quite well proportioned edifice, of brick, with "circular" pews, an elegant marble pulpit and galleries; and it will be quite cheerful and pleasant when they rub off the lying pillars and recesses evidently colored in imitation of each shade of dirt in the valley. The house was well filled, hundreds of soldiers being added to the congregation of citizens. There was no organ, or other musical instru-

---

114 Benjamin F. Brookes (1820 – 1882) was a native of Fauquier County, Virginia and was a graduate of Dickinson College (1841). Between 1860 and 1864 Brookes was pastor of the Market Street Methodist Church. Holsworth; *Civil War Winchester*.

ment, but a choir of perhaps twenty singers excellently led the congregation. I wondered, on entering, for what dignitaries the alternate tiers of pews were reserved; but they were soon occupied by women. I had never seen this silly custom before.

Rev. Mr. McReading, formerly in Boston, now Chaplain of an Illinois Regiment, offered prayer in a most appropriate, rich and earnest manner.[115] It was a *good* prayer. The pastor preached from these texts: "We preach Christ crucified." "God forbid that I should glory," &c. "I determined not to know anything," &c. His theme, as announced, was, "Christ crucified the center of the Christian system." The discourse, which was extempore, had in it a great deal of thought, put forth in very rash language, and mixed up in heterogeneous manner. It would do him a world of good to be put under our revered and beloved Professor of Pastoral Theology at Andover for a year. The preacher's evident sincerity was impressive. I could endure his pronouncing *soi-disant* "sawy-dizzen," for he did not call "guard" "gorrd," here," "yur," as people here generally do. I could even be willing that he should suddenly wheel around and address the minister in his pulpit. But one thing spoilt the sermon for me. He told four falsehoods.

These: with a plan which could not be decently developed in less than an hour and a half, he said he was going to address us "a few brief remarks;" he *knew* better. Further on he said, "but I promised brevity, and will come to an end;" he was only one-third through! Still further on, be begged our "attention to this remark, with which he would conclude;" but after the remark was attended to, he began on a new set of exhortations. By-and-by, "one word more, which is all I have to say;" "one word!" he talked on to the amount of at least five pages of sermon paper, and had an application after that. I presume that this preacher is an estimable citizen, and, in private life, honest. It is truly to be regretted that he, or any other preacher should thus utter falsehoods while presenting the most solemn truths. "One word more!" How often that is said without the slightest regard to fact.

---

115 Charles S. McReading (1811 - 1866), a Methodist minister, was commissioned in October 1861 in the 39th Illinois infantry and resigned in August of 1862. He was re-commissioned in the same regiment in December 1864 but he never rejoined the regiment. He served in many posts throughout Massachusetts and Illinois. Apparently, Benjamin Brooke, the usual minister of Market Street Methodist Church, had a different take on this sermon than Quint, which observations he wrote in his journal. Holsworth; *Civil War Winchester;* and, Brinsfield; *Faith in the Fight:*

Of course, the Gospel hereabouts is set in a pro-slavery frame. Ministers occasionally own their fellow beings. I used to think that I would admit a brother minister into my pulpit careless of the question whether he was a slaveholder or not. I would not do it now. I will not say that there are not many slave-owners who are Christians; I know some whom I do respect and love; some who labor and pray for the conversion of their slaves as those for whom they must give an account at the day of judgment. But a slaveholding minister – I could not endure that. I am no fanatic. I never even voted a Republican ticket. I would treat tenderly those thus perverted. But this eight months' campaign on slave soil, in localities where slavery assumes its mildest type, has made me feel – and I do assure my conservative ministerial brethren – that the whole system is infamous. "The sins of slavery?" There are none; it is slaveholding *itself* that is the sin. Its effect on the masters is one of its greatest evils; it perverts the conscience, warps the intellect, brutalizes the heart. Believe no such nonsense as that "the slaves are contented." They, with no noticeable exception, *long* to be free. Nor is there any difficulty in settling the slave question so far as our armies go. The property is thenceforth good for nothing. Crowds of blacks forsake their masters at the first opportunity. In this very place, over and over again, do they say, "I have worked so many years for my master, now I want to work for myself." They are docile, peaceable and industrious. They say, "only *hire* us, and *try* us." *Can* it be that Government means to remand these now happy fugitives again to their oppressors? As an army we have nothing to do with slavery. We neither entice, nor drive back. The blacks take care of themselves. I was amused with one case at Charlestown. A master refused to sell any chickens, even, "because," said he, "I must feed my poor servants, who will never leave me;" and he wanted a guard over his property. In a few days his "poor servants" were all gone, and this aristocratic son of one of the "first families of Virginia," was himself taking care of his solitary cow and pig.

A.H.Q.

April 11, 1862

The Hospital after a Battle.

Across the main street in Winchester, in front of the Court House, on Monday last, was suspended the sentence "Theatrical performances here every evening." But within the Court House, in every available spot lay the wounded, the dying, and the dead. On Tuesday, was suspended a notice, "No performance this evening." But within, the surgeons were using the knife and the saw, nurses were dressing ghastly wounds, and, in spite of all care, scores were passing into eternity.

This was but one of four hospitals.

It was sundown on Friday when our Brigade returned to Winchester, after a fifteen mile march, called back by the battle, and I went immediately to the hospitals. It was our great misfortune not to be near the contest. Had our Brigade been there, with its good fighting blood, and the military abilities of some of its officers, with Col. Gordon at its head, there is every reason to believe that Gen. Jackson's force would have been cut to pieces, instead of retiring in very tolerable order. It is a great disappointment to us; but we had gone where ordered.

The battle was fought about three miles below Winchester, on the Strasburg pike. Gen. Jackson's policy had been to keep this whole corps in the Winchester valley, and with constant annoyance by Ashby's[116] cavalry, and the skillful strat-

---

116 Turner Ashby (1828 – 1862) was Stonewall Jackson's cavalry commander. Ashby had been a member of a mounted militia unit prior to the civil war and his unit performed guard duty following the surrender of John Brown at Harper's Ferry. Ashby was killed at the Battle of Good's Farm near Harrisonburg, VA. Ashby; *The Life of Turner Ashby*.

egy of his other forces he succeeded. We had entered Winchester after *very* slow approaches, without opposition, Jackson retiring to a safe distance with his inferior numbers. Whether a different plan would not have captured, or at least broken up, his force, it is for others to say, if they would. Jackson made a great mistake when he risked the battle. He was led to suppose, by information from the secessionists there, that Winchester had been evacuated by all our forces excepting a provost guard, while in reality the whole of Gen. Shields' division lay sheltered by the hills. The information went mainly from secession women, whose bitter zeal led to the melancholy slaughter of many of their own relatives.

Soon on Saturday, a portion of his cavalry drove in our pickets. It was not supposed that is was more than Ashby's lively troops, with a couple pieces of artillery. Some little fighting took place on Saturday afternoon, in which Gen. Shields' arm was broken by a shell. Desultory shots were exchanged all Sunday, and it was not until the afternoon that it was found that Jackson was present in force. Our troops then, at about four o'clock were sent out to the amount of eight regiments, with several batteries. Jackson's, as it appeared from rolls captured, comprised twelve small regiments, five hundred cavalry, and twenty-seven pieces of artillery, of which two-third appeared to be kept in reserve. As you go out of Winchester, the enemy had posted some artillery on the left side of the road, supported by infantry, but the bulk of his force was stationed on a commanding wooded ridge, running at an angle with the road, which is low. Our troops were formed a short distance towards Winchester, in a corresponding curve, our artillery principally on a ridge unfortunately a little lower than theirs, and our infantry somewhat sheltered behind it. Our troops drove them back at first, but they regained and strengthened their position on the wooded ridge, whence they poured their destructive fire. It was necessary to end this artillery engagement, and at the end of one or two hours' hard fighting, our infantry were ordered to turn their left flank. It appears that Jackson had similarly ordered an attempt to turn our right. Our infantry, therefore, encountered theirs, and with hard fighting drove them back. Theirs was sheltered by a stone wall, and did great damage. Their battery there was making havoc, and two regiments charged upon it, and, with much loss, captured it. A charge was made upon the center, the enemy broke, and the field was ours.

But Jackson retired in very tolerable order. He has since kept so. The pursuit commenced the next day, has never, I believe, encountered anything more than his rear guard, skillfully fighting and then retiring. He is now doubtless safely encamped some dozen miles from our advanced force. I read in the papers of the 26th, the following:

> "The loss of the rebels must have been enormous. They have abandoned their wagons along the road, filled with dead and wounded, and the houses on the route are found crowded with their wounded and lying. The dwellings in the town, adjacent to the battle-field of Sunday, are also found filled with wounded. The inhabitants aided the rebel soldiers in carrying off their wounded during the day, and burying them quickly as soon as dead. Our artillery makes terrible havoc among the enemy in their flight, and the rout bids fair to be one of the most dreadful of the war."

Two-thirds of this is pure invention. The rebels suffered, and worse than we did. Success remains with us, and the enemy have retreated. And that is all.

Not all. The battlefield is there. I visited it for a few minutes on Tuesday morning. Whatever excitement there is in the time of action, the next day's look excites only melancholy. It was a raw and chilly morning, and there lay, soon to be buried, more than two hundred corpses. Most of them were as they had fallen, in every position, but most with their faces upturned. Here were the dead, shot in the head; there a limb shattered; there a slight hole in the breast; and, again, a shell had shattered every feature. In one spot was a pile of over twenty, mainly from the accurate bursting of a shell in their midst. In another place, their concentrated infantry had suffered terribly from our musketry. A few soldiers were guarding the spot from all depredation. Women were there searching for dead friends and relatives. It was hard to realize, in that calm and silent air, that a few hours before the scene had been terrific with conflict, and full of slaughter. But the silent and mangled dead bore witness, and I wished that Jefferson Davis could have been brought face to face with every corpse, and it be said to him, "*your* infernal ambition killed this man."

The hospitals remain also. Four places were thus occupied, -- the Court House, the Union Hotel, and two smaller buildings. I was able to visit three of the four, on Monday evening and until we moved on at six o'clock on Tuesday. As you entered the Court House, the outer room was occupied with dead laid side by side, and reverently covered, and each, so far as could be, with a little slip of paper bearing his name and that of his regiment. Passing in, every spot save room for the attendants to pass, was occupied by the wounded, and now and then one was carried to the dead-room. Owing to some strange management, for twenty-four hours, neither hay nor straw was procured, and the wounded men lay upon the floor. When our Brigade came, our surgeons immediately volunteered their services. They were declined! The surgeon's of Gen. Shields' Division "needed no help," when I saw soldier after soldier waiting impatiently for necessary care. The spirit seemed that of some third-rate physicians in small towns, who are afraid somebody is trying to get away their practice. It was only until a most formal application was made Tuesday morning, by our Brigade Surgeon, that the services of ours were reluctantly accepted. Nevertheless, with or without formalities, our surgeons made themselves useful. The two of our own regiment proved of the greatest service. Our senior surgeon remained all night and all day in the Court House, reduced things to order, and proved himself most admirably qualified for his post. Our assistant surgeon did similar work at the Union Hotel. Our Hospital Steward, with his medicines and apparatus, was there, and of the greatest use. Our nurses were indefatigable. Our litters did most of the work of moving the injured from place to place. However much disappointment our Second felt at having no share in the fight, our hospital officials did noble service in relieving the unfortunate sufferers.

It was pleasant to see the gentleness and activity of the attendants. Hardy men seemed like women in the care of children. By and by delicacies came from the people. Monday evening, many people were called upon for beds. To the eternal infamy of this rebel town, it was hard to procure even a few. One man, living in a fine house, had "no beds for damned Yankee soldiers; let them lie on the ground." Women, on Tuesday morning, brought luxuries "for *Southern* soldiers," while with us there was no friend, no foe, only wounded men laying there indiscriminately, equally cared for. Women came there to abuse and insult us, with ultra rebel attacks in the hearing of our wounded men; but they were speedily sent off. I think the kind treatment of their own wounded shamed them into decency; or perhaps a refusal to receive anything for one class exclusively. By and by they came with supplies without specifying for which men. The inhuman feelings of these people is painful. They are full of lies, too; and they have made many believe them. One Confederate soldier was asked, "Do you have kind treatment here?" "Yes," he answered, as it wondering at it. "Why, didn't you expect it?" "No, I thought you would kill us." "What made you think so?" "We were told so." Such is Southern honor.

I had the privilege of speaking with many, many soldiers. Many were terribly injured. Many were soon to die. Some died but a few minutes after. There were various feelings. Some few were hardened, but most were glad to see a Christian minister. Many more than I expected had a good Christian hope, and some who knew they were soon to die, were happy. One man, from a Western regiment, was *very* happy, though fatally shot in the neck. He asked me who I was. "A chaplain." "Of what denomination?" "Congregationalist." "Ah, I don't like them much." "Why?" "Well, I've met some I didn't think much of. I'm a Methodist; been a church-member this long while." "But *I* love the Lord Jesus Christ." "Well, then, I guess you are all right; now pray with me."

One poor fellow of sixteen, from the South, wanted to take the oath of allegiance. He knew he must die, but he felt he had been in a wrong cause, -- his mother had made him go, -- and if he could take the oath, he should feel better, and die happier. He needed something better than that, however.

Others hoped to get well and go home. They would never engage in the Southern service again. But I told them to engage in Christ's.

One man I can never forget. He was a Southerner. One deed had struck him with remorse. I found his story at last. A few days before he had gone out with a white flag, enticed one of our soldiers near, and then deliberately shot him. Wounded now, his mind dwelt only on that. He felt that it was murder. He would not have his wounds dressed. Horror-struck, he was determined to die. He would admit no hope of pardon. But there was an opportunity for forgiveness. "The blood of Jesus Christ his Son, cleanseth us from *all* sin."

Then there were poor fellows whose thoughts were all of home. One mere boy, from Texas, talked of his sister; and he wanted her informed, and sent his dying love. One man, a rebel officer, wanted his wife – in Southern Virginia – to know he died happy, and his blessing to go to his little children. And one had longings for his mother. And so on, on, through the long rows and many rooms. But most were ready to hear the assurances of free forgiveness for sinners through Him who died for us.

Strange to say, I felt not the least shrinking in looking on the most terrible wounds. Others tell me they felt the same. But, more to the purpose, I never felt so strongly the value of the way of life which offers forgiveness to sinners in reliance on the expiatory sacrifice of Christ our Lord. What else could one have to say in such circumstances? Tell them to amend their lives? Many would end their lives in a few hours. Tell them that sin would not be punished? Their own dread falsified that. But the simple words "repent and believe on the Lord Jesus Christ" meets all times and all circumstances. He who said to the dying criminal, "This night shalt thou be with me in Paradise," is able "to save unto the uttermost all those who put their trust in Him."

Strasburg, Va., March 28, 1862.
A.H.Q.

Clockwise from the top left image: Surgeon Lincoln R. Stone; Surgeon Francis Leland; Surgeon Lucius M. Sargent; Surgeon William H. Heath

(Images courtesy of the United States Army Historical and Educational Center; MOLLUS Collection)

April 11, 1862

Letter from the Army.
Edinburgh, Va., Friday, April 4, 1862
Outpost Duty.

I began a letter to tell of our sudden movement to Strasburg; how gaily, at evening, March 25, our band led off with "I wish I was in Dixie;" how cold the night became; how we bivouacked by the roadside about one o'clock, five miles above Strasburg; how, the next day, we forded Cedar Creek, a rapid and beautiful stream, where the villains had destroyed a fine bridge, and were placed just outside of Strasburg, in a rough and delightful pine wood; how, the following day, a "scare" sent us forward four or five miles below Strasburg, where we camped again. But I did not finish it, because I thought a letter on "outpost duty" would be preferable.

So I began to write about "twenty-four hours on outpost;" how, last Saturday afternoon, our regiment relieved another as outpost; how we reached the spot about sundown; how the reserve, the grand guards, the pickets, and the sentries, were stationed; how a patrol went out at daybreak, and a larger one in the forenoon; how the rebels spitefully threw a couple of shells at our pickets; how it rained all night and was wet all day, and how we "hutted" the best we could with boughs and rails; how it was the strangest Sunday I ever spent, barring the preceding, when we watched, at Snicker's Ferry, the repairs making on a "scientific" bridge which had broken down from defects a New England carpenter, earning a dollar and a half a day, would have been ashamed of, -- by which breakage our regiment was kept back, and its subsequent direction changed. But we moved so suddenly, that I got beyond the letter, as we did the outpost.

We moved thither last Tuesday, April 1st. Early in the morning came orders to go without tents or baggage. The whole corps was to move, -- each division. Everybody knows that Gen. Jackson's headquarters are at Mount Jackson, seven or eight miles below here, where they have been all along, and whence he has made his sudden forays. But a very skillful rear-guard, -- Ashby's Cavalry, with some artillery and infantry, -- have been close up to Gen. Banks' lines. This was all that was to be encountered. As the advance of our corps, Col. Gordon's brigade was selected, and the whole was under his management, -- Capt. Corthren's fine New York battery being added, with some cavalry.[117] The next brigade was a mile behind.

Two miles from our camp we halted. The rebel scouts and guns were in plain sight, on an opposite ridge, sheltered in a wood. A couple of our Parrot guns were put in position with great rapidity; two or three shells were fired, and the rebels suddenly left.

From that point, the advance was made in regular order. Skirmishers and flankers were thrown out, a reserve following, a section of artillery next, and then the next regiments of our Brigade. It was new to me in certain particulars, as, although two or three of our companies had exchanged lively shots with the enemy, our regiment, as a whole, had never encountered the fellows. And so it may interest somebody's mother, or wife, or sister, to see the order of moving:

---

117 George W. Corthren (or Cothran) (1834 - 1898) was a lawyer of Lockport, NY and was Captain of Battery M of the 1st New York Light Artillery. Battery M was raised in the Rochester, NY area and served with the army of the Potomac through Gettysburg before joining Sherman's army for his Atlanta and Carolina's campaign. Cothran got into a scrape over defrauding the U.S. Government for moneys paid during the raising of his company. Gen. McClellan dismissed Cothran due to the outcome of a court martial. President Lincoln reversed the findings and restored Cothran to service. Cothran resigned his commission before the battle of Gettysburg. "1st NY Light Artillery Regiment Battery M Civil War Newspaper Clippings;" *Unit History Project*.

```
                    ♀ ♀ D
                    ____ ____
                    ____ ____
                    ____ ____ A


____ ____              ____ ____              ____ ____
____ ____ B            ____ ____ B            ____ ____ B


           * * * * * * * * * * * * * * C
```

A. Three companies, reserve, under Major Dwight.
B. B. B. Five platoons, as represented, with Lt. Col. Andrews.[118]
C. Skirmishers, reaching about 200 yards each side of the road, A being in the road.
D. Artillery

In advancing, C is about 130 yards before B, and B about 300 yards before A. On the skirmishers go, at a cautious but steady pace, over fences, walls, or brooks, -- keeping their distances, each a few paces from the next man, and their officers in command, when nearing the enemy, still they must press on, though in open sight. As we moved forward, the rebels stopped in the woods, scattering as far out as our skirmishers, hiding behind walls and trees, and getting a shot as often as possible. It was the first time our regiment had been really under fire, but it was beautiful to see how steadily they moved on, keeping their distances admirably, and firing at the scoundrels as coolly as though hunting partridges. Both their bravery and their splendid discipline

---

118 George Leonard Andrews (1828 - 1899) took a degree from Bridgewater Normal School (now Bridgewater State University) and West Point (1851) at the top of his class. Worked on the construction of Fort Warren for three years before becoming a professor at West Point. Andrews resigned his commission in 1855 to accept a position with the Amoskeag Mills in New Hampshire as an engineer. Andrews turned down his own Colonel's commission to accept the Lt. Colonel's commission in the 2nd Massachusetts Infantry. Andrews commanded the 2nd Mass., from Bank's retreat to Antietam. Following Antietam Andrews accepted a commission as Brigadier General and Chief of Staff for General Banks as he prepared his expedition to New Orleans. Andrews spent the rest of the war in Louisiana, eventually rising to command the Corps d'Afrique. Quint; *The Record of the Second Massachusetts*; and, Adjutant General of Massachusetts; *Massachusetts Soldiers, Sailors and Marines in the Civil War*.

told admirably; for it was evidently not a pleasant position to be an open mark for concealed rifles. But not a man flinched, and a good Providence preserved every life in our regiment; though blood flowed, not a serious casualty occurred on this contested march of fifteen miles. The nearest to anything fatal occurred to Bonney, of Co. I, whose brass plate on his cross belt was indented by a ball, which, glancing, tore the belt, penetrated three or four thicknesses of clothing, and made a slight wound; the force of the bullet of severe, but the plate saved his life.[119] A rebel dragoon was observed taking near and deliberate aim at one of our officers, but a private seeing it emptied the saddle and so spoilt that shot. In fact, the bullets evidently buzzed thick enough, in the early part of the march, but the rebels seemed to see quite speedily the beauty of our Enfields; and in fact, we learned from friends, in a village through which we passed, that the rebels swore terribly about those " _____ long-range Yankee rifles." Of course we met soon with a bridge torn up, and the beams partly cut. The Yankees of the Second went at it, and in five minutes it was made passable.

At three places they made a stand, each time on a capital spot. They know every inch of ground here, and it is a great country for fighting, as it is beautiful in scenery. The first was a little outside of Woodstock, which is quite decent looking for a Southern village. As we came near the town, the rebels had planted their guns on a hight just beyond, and suddenly opened with whizzing, screaming shells. But it was no surprise. Col. Gordon's experienced eye had seen the capacities of the ridge, and had halted. We open ranks; down gallops the artillery; up to the near ridge; quick as thought our guns were in position, sighted, fired; "whizz" goes the savage missile, flying through the air; then, it two or three seconds, a sullen sound shows that it has exploded, and the pieces are flying in every direction. Then another, another, and so on, in immense rapidity, and in a few minutes the rebels are driven. We entered Woodstock in quiet, and the alarmed people, over whose heads the shells have been flying, came to the doors relieved. Fragments are lying about in the very streets, and one house shows the long scar which a shell scratched, as it fell to the spot where it exploded.

---

119 Wallace Bonney (1838 – 1922) is listed as a painter from Boston on the roster of the 2nd Mass, but in fact he was from Southeastern Massachusetts. Bonney would be taken prisoner at Winchester in May of 1862 and discharged with disability in August of 1863. Quint; *The Record of the Second Massachusetts*; and, Adjutant General of Massachusetts; *Massachusetts Soldiers, Sailors and Marines in the Civil War*.

Then the same long line of skirmishers, for several miles again. Then we approach the "Narrow Pass" – where the river, suddenly bending, leaves only room for a road. You descend the hollow, cross a swift creek, and then ascend the "Narrow Pass" – completely commanded by a ridge stretching up above. There, again, our commander saw the thing needful. He did not hurry up his artillery, but ordered it back, and hastened the Second into the valley to the bridge, halting the other regiments behind the ridge we have just passed, and on which he had stationed his guns. It was just in time. The rebel guns had not fired their second shot, when Capt. Corthren opened with half a dozen replies, and for a little while, the scene was noisy. The Blue Hills echoed back the reports, and the sound rolled up the valley in long thunder. The bridge is on fire, as the rebels left it, and our men go to work to put it out, and succeed. Meantime the storm fell so thick about the rebels, that they were driven from their guns, but the hight and the distance prevented any capture. Then the heathen are silent, and finally are running again, and on we march.

Near Edinburgh we move cautiously. Another stream is there, with high banks, and lofty ridges on either side. The bridges, railroad and common road, are on fire, and the enemy have planted their guns again. Again our guns are hurried on through hastily torn fences, over hollows and rocks, and up on the eminence. Soon both sides are at work; the skirmishers are drawn in; the second is ordered forward at "double quick;" fortunately, for the range of the enemy's guns commands the spot where they had been, and death comes where others loiter. There is a sharp fight now, but the bridge is ours. It is near night, however, and though the opposite hight is ours when we want it, it is useless.

Again a bivouac in the woods, after a day of labor. The Second has been under fire, and did its duty. Its officers have shown their pluck. Its Lieut. Col. in command has handled it beautifully. Its Colonel in charge of the Brigade has led the advance, being everywhere at the right time. It lies down to rest feeling that "the old folks at home" will be satisfied, and longing for a time when it can use the steel. And, doubtless, many hearts remembered that God was their guardian and shield.

Next day was noisy, but that was all. The bridge was rebuilt, while the guns on either side are firing at rapid intervals above. Pennsylvania men did it, and did well. The other Brigades came up, but of their number, or place, or destination, I must not speak even the very little that I know.

A. H. Q.

April 25, 1862

Letter from the Army.
It is a rainy day in camp.

Sometimes I used to enjoy rainy days, at home, and sometimes I did not.
    They were pleasant when one had a heap of odds and ends of work, and a rainy day was so good a time to finish them up. Or, one wanted a clean day for some special object, and had it then, beginning as soon as breakfast was over, hardly stopping for dinner, and not caring whether "The shades of night were falling fast," or slow. But sometimes the rainy days seemed dismal; by reason, doubtless, of a moderate fit of the indigoes, warranted not to fade; or possibly sometimes from some depressing influence of the air. But, on the whole, I used to like rainy days; not merely for the opportunity for work, but because it was pleasant to make a real visit on one's family, which is rather a rare event. I could both work and have the visit. Some people have an exclusive and forbidden study. I could not. If I locked the door, soon little feet pattered up, and little hands tried the handle. Suppose I said, "busy now;" then I heard a good-natured, but self-satisfied and triumphant voice, "papa, its ME!" Who could resist that? ME always came in, and ME and papa had the best time imaginable, to the detriment – no – the decided improvement of writing; and then ME would sit down quietly to play and not disturb papa. Children improve sermons. Besides there are two ways of thinking and writing. Some people think as the horse-cars journey from Jamaica Plain to Boston. From the stables to the office at Eliot street is the Introduction. There comes "first." They jog along to Hyde's corner, and the conductor sings out that name, which means "secondly." At Roxbury is the stopping for "thirdly."

"Dover Street" means "fourthly." And from Boylston Street, various halts let out the different parts of the Application, and the office opposite the Tremont House is "To conclude." And all the way along, you must keep on the iron ruts. Get off the track, and there is a terrible jolting over the rough pavement before you get on again. Indeed, on the track, every stoppage loses impetus; and a stop at rising ground is sometimes terrible. That's a good way for those that like it. But I would rather take a seat with some of my good people who have fleet horses, as I used to do. You can then start when you please; you can stop errands; you can take the smoothed roads and dodge the pavements; you can see a little speed on Tremont Road; and your friend drops you at just such part of the city as you wish. However, different people may have different ways, to advantage. And my way was to have few secluded study hours, but to let all hours be study: and to have the freshness of life illuminating the cold rows of books – which books are capital things for a little girl to make houses of, in such times as they are put to no other use. I would as soon think of shutting sun and air out of my study, as of keeping out my wife and child. There is a salutary warning in the case of that good minister whose grandchild was always driven from his study. "Mother," said she, "will grandpa be in heaven?" "Why, Certainly, my child." "Then it's no use for *me* to go; as soon as he says me, he'll say, what's that child here for? Go right out of my study!" I fully believe that that divine's accurate "scheme," would have the same resemblance to the real living doctrines of the Gospel, as the dry, pressed, squared and labeled, roots and herbs in an apothecary shop do to the blooming, fragrant, lovely plants out of which they were manufactured.

However, I will go back to the "track" again. Rainy days are *not* pleasant in camp. To-day, it snows, it sleets, it hails, it rains. The trees are covered with frozen snow, or half melted ice, and every now and then they shake off heavy pieces which rattle down like fragments of shell. The huge tops of the pines, away up above their limbless trunks, frozen into masses, sway heavily to and fro. Drip, drip, from every bough. Pour, pour, in every open spot. The forlorn horses stand with drooping heads, looking ashamed of their condition and disgusted with Virginia -- immovable except when eating their breakfast or dinner. The pet dogs keep inside of tents. The fronts of our canvas houses are drawn outward and open, and great logs support a struggling fire just in front, and live coals are placed in holes within the tent, provided the holes do not speedily fill with water. Ditches are dug all around the tents, and now and then a ditch runs *through* the tent, as a necessary resort. Dripping individuals are solemnly chopping wood. Dismal people go about their duties hoping to have as few as possible, but of course feeling that, in military service, "to hear is to obey." Rubber coats are in active service, and cap covers and appended capes shelter the head and neck, in the absence of umbrellas, which the government has neglected to furnish. Boots will get wet; the soft ground yields to every step, and the leather greedily drinks up the moisture. The sentinels in overcoats, pace up and down, as steady as ever, but wet, very wet, and with arms sheltered as much as possible from the rain. Off on picket somewhere is a company, and we talk over their shelterless, fireless, condition. The enemy with their insulting, but useless artillery practice from the opposite ridge, are doubtless wetter than we are. All soldierly precaution is taken, and officers and orderlies ride away on duties, but with somber countenances. "Hard business, sir, this soldiering," says John to my nearest neighbor. "Yes, John." "It's aisy for them as sits at home with their good fires, to read of this victory and that, but it's hard for them as has to do it, sir." "Yes, John." "It would do them good to come out here, and try to warm themselves by a hole in the ground, sir." "True John."

The rain, however, does not keep us here, but the plans of authority. Going forward, we could sweep before us everything of Jackson's command, which probably consists of no more than six or eight thousand. His main camp is said to be at Mount Jackson, a little village about seven miles onward; but he will hardly remain there when we go on, at least no more than to annoy and delay us. A small force, his rear guard, under Col. Ashby, remains opposite us, but is of no particular account at present. *Why* we wait, of course, I do not know, but I have no doubt that it is a part of the plans working out. Nevertheless, our men want to do something; their little fighting the other day sharpened up their appetite.

Last Sunday we had public worship again. We had had none by reason movements, since we were at Charlestown. But last Sabbath was a most beautiful day. The air was mild and sweet, the sun warm. So, in a little hollow, near us, we met in one of "God's first temples." Sunday in our camp, when we are allowed to remain, is always quiet. I have repeatedly noticed how still and homelike it seems. Our commander never has any work not absolutely necessary; and although there may be as much evil, yet the stillness is always refreshing. Last Sunday, even the rebels opposite left off their gunnery Saturday night, and waited till

Monday morning, though I do not know why. For whatever reason, not a single piece of artillery was fired on either side, though here and there one could hear the distant sound of a musket. God hasten the time when all Sundays shall be as ignorant of shot and shell through our whole land, by the suppression of this wicked rebellion.

Sunday afternoon I called upon a Presiding Elder of the "United Brethren in Christ," who lives in the village a mile away. He had returned only a day or two before from his visits to the churches in his circuit. I was very hospitably entertained by the by the worthy United Brother, and the excellent United Sister, his wife. This denomination, which was novel to me, seems exactly like the Methodists in doctrine and government; with Bishops, Presiding Elders, Itinerancy, (less restricted as to time.) It is anti-secret society; will not have a Free-Mason in the church. And it is anti-slavery fully. No slaveholder can be admitted to this membership; yet they have about thirty churches in this Valley. They are opposed to war, but many of their members were pressed into the rebel service, and some were swept away by the torrent of secession; still we have many friends among them, and the denomination opposed secession to the last. Since the John Brown affair they have met with a good deal of persecution, which is not strange, when they will refuse admission to the master whose slaves they welcome to the church. Their spirit – and I have seen several members – I like exceedingly, as being meek, humble, laborious, devout.

Anti-slavery, and yet spreading here for years, and with thirty churches in this limited locality. Who can say that slavery could have lived, if the powerful Presbyterian, Episcopal, Baptist, Methodist, denominations here, had resisted it like these poor United Brethren? Who can deny that the Southern churches therefore are the bulwark of slavery, and that Northern churches which silently or actively fraternize with them, are, so far forth, participants in the giant sin of the age?

You alluded, a few weeks ago, to my "conservative" proclivities. Other papers have done the same, but they erred in supposing I ever believed slavery to be right. I only objected to "agitation," as meddling with that was neither politically nor religiously our business. Therein did I err, both politically and religiously. And still, that very error, the very going so far in defending what seemed the constitutional rights of the South, has made swarms of old Democrats now the bitterest foes of the oligarchy which dared lay its hands on that constitution, in defending whose apparent guaranties, they had been left in a hopeless minority, been censured and reproached, and been placed even in a false position as to their real sentiments. Religiously, we have no right to ignore the claims of suffering millions; we never had. Politically, the existence of a republican government over its thirty-four States, necessitates the destruction of slavery; whether immediate or future, the result the commencement of its destruction must be *now*. What measures are necessary, I am not qualified to say. It is a hard question. But pardon me this new reference to the great cause of the rebellion, while I say a few things more.

I quote now from words of a commander of ours:

"Said I to a girl about sixteen, at the house of whose master I passed the night, "Do you know what we are here for?" "I specs you's here to free us." "Do you want to be free?" "I does." "Don't you like your master?" "No, sir." "Why?" "He sold my mother." "When?" "Twelve years ago." "But your master looks like a kind man, and treats us kindly." "I know he looks so, but he ties *me* up and whips me with a cowhide." The tones of the girl were inexpressibly sad; I have never found but hopelessness and utter despair."

I quote again, of a conversation I witnessed:

"At the house of a Virginian near _____, the proprietor's apparent cordiality was induced by fear. While at table, we were waited on by a bright looking yellow woman about twenty-five years of age. I questioned her of the rebels; she spoke intelligently but hurriedly, and in low tones, as if desiring to communicate with us, and yet afraid her master might hear. She told me among other things that the rebel.........I asked her if she liked to live with her master. "*No* sir." "What will I do with my family, and how shall I leave my friends; we can't all go, and how can we be separated? Besides, we thought we'd better wait for the law." "What law?" "Why, the law that is going to be passed to free us."

She added, also, "this is our *home*. We don't want to leave it. We are willing to work."

There was a man near Snicker's Ferry, who made many abolitionists. Nobody suspected he was a slave. He was no darker than a browned soldier. His hair was straight, just turning grey. He was the son of his own master. His wife was the daughter of her master. A more pious man it would be hard to find. As he told of his early dissatisfaction with his lot, there were tears in men's eyes. Now, he was resigned. He thanked God that his children had not been sold away from them. But, hopeless as he now was, in approaching age, he did wish his *children* might be free, and live in a different sphere. Sad, yet religiously happy – resigned, but ambitious for the children, so fair, so white, so intelligent.

Now I select these three cases out of many, as *fair* illustrations, and for several principles, asking you to remember that these answers came in connection with inquiries for military purposes.

1. In the mildest type of slaver, girls of sixteen are tied up and flogged by their masters with cowhides.
2. Men hold their own children in slavery.
3. The slaves do not want to leave their homes, but profess a readiness to work for wages; and if the resources of this section were decently developed, they could not do half the work.
4. The slaves exhibit the strongest family attachments; repeatedly preferring to remain in a slavery they dislike, rather than leave a husband, wife, or children.
5. They are peaceably disposed, but sad and depressed.
6. They are, as a class, more intelligent, more industrious, more civilized, than the "poor whites," though with less natural vigor of character.
7. They are looking with intense longing for legal redress.
8. They are our faithful allies; they give us ready information; they have brought to us scraps of writing left with them by men pressed into the *rebel service,* who were anxious we should so succeed, and which we have found correct.

Of course these views are based upon, and refer to, facts in this section only. But in this section, let me add, Christian "professors" are often the hardest masters; and if I had a personal friend a slave, I would pray especially, "Lord keep him out of the hands of a Christian minister!" The more light, the greater blindness; I speak that which I have seen.

Edinburg, Va., April 8, 1862
A.H.Q.

May 9, 1862

Letter from the Army.
Near Newmarket, Va., April 24, 1862.

We move by fits and starts. A week ago this morning, after – I don't know how long a residence, we left Edenburg. We had remained there I suppose as long as we did, only because the corps lacked provisions and shoes. The intended, and partly accomplished, removal of Gen. Williams' Division to Centerville, had sent on the Division supply train, and that had to come slowly back. In addition thereto, the miserable railway from Harper's Ferry to Winchester used to give out once a day or so. And still further, it was, of course difficult to foresee that men would need shoes; nor is it very wonderful that nobody supposed that shoes, given out new on the morning of a march over a plain, smooth road, would have holes clean through the soles at night, as various pairs did. But the various vexations overcome, we were to follow up Jackson; and now a General Order congratulates the corps that the Virginia Valley is cleared of an armed enemy.

Gen. Shields' Division moved in the night. Ours in the morning following. Reveille beat at a quarter past two; the regiment was in line of march at four. There was no excitement in following another Division; the advance is far pleasanter. So we could enjoy the scenery and the day. The faint light in the east was struggling with the clear moonlight, soon to overcome. The denser column of fog, along the river, half hid the mountain range, rising beyond it clear and sharp in outline. We crossed the creek at Edenburg, after waiting till near sunrise, and moved onward in the most delightful scenery and air imaginable.

It is hard to imagine more beautiful views than one meets in this valley. Varying from ten to thirty miles, bounded by lofty and rude mountain ranges, watered by rapid rivers or foaming creeks, the undulating lands, now wooded, now gently swelling fields, now green meadows, change the landscape almost constantly. The winter wheat was clothing many an acre with the liveliest green. Peach trees were just making ready to bloom. Now and then one saw hyacinths and hearts-ease by the roadside. And robins and swallows were flying about in the greatest glee. Such it was as sunrise bathed the whole scene in richest glory. But for the occasional roar of artillery miles onward, and the succession of burning bridges which we regularly met, it would have seemed the embodiment of peace. But the plow was idle in the field. The fences were broken down. The relics of straw and brands showed the recent bivouacs. The men were away at war. The past thirty years of retrograde were rapidly accumulating the ruin of the valley. Beautiful, but decaying. Beautiful, but deceitful; consumption and fever are the bane of this lovely spot; and tyranny and ignorance are ruining its population.

Every bridge, for miles, was burning. The hurrying enemy foolishly supposed this would delay our march; but there was a ford at every place, and where our artillery was stopped, Yankee eyes saw the railroad crossing few rods above, and dashed over safely. So we went on to Mount Jackson.

There we waited for several hours. Why, I do not know, nor was it any of my business. Two or three miles onward was Rood's Hill, the place which Jackson held in force. Mount Jackson itself is not a hill, but a village. Here the enemy had built large hospitals, and evidently expected to remain. While waiting I went into them. The hospital flags were still flying, those little safeguards which are a sure protection in all civilized warfare. But the sick had all been removed ten days previous, to the number of nearly five hundred. The buildings were admirably contrived, and constructed. In addition to two or three small ones, there were two completed and one nearly so, of perhaps a hundred and fifty feet in length, two stories in hight, perfectly ventilated and yet warm. The upper stories were entered from the outside, by plenty of broad and easy stairways; and the whole showed better skill than usual.

Near by were two graveyards. In one there were some fifty or sixty graves of soldiers, each with headboards distinctly lettered. I noticed that there were buried there, in addition to Virginians, men from North and South Carolina, Georgia,

Alabama and Louisiana. Poor fellows; to die away from home, and in an unjust cause!

Near by was the railroad station, the terminus of the Manassas road. The rebels were determined we should have no use of it. The rebels were determined we should have no use of it. The engine-house was in smoking ruins. The engine was as well broken up as they knew how to do it. Remnants of passenger cars, and a long line of freight cars were still burning. I cannot understand the love of the rebels for the destruction of property. The bridges on the common roads they destroyed, the bridges their own South must rebuild, when it could not delay our forces ten minutes. And these cars they burned belonging to a private corporation, while their uselessness, if left unhurt, is clear from the fact that on the line of the road every wooden bridge, many a one of great cost and labor, is destroyed. And if the bridges were to be rebuilt, it is perfectly easy to obtain rolling stock from the other end of the road. But they seem to have a passion for destruction, even when at their own expense, and when perfectly useless.

Our waiting at Mt. Jackson ended. Gen. Shields' Division was to advance on the main road; but to us was given as hard toil as we had ever had. Col. Gordon's Brigade, with two or three regiments of Col. Donelly's,[120] was ordered to make a flank movement to the right. Now we left our good turnpike traveling, and took a "dirt" road. Dirt road it was; muddy, stony, and rough. For two miles it led Westward by the side of a rapid stream, whose power is wasted on the few little mills. Then we crossed it. It was fordable – that is, wade-able, and our soldiers emerged thoroughly wet to the knees. Bending Southward, we were soon opposite Rood's Hill, and now and then a cannon shot came to our ears. They were speeding courtesies to the rebels, who, of course, saw the flanking process, and knowing that if it succeeded they were prisoners, left in disgust.

You suggest a doubt whether the report is true that many of Jackson's men being forced into the army, will not fight. There is every reason to suppose that it is

---

120 Dudley Donnelly (1825 - 1862) was a magistrate in Lockport, NY and came out with the 28th New York Volunteer Infantry. Similar to Col. Gordon of the 2nd Mass., Donnelly had been promoted to command the 1st Brigade of Banks' army. 1st Brigade consisted of the 28th New York, the 5th Connecticut Infantry and the 46th Pennsylvania Infantry. Donnelly would be killed at the Battle of Cedar Mountain. "Niagara County, New York in the Civil War;" *Unit History Project;*

true, so far as this, that he cannot rely on them. It is stated on good authority, that Jackson asked the opinion of his officers whether to stand at Rood's Hill, which is a narrow ridge commanding open ground for a mile or two, itself guarded by a river on each side, and not overlooked by any accessible position. His officers favored a fight, but he overruled them, on the ground that he could not depend upon a portion of his force.

However we plodded on, turning more to the East. We passed through a mean and dirty village called Forestville, probably because there is hardly a tree there; crossed another stream, where Major Dwight, with twenty pioneers from our regiment, had made a slight bridge; ascended and descended ledges; waited for artillery stuck fast every now and then. It was bad enough by daylight; but when the sun had set, the march was execrable. It became *very* dark; the road let through woods; some of our men were even barefoot; and when, at half past eight, we turned into a wood, and built fires, and had our supper, and piled up leaves, and spread out blankets, everybody was ready for the slumber that awaited all but the guard. It was a beautiful night to sleep, and few, after eighteen miles of the hardest travel, moved till reveille.

The next morning we went on to rejoin the corps. The march had nothing noticeable save one ford. It was through the North fork of the Shenandoah. Water was high; the bottom rough; the river too wide; the current exceedingly rapid. IT took two hours to pass. Now and then a man was down; and now and then a horse. Six horses found it difficult to take a gun through; and one caisson obstinately refused to budge from the middle of the stream until horses were changed, and ten of them exerted their strength. It was a scene of order, but of exceeding bustle.

Two miles more brought us to Newmarket. For a description of this place, turn to any of my allusions to Southern villages. This one had, however, a rather pretty church, Lutheran in name. It had also a graveyard, from which, as we halted by it, I took from one of the best marble stones, the following mixture of fact and piety:

> "He was taken sick the eleventh of June
> And only lived ten days ;
> But he's gone to rest in heaven above,
> And sing his Saviour's praise."

From which I gathered that it is considered extremely remarkable here that a man should go to heaven who was taken sick on the eleventh of June, and who had so short a sickness.

Yankee Doodle brought out the population of Newmarket extensively, but we could not wait. There is a strong Union sentiment here, as there is all through the valley, and of the most intelligent class excepting the few wealthy proprietors. This sentiment only needs to be favored, to make it extremely powerful; that it has not been more attended to, I suppose is owing to the fact that the Union class is dark-colored.

Two miles out of Newmarket we went into camp. It had begun to rain a little before we reached the camping place, and we were glad to be located. Do not, however, have too exalted ideas of the shelter; we had no tents, nor have had any until yesterday, although saving yesterday, it has rained steadily. The shelters are improvised of rails, straw, and such like. Two rails fastened together near the top, with legs spread out, form one support; two more form another; a rail is laid on top between the two, and from this horizontal cross rail, other rails slope to the ground; straw is laid on, often plastered with mud; some rubber blankets are hung up inside; and if the wind happens to be right, the shelter will keep off about half the wet; if the wind is wrong, it doesn't keep off any. Outside, is mud, mud, mud. Yet our men are cheerful and manly. Notwithstanding they have done more work and borne more hardship ten-fold than regiments sent by steam direct, and then allowed the opportunity to show themselves brave, notwithstanding the exposure to disease and bullets for months and months, which the 2d, the 12th and the 13th have had to endure, and for which they get no name upon their banner, while others, newer in service get the glory of some fortunate opportunity, which our men are not allowed, yet they feel that the work they do is still for their country and necessary, and they bear it cheerfully. Though not always able to see why a rich Government leaves them exposed to cold storms without shelter, for days, while their tents are but a few miles off, and no enemy near, yet they endure hardness as good soldiers.

Contrabands are frequent. All tell the same story, all desire to be free, all seem ready to work. "Can you take care of yourself?" is a frequent question. "I should think I might," was the sound reply of one; "I hire myself out, make my own bargain, and carry the money to my master." Said another, "we take care of ourselves and our masters too; it would be strange if we could not take care of ourselves alone." All are happy to be free. But they will not leave without their families. Shame on the fools who say that slaves have no natural affection.

    A.H.Q.

May 23, 1862

Letter from the Army.
Harrisonburg, Va., May 1, 1862

Harrisonburg, shire town of Rockingham County, is superior in appearance to any town in the valley which we have thus far seen, though quite inferior in size to Winchester. Its people certainly behave a great deal better. Winchester people, especially most of the women, act as though their hearts were "set on fire of hell." In addition to an evident lack of decent breeding, they show a want of all those humanized feelings which civilized nations show even to enemies. The barbarous institutions under which they live, keep them down to barbarous levels. But in Harrisonburg, the inhabitants are decently courteous; and, indeed, there is, if true sentiments could be spoken without danger, a great deal of Union feeling. But who can wonder that they are afraid to speak openly, when they fear to be again deserted to the cruelties of the rebels, as the Union people were last summer by Patterson, in the upper part of the valley?[121] The evil result of Patterson's failure was

---

121 Robert Patterson (1792 – 1881) was a native of County Tyrone Ireland who immigrated to the United States at a young age. Patterson volunteered for the War of 1812, eventually rising to become Colonel of the 2nd Pennsylvania Militia. During the Mexican-American war, Patterson was commissioned a Major General of Volunteers and he saw service at Veracruz and the Battle of Cerro Gordo. After the war, Patterson returned to his very successful cotton mills until the American Civil War when he was, once again, appointed a Major General of Volunteers. Patterson's failure to keep Confederate General Joseph E. Johnston engaged in the Shenandoah Valley aided the Confederacy in their victory at the Battle of Bull Run. Patterson was mustered from service in April of 1861. General Abercrombie is Patterson's son-in-law. Warner; *Generals in Blue*

not merely the loss of Bull Run; his leaving Union people to the terrible vengeance of secessionists, left a sad distrust and fear. Better lose a battle than to abandon loyal citizens.

Harrisonburg is the center of probably the best wheat county in Virginia. Nothing can be more beautiful, agriculturally, than the broad fields now covered with living green. The town itself has very good shops, a court house, two or three hotels, and six churches, viz: two Presbyterian (New and Old School), two Methodist (North and South), a Lutheran, and an "Ironsides" Baptist, besides other civilizing institutions, which I will not venture to mention.

For this place we left our camp (I mean our regiment did) on Friday last. We were glad to get away from the mud, though with little prospect of improvement. Still any change would be for the better. Some of us had had our meals at a house near by, owned with, I believe, eighteen hundred acres of land, by a present Brigade Quartermaster in the rebel service. The family, except the head, were there, and the conflict between hospitality and enmity was entertaining. A guard was allowed the premises, as is very common; and the good lady, on our leaving, felt bound to say that the men of our regiment had treated her and hers with courtesy; in fact, she said, Virginians could not have acted more like gentlemen. Our men always bear that character. The thirty or forty slaves of the place she notified to take care of themselves in future, as have others in the valley. She might as well, as the slaves evidently intend to do so, with or without permission.

It was a raw day when we made our march of fourteen miles, but it did not rain, for a wonder. We are now in camp a little above Harrisonburg, in a pleasant, open wood. It rains now, of course. Of course it is muddy. Of course any number of brooks run across the roads. But we are well sheltered now, and the regiment is in very good health. It is a curious fact that wet feet hurt nobody, if you keep them wet all the time.

Sunday was a beautiful day. I felt glad, because we could have public worship. But after arrangements were all made, suddenly there came an order to go out on reconnaissance, towards the Shenandoah. On the other side of that river is Jackson, said to be reinforced. The bridge is piled with straw, and everything is ready to set it into a blaze as soon as we should attempt to cross. The road we took on reconnaissance is a "dirt" road, of a very mean kind, and very mean of its kind. Mud, brooks, and rocks, are its constituents, with here and there a rod or two of decent road to hold the rest together. I have seen hard roads in New Hampshire, but never anything equal to a Virginia dirt road. Their only redeeming feature is rail fence, which makes a most beautiful fire when you stop for the night.

On this road we advanced until we were eleven miles from camp; we, the 27th Indiana, and somebody's battery, and somebody's else, cavalry, -- Vermont cavalry, I think, which, for goodness of horses, and dash of men, beats any other cavalry we have seen.[122] Soon after leaving Harrisonburg, we met Col. Donelly's brigade, which was coming in from an advanced camp. I do not exactly understand what a reconnaissance was intended to discover, made to the same spot which regiments had just left; but I have no doubt there was some brilliant result obtained. A little brush between our cavalry and Ashby's took place, resulting in an exchange of one of our men for two of theirs. The day before their cavalry drove in our pickets; one man, I forget his regiment, did not reach cover, in consequence to taking the wrong direction; he hence was virtually a prisoner, but the rebels preferred to shoot him, and as he lay wounded, shot him again. This is rebel chivalry.

In Col. Donelly's Brigade, on the road, I had a great pleasure. It was meeting my brother Winslow, late of Great Barrington, now the excellent and beloved chaplain of the Connecticut 5th.[123] We were, of course, instantly acquainted, and I delayed to talk with him, until a rapid gallop was necessary to overtake the Second. In your ministers' meetings you do not conceive the pleasure of greeting a brother. But be a hundred miles into Virginia, in a hostile land, with no "exchanges," no "Monday meeting," no Sargent's, or Crosby's, or Tilton's, or Piper's, for Monday greetings, and you would count it a luxury to spend a few minutes with a Massachusetts brother. Keep up the "meeting" brethren, and make it a hearty fellowship.

---

122 The 1st Vermont Cavalry was organized in Burlington, Vermont in November of 1861 under the Command of Colonel Lemuel B. Platt. The unit remained in the Eastern Theater the entire war, serving through the surrender of General Lee at Appomattox. Notably, the Vermont Cavalry made an unsuccessful attack on the Confederate at the Battle of Gettysburg on the 3rd day. It lost over 400 men during the war, including 159 in Confederate prisoner of war camps. Fox; *Regimental Losses.*

123 Horace Winslow (1814 – 1905) was a Presbyterian minister who was a graduate of Hamilton College and Union Theological Seminary. Winslow was an active participant in many of the same organizations as the Reverend Quint, including the American Tract Society, American Board of Commissioners for Foreign Missions, American Bible society, etc. At the time of his commission as Chaplain of the 5th Connecticut, he was minister of the Congregational Church in Great Barrington. However, Winslow resigned his post late in 1862 and accepted the call to a church in Binghamton, N.Y. Gillett; *General Catalogue.*

From the Potomac to the Etowah

Farther on, a few of us stopped for dinner. The men of the companies carry food in their haversacks, but some of us have to trust to the road. We stopped at a good looking house; speedily obtained our dinner, and fed our horses. It was a very intelligent family; books were quite plenty; and flowers were far more common than usual. Many of the books were religious, and Presbyterian papers abounded, though few of late date. I should not mention, perhaps, this wayside dining, but that one thing carried my mind back suddenly to home. It was a "balm-of-gilead tree."[124] Don't laugh at it, anybody. At the farm of my birth-place, there used to be, by the gate, a noble tree of that kind. It had stood for many years, and there I used to love to sit or play. When a boy I went once a year to see grandparents, uncles and cousins. There was a house full of these. But one day there came a hail storm of unprecedented fury, and in it the old tree was killed. Out of the root, it is true, there came up little ones, but they never grew to be large and beautiful. When I saw this one in Virginia, my mind was full of the old homestead, grandfather then active, grandmother, a minister's daughter, meek and pious, and all the numerous household who made the home so happy. Gone the older; gone or scattered almost all the middle generation; gone, not a few of the youngest, into the world of silence; and the old place is different now. So do we often think here of home, at slight provocations. When rising from a prayer in hospital once, I heard "that seems just like my *home,*" murmured almost dreamily by a very sick and weak man. Home! Happy those whose thoughts of home are so linked with prayer and praise.

We turned about. And a little after dark had reached camp again. Our men were sadly fatigued, but they had marched splendidly, over a road of twenty-two miles, equivalent to a good road of at least thirty, in little more, if any, than ten hours. Here we still are; and in this vicinity I doubt not we remain until Yorktown matters progress for the timing of our movement. But I *know* nothing about it. In the meantime, we are eighteen miles from the Post Office of the corps. Think of that, you who have mails two or three times a day.

A.H.Q.

---

124 A "balm-of-Gilead" tree is a hybrid between a balsam poplar and the eastern cottonwood. It's leaf buds are coated with a sap that has a strong turpentine odor and are used in pot-pourri or herbal medicines.

May 23, 1862

Letter from the Army.
Strasburg, Va., May 16, 1862

We learn from the newspapers that our corps is now at Staunton and aiming for Richmond. We learn also that Jackson has evacuated the valley. Neither statement is true. We advanced; Jackson retired. We reached Harrisonburg; Jackson crossed the middle Shenandoah, and rested at the opposite end of the bridge which he had piled with combustibles, towards Swift River Gap. We threw out forces towards the bridge; Jackson watched them with cavalry scouts.

Then the corps retired. Gen. Banks' headquarters had never advanced beyond Newmarket, eighteen miles north of Harrisonburg, and have now come back to this place, thirty-one miles north of Newmarket. Jackson has been reinforced, and appears to have re-occupied Harrisonburg, and even farther north. From Gen. Banks' corps, Gen. Shields' division has been detached and has gone over – somewhere. Gen. Williams' division remains here, where fortifications were begun some time ago. This place is the key to the valley; the practical termination of the Manassas Gap railway, over which road trains now run to within two miles of this place, and will run in on Monday next; and a very strong natural position.

The slow advance of this corps is apologetically attributed in newspapers editorials, to bad roads and deficient supplies. As to roads, your *Spectator* said, May 5, that Gen. Banks' found them in "shocking condition," in the same paper in which I spoke of "plain, smooth" roads. Now there is no part of New England whose main avenues are better than those of this valley. By-roads are bad; but the principal lines are direct, macadamized turnpikes, built in large part by the State.[125] An army could advance with perfect ease and great rapidity. So far as the matter of supplies is concerned, there has been no difficulty which energy could not have easily remedied. The reason, therefore, of the exceeding slowness of movements, and the present retrograde, is to be found in other directions; and is in all probability, attributable to directions from Washington. Weeks ago, had it been desired, we could have been beyond Staunton, and have swept every foe out of our path; but at the risk of having our communication cut off.

Our regiment remained in camp at Harrisonburg, until, on Sunday, May 4th. About sundown that day, tents were struck and every one packed. We were ordered out to the road, and half a mile towards Harrisonburg, and there had the comfort of a sudden bivouac. At grey morning we marched – not southward as we expected, but northward, eighteen miles or thereabouts; passed through Newmarket village, and had tents pitched by about eight in the morning.

But, at one o'clock in the morning, we were ordered out. A mile or more east of Newmarket is the Masanutten range, or part of a range which reaches from Strasburg just fifty miles southward, dividing the valley in two long parts. On the other side of the range was Gen. Sullivan.[126] In the evening we had noticed the lights of the signal corps on top of the gap, flitting backward and forward. They were telling some scare-crow story about the needs of Gen. Sullivan against a threatening force of twelve thousand men; and our brigade, tired as it was with an eighteen

---

125 The Macadamized road or "Valley Pike" (now Rt. 11) was a topic of frequent comment among Northern soldiers due to its uniformity, length and easiness of travel. The road is often given credit for Gen. Stonewall Jackson's swift movements of troops through the valley. The road was built in two sections by two different public-private partnerships. The first company built the road from Winchester to Harrisonburg, and the other from Harrisonburg to Staunton.

126 Jeremiah Cutler Sullivan (1860 – 1890) was a graduate of the United States Naval Academy (1848) and spent six years in the United States Navy, mostly in support of American forces in Mexico. He resigned his commission in 1854, returned home to Indiana where he studied law and passed the bar exam. Sullivan helped raise the 6th Indiana and served with them for 3 months as a Captain. Governor Morton commissioned him Colonel of the 13th Indiana and fought in some early battles alongside General McClellan. Commissioned Brigadier General in April of 1862, Sullivan was transferred to the Western Theater where he served on the field staff of General Grant. In September of 1863, Sullivan returned east but during the Valley Campaign of 1864 a disagreement with General Hunter found him without a command. Sullivan resigned from the army in May of 1865. Warner; *Generals in Blue*

miles march over a dusty road, must climb up the hills and down the other side. There was no help for it.

Turning at right angles from Newmarket, the road gradually descended for a mile or more towards a rapid river. The air was damp and chilly; the misty darkness allowed only vague and spectral views; and to enjoy both, an artillery train, ordered to report at the covered bridge, stopped us for a detestable hour, until some piece of red tape somewhere could be accurately measured.

But we climbed the hill. There was no *hard* climbing, however. The road over the gap was as smooth and firm as any in Roxbury or Dorchester, and was make [sic] up of so many acute angles as to give a grade of exceeding ease. Indeed, it is a beautiful specimen of engineering and evidently costly – built on the principle of getting as much road into the given distance as possible – and so contrived as to make you believe you are going down hill instead of up. Another brigade was bivouacked for a mile or two by the road, and their brilliant fires crackling all along on either side, now against a wall of earth left by excavation, and now bringing into relief the wild woods over a precipice, while a brook near by was rolling, scolding, or singing by turns – made a bewildering and fascinating scene. At the top we rested, and turning to look behold a view of the utmost beauty; a lovely valley of great breadth confined by the distant Alleghanies, whose tops the rising sun was just tinging.

Down the other side; a halt at the base, in beautiful scenery; a dispatch; the pleasant information that either the signal officer had blundered, or else somebody had – made a mistake; two nights bivouac in delightful woods; and on one of them a magnificent spectacle, in the "woods on fire" near the top of Masanutten.

Then we returned. Up the hill and down again, and back to camp. On the way up, a few of us took short cuts from angle to angle once or twice, to gather wild flowers. There was great abundance of several kinds. Wild cherry was in blossom, and laurel, and what they call dogwood here, which I think is found in Milton, Massachusetts, and "red bud," without leaves, but gorgeous in its wealth of flowering; and, of lowlier plants, the red columbine, May flower, much like the New Hampshire one, which is more beautiful than that in the Plymouth woods, (I have gathered both) the anemone, the iris, far more delicately lovely than any I ever saw wild before, -- and above all such profusion of wood-violets as one rarely finds, of which many were colored so like pansies, that they were easily mistaken for them at a little distance. Sitting upon a rock to rest, the sight of belted men with swords at their sides and pistols ready, gathering flowers, awakened strange sensations. But these "wood violets are the same we have at *home*," they said.

On Saturday, at sundown, tents were again struck; but orders soon came to stop the wagons; and so with tents less than half a mile off, we had two more nights and the whole intervening day of shelterless waiting. What for, do you ask? Shrug your shoulders and keep quiet.

But on Monday morning at half-past two, we were in the road; fourteen miles that day, and woods at night, with plenty of luxurious leaves for beds, which, with good weather and a few blankets, make just the pleasantest summer residence imaginable. Tuesday morning at three o'clock, we rise again, and make fourteen miles more, -- to this dirtiest, nastiest, meanest, poorest, most shiftless town I have yet seen in all the shiftless poor, mean, nasty, dirty towns of this beautiful valley.

There is considerable force – perhaps fifteen or twenty thousand, of rebels down the valley. That they will be fools enough to come up, is not possible, while Fremont is at Franklin. So our chance to do something active seems small. Rumor has it that our Division is to remain here this summer; to hold this place, which is a very important one in reference to operations in the valley; and to look after the Manassas Railway. We are all terribly chagrined at such a prospect. It would be too humiliating to a large, well equipped, finely organized, brave, admirably led Regiment like ours. To sit down virtually to garrison purposes, while troops which came into the field far later are placed in posts of honor, would be hard to bear. To read the brilliant despatches from this place by the reporter to the "Associated Press," [127] which have become here a laughing stock for their stereotyped beginning "Great rejoicing is exhibited in this corps on hearing of the brilliant victory at ------" one place after another – would be rather tough for summer employment. If this be the settled plan, I shall relieve you of one "army correspondent," as what is going on this summer in this quarter would not be worth reading; and I would not insult your kindness by writing. But we hope better things.

---

127 The Associated Press, or New York Associated Press at this time was entirely a New York cooperative between the New York Sun, The New York Times, The Tribune, the Herald, The Courier, the Enquirer, the Journal of Commerce and the Express. There was also a Western Associate Press and a Philadelphia Associated Press. "Journalism in New-York;" *Courier*.

In the mean time there is plenty of guerilla business. One of our men was captured not sixty rods from the road side by the woods where we had halted; but after four or five days captivity shrewdly escaped from a rebel camp of thousands of men, and after two days travel in the woods, reached Union pickets. Another, in advance, on a march, was shot at and very severely wounded. It is learned that citizens and soldiers in citizen's clothes are roaming the valley to pick off any one they can find outside the lines, as well as pickets. This is in accordance with Gov. Letcher's proclamation.[128] There is but one way to treat those gentry; hang them when caught; burn every house from which they shoot; and in default of catching the scoundrels, seize secession residents as hostages, and hang a man for every man shot in this murderous way. This would stop it. But this will not be done; we must *conciliate* the greatest scoundrels that ever went unhung!

A.H.Q.

---

[128] John Letcher (1813 – 1884) was the Governor of Virginia during the American Civil War. Quint is probably referring to the Proclamation that was issued on 10 March 1862 in which Governor Letcher says "The loyal citizens of the West and Northwest, in counties not herein named, are earnestly invoked to form guerilla companies and strike, when least expected, one more for the State that gave them birth…..Scorn the misrule of traitors, who, with usurped authority, are desecrating our soil with a pollution worse than that of the direst enemy, and execute vengeance upon the foe who acknowledges and sustains their treason." Wright; "John Letcher (1813–1884);" and "Governor Letcher's Proclamation – It's History;" *Richmond Examiner*.

June 6, 1862

Letter from Chaplain Quint.
Williamsport, MD.
The retreat of Gen. Banks.

On the night of the 11th of July, last year, our regiment camped in this town, by the river side, having left Camp Andrew[129] in West Roxbury, on the 8th, and now, after over ten months of campaigning, we have come to the same place again, very unwillingly.

I wrote you last that Jackson could hardly be fool enough to come up the valley again. He has been, however; and if government is wide awake, as I think it is, Jackson's folly will soon be made apparent. Good generalship cannot fail to annihilate him.

Nevertheless, in the meantime, we have had to retreat, and to retreat in circumstances which ensured disaster. But when the country learns full the history of a retreat made by less than five thousand, while an enemy of twenty-five thousand moved at the same time on a converging road, -- a retreat of fifty-three miles, encumbered by five hundred wagons – a retreat marked by fighting for miles upon miles, and by repeated stands to enable the trains to gain in distance – a retreat which ended in a successful passage of a wide and rapid river, in which the horse had often to swim – this retreat will take its place as a masterly movement; and

---

129 Camp Andrew was established on the site of Brooks Farm, the Transcendentalist community in West Roxbury. The property was given to the state for its use by James Freeman Clarke. Quint; *The Record of the Second Massachusetts*;

Gen. Banks, with his gallant little corps, will take a high rank in the esteem and affection of the people.

When the plans were fully consummated between separated forces to attack and destroy or capture Jackson near Harrisonburg, the very night previous to the intended movement there came positive orders to our corps to retire to Strasburg, and to detach Gen. Shields from this command. Disaster was then foreboded. Remonstrances were useless, and we retired. We had then left but two infantry Brigades of four regiments each, and a regiment of cavalry, with sixteen guns. The Manassas Railroad was opened to Strasburg, and must be guarded. Col. Kenley's[130] regiment, the 1st Maryland,[131] was spared to guard it at Front Royal, ten miles east of Strasburg. The remainder of the force was mainly at Strasburg, detachments being constantly on outpost duty.

On Friday, May 23, Col. Kenley's force was overwhelmed. News came by an orderly, too late to help him, even if it had been possible. About midnight the wagon trains were put in motion, but the men, though under arms, were not moved until Saturday morning at about 11 o'clock. It did not appear certain until then that the attack on Front Royal was more than a mere raid. But it soon appeared that Jackson had been very heavily reinforced, and instant retreat was needful.

Gen. Hatch, with cavalry, and some few guns, were rear-guard.[132] Col. Donnelly's Brigade led; Col. Gordon's followed. The train was far on the road, but the forces,

---

130 John Reese Kenley (1818 – 1891) was a Baltimore lawyer who served in the Mexican-American war as a lieutenant of volunteers and worked his way up to the rank of Major. Kenley was wounded at this fight at Front Royal and was taken prisoner. Kenley was promoted to Brigadier General and he led a brigade for the rest of the war. Warner; *Generals in Blue*

131 1st Maryland Regiment was organized in May of 1861and assigned to Banks' force in the Shenandoah Valley. At Front Royal, the 1st Maryland (Union) held off an attack by Gen. Stonewall Jackson's forces losing 57 men killed and wounded and five hundred and thirty-five captured. When they were attacked at Front Royal, the regiment which headed the attack was the 1st Maryland Regiment (CSA). The 1st Marylanders would see service right through the end of the war. Wilmer, Jarrett, and Vernon; *History and Roster of Maryland Volunteers, War of 1861-5.*

132 John Porter Hatch (1822 – 1901) was a graduate of West Point (1845) and served with the 3rd U.S. Infantry during the Mexican American War. Between his service in Mexico and the Civil War he served in the West at posts from Oregon to New Mexico and at the outbreak of the war he was assigned to lead the cavalry under General George B. McClellan. Hatch was promoted to Brigadier General in September of 1861 and led the cavalry until he

excepting the rear guard, reached some of it, near Middletown, about six miles above Strasburg, and passed it.

The Second Massachusetts, in Brigade, had gone about a mile and a half above Newtown, (sometimes called Stephensburg) and about twelve miles from Strasburg, when reports came that the wagon train had been cut by the enemy. Gen. Hatch was thus intercepted, and it appeared afterward, had crossed over to a road westerly, and came round. Col. Gordon was then ordered to go back with the 2d Mass., the 28th New York,[133] and a section of Best's Battery to relieve the train.[134] On approaching Newtown, they found the 27th Indiana (of Col. Gordon's Brigade) drawn up across the road in line, with four pieces of Corthren's N.Y. Battery. 28th New York was halted, and Lieut. Col. Andrews, with the 2d Mass. was ordered by Col. Gordon to take and hold Newtown. They passed the wagons along the road, in every conceivable state of confusion, abandoned by the drivers. The enemy had posted artillery in the street, but the Second advanced without firing a shot,

---

was transferred to the Infantry by General John Pope. He was wounded in the leg at South Mountain for which he was later awarded the Congressional Medal of Honor. He spent much of 1863 in light administrative duties but in 1864 he led Federal forces in the Carolinas in coordination with General Sherman. Hatch continued in the army until his retirement in 1886. Warner; *Generals in Blue*

133 The 28th New York was organized at Albany for two years' service under Colonel Dudley Donnelly, although there were a few companies of three year's men. The 28th saw service until Chancellorsville and mustered out having lost 68 members killed or died of wounds and 49 from disease and other causes. The regiment lost heavily at Cedar Mountain and Chancellorsville. "28th Infantry Regiment;" *Unit History Project;*

134 Clermont Livingston Best (1824 - 1897) was a West Point graduate (1847) who commanded a battery in the 4th U. S. Artillery in Banks' Army. Best served against the Seminole Indians in Florida, as well as on the frontier before the Civil War. During the war, Best rose from the command of a battery to chief of artillery of Fifth Corps and later a position of Assistant Inspector-General of 12th Corps. Best also served as Division commander of the Artillery Reserve in the Department of the Cumberland until October of 1864. Best returned to Washington to act as an instructor of artillery and a recruiting officer until the end of the war. After the surrender of General Lee at Appomattox, Best served in many posts, mostly throughout the Northeast. Bradbury; *History of Hudson*.

(companies H, Capt. Abbott,[135] and C, Capt. Cogswell,[136] as skirmishers) under a fire of shell; the enemy did not wait to be closed upon, but retired to an eminence near by. There the artillery was posted, and constant firing was kept up for an hour, during which the Second held the town. Col. Gordon endeavored to procure mules to save the wagons but none were sent, and he ordered the 27th Indiana to burn them, which was accomplished. When this was done, Col. Gordon ordered the forces on again. It was now twilight.

From that time the Second was rear-guard during the retreat. A and C still followed as skirmishers, with Co. B, (Capt. Williams)[137] as flankers, two hundred yards each side of the column – three companies also being attached to the battery just in front.

No annoyance was then experienced for the two miles which the regiment had just retraced. There, when it had been ordered to return to Newtown, it had, in order to relieve the fatigued men, left knapsacks in a field by the road. The regiment here halted to take them. While this was being done, on came the enemy. It was now quite dark. Companies A and C were immediately formed to resist cavalry – under Major Dwight. Capts Abbott and Cogswell formed on the sides of

---

135 Fletcher Morton Abbott (1843 – 1925) was a 2nd Lieutenant in Co. D until commissioned Captain of Co. H. He later served on the staff of Brigadier-General William Dwight. Abbott went with Dwight to Louisiana as part of Banks' expedition and served with him until December of 1863 when he was forced to resign due to disease. He took an MD from Harvard in 1876. Quint; *The Record of the Second Massachusetts*; and, Adjutant General of Massachusetts; *Massachusetts Soldiers, Sailors and Marines in the Civil War*.

136 William Cogswell (1838 – 1895) was a graduate of Harvard Law School (1860) and lawyer from Salem and was commissioned Captain in May of 1861. He was wounded at Chancellorsville in May of 1863 and commissioned Colonel the next month. He remained Colonel of the Regiment until the end of the war. After the war he went on to serve as Mayor of Salem, a State Representative, State Senator and to five terms as a congressman. Quint; *The Record of the Second Massachusetts*; and, Adjutant General of Massachusetts; *Massachusetts Soldiers, Sailors and Marines in the Civil War*.

137 William Blackstone Williams (1830 - 1862) was a civil engineer who worked on the Cleveland and Columbus Railroad and as a surveyor for a route across the Isthmus of Tehuantepec. Williams also worked on several Southern railroads, including Maysville and Big-Sandy Railroad (KY) and the Mobile and Ohio Railroad (AL). Williams was killed at the Battle of Cedar Mountain. Quint; *The Record of the Second Massachusetts*; and, Adjutant General of Massachusetts; *Massachusetts Soldiers, Sailors and Marines in the Civil War*.

the road, while Lieut. Grafton,[138] with two platoons formed in square in the road itself. Down came the enemy's charge; but our men waited until they came to within seventy or eighty yards, when from the three directions, and admirable volley was poured into them. They did not wait for a second, but wheeled in dismay. Again their officers tried to rally them. So near were they, that their orders could be heard, and when they were disobeyed, the word "cowards!" was audible. But in vain. They would not risk themselves against such musketry. They brought up artillery, but it had no effect, except to stampede some of our cavalry. To finish the recovery of the knapsacks, Co. I relieved A and C, and Co. D, (Capt. Sanger,)[139] took the place of Co. B.)

This was hardly done when the enemy's infantry appeared. Co. I had the brunt of the attack. The enemy's fire was severe, but Co. I flinched not, but fired with perfect steadiness. Part of C and B were sent to their assistance, being deployed as skirmishers on either side of the road. These three checked the enemy.

Everything being ready, the troops moved on. The enemy moved followed, but our fire was too hard for them, and they were wary. The Regiment reached Kernstown and halted, both to rest the men, and care for the wounded which had been unfortunately taken to that point only, instead of going on to Winchester. Ambulances were sent for, but they did not return. Half an hour passed. Again the enemy crept up in the darkness, and opened fire. It was returned with spirit. Capt. Underwood's company again suffered.[140] It was useless to wait. Artillery could be

---

138 James Ingersoll Grafton (1841 – 1865) was a student at Harvard when the war broke out and he left to accept the commission of 2nd Lieutenant. He was wounded at the Battle of Cedar Mountain and seriously wounded at Chancellorsville. He returned to the regiment and was killed in the last battle the regiment fought in, Averysborough, NC. Quint; *The Record of the Second Massachusetts*; and, Adjutant General of Massachusetts; *Massachusetts Soldiers, Sailors and Marines in the Civil War*.

139 The mistake here must be Quint's as it appears in both the *Congregationalist* and "From the Potomac to the Rapidan." There was no Captain named Sanger in the 2nd Massachusetts, and the Captain of Co. D at this point was James Savage, Jr. (1832 - 1862) who was a graduate of Boston Latin School and Harvard (1854). Commissioned Major in June of 1862, Savage was wounded at Cedar Mountain and taken prisoner. He died in a Confederate hospital in Charlottesville, VA. Quint; *The Record of the Second Massachusetts*; and, Adjutant General of Massachusetts; *Massachusetts Soldiers, Sailors and Marines in the Civil War*.

140 Adin Ballou Underwood (1828 - 1888) was a graduate of Brown University (1849) and involved in manufacturing and law. In July of 1862, he accepted a commission as Major of

heard rumbling in the rear. The Macadamized road brought our men out into relief, and the Regiment moved on, in good order.

About 2 A.M., the tired soldiers reached Winchester, and lay down to rest. They needed it badly. But Co. C was sent out as outpost, with companies from other Regiments. Firing was steadily kept up. Capt. Cogswell was skirmishing continually, while all other pickets of this Brigade were driven in. In two hours, he returned, falling back, in good order before the enemy's advance.

Col. Gordon immediately chose position for his Brigade. It was just out of town, on the right of the road going Southward. A long ridge running nearly parallel with the road is broken by a cross gully. On the eminence nearest the town, a little sheltered by broken ground was placed the infantry, the Second Massachusetts, on the right, then, in other the 3d Wisconsin, the 27th Indiana, and the 29th Pennsylvania; and several pieces of artillery were posted in the rear. The other Brigade was on the left of the road, where they fought bravely, particularly the 5th Connecticut.

On the opposite hight was the enemy. As they showed themselves, there were immense masses, dropping them mainly out of sight. As Col. Gordon's Brigade ascended to its place, a fire of grape was opened to them at a few hundred yards distance. The men were ordered to lie down, rising only to fire; and the artillery was kept constantly at work. Co. D was sent to the right as skirmishers to pick off the enemy's horses and gunners; much exposed, they were soon ordered sill nearer the enemy; where they could be sheltered by a wall. So accurate was their fire, with that of the troops in line, that one gun was completely silenced, the enemy not daring to attempt even its removal.

The troops fought bravely, cool and determined as ever, the Second firing only as commanded, and firing with deliberate aim, and in one report. Every man did his duty. But by-and-by a movement of the enemy threatened the two companies

---

the 33rd Massachusetts from which post he rose through the ranks to become Colonel, commanding the regiment at Chancellorsville, Gettysburg, and Lookout Mountain, where he was wounded at Wauhatchie in October of 1863. Underwood was commissioned Brigadier General in January of 1864 and he was posted to Washington, DC until he accepted a Presidential appointment to become surveyor of Customs at Boston in 1865. Quint; *The Record of the Second Massachusetts*; and, Adjutant General of Massachusetts; *Massachusetts Soldiers, Sailors and Marines in the Civil War*.

of skirmishers, and they were called in. Then heavy columns were seen moving to turn the right of the Brigade. Col. Gordon ordered the 27th Indiana and 29th Pennsylvania to take position on the right, in an oblique angle with the other two regiments. They rushed thither, and with shouts began a rapid firing. But seeing the force approaching, they fell back. What could valor do against such odds? Then the guns were seen to be limbered. It was useless to remain. Orders came to retire. The 3d Wisconsin and the 2d Mass., near together, would otherwise have been sacrificed. The former moved off in line. The Second was formed by companies, and moved off by right flank, in perfect order, under heavy fire.

So they entered Winchester, the enemy in pursuit. The exultant foe pursued. But in a side street Col. Andrews halted to reform, as, though steady, two companies were not in position. The regiment was formed in line; guides were posted; the men dressed up. Then the enemy appeared and fired, and the regiment at double quick turned the corner. Then it again marched at common time, disdaining to break. They were the rear. Cavalry dashed against them. Citizens fired from houses. Women shot from windows, and threw hand grenades at them. Yet not a break occurred. Volleys were poured into the houses fired from. Riders were unhorsed. Past burning buildings, intensely hot, reckless of attack, the noblemen stood steady. Then the discipline of the Second told.

So on to Martinsburg. Shells bursting over them; cavalry sweeping round; but unbroken still. And unbroken this rear regiment, before a foe of twenty-five thousand men, it retreated. So on to Williamsport, fifty-three miles from the place it had left thirty-three hours before.

It the action at Winchester this corps stood for three hours and a half from the time the pickets were driven in; four thousand men against twenty-five thousand; seven regiments against twenty-eight actually counted at once. Escaped prisoners tell us that the enemy suffered severely. They were astonished at the daring of this little force, and at its escape. They expected its entire capture. Massachusetts should give Gen. Banks the credit due him, and his corps; and Col. Gordon, who admirably handled his Brigade; and Col. Andrews, a trained soldier and firm commander; and our Second Regiment, which stood like iron, never flinching, firm as veterans; and its gallant dead, who have sealed the cause with its blood. Our Regiment is now acknowledged to be worthy of Massachusetts.

The passage through Winchester illustrates again the infernal influence of Southern education. Men were repeatedly shot after having been captured. Women had accumulated pistols and hand-grenades, and used them on *helpless* men. What causes this? The education of *slavery. That* brutalizes the people it curses. In this town of Winchester, when we occupied it, not a house was robbed; not a woman insulted. Such is the return. Woe be to that town when our troops see it again! As Sodom was, it is; as Sodom is, I trust it will be. But what else is to be expected? "Conciliate!" Conciliate rattle-snakes, if you will. The spirit of a slave-holder, as such, is the spirit of hell.

Our beloved Major Dwight, a splendid officer, is missing. Dr. Leland, our Surgeon, a man of great skill, and universally esteemed, would not abandon his wounded, and is in rebel hands. Dr. Stone met the same fate in similar circumstances. Our loss is, known to be killed, 13; known to be wounded, 43; missing, 105. As stragglers have ceased to come, and as the enemy were seen to kill indiscriminately, there is too much reason to fear that many of the missing we shall never see again. But the names of our gallant dead will be honored.

A.H.Q.

July 18, 1862

Letter from the Army.
(The following letter has been delayed in reaching us, as it was not received till Wednesday last.)
Near Front Royal, Va., June 19, 1862

We have been greatly gratified to find that the Second is praised at home. I have always felt that all which was wanted for the regiment was opportunity to show the character of its material, and the results of its drill and discipline. Few know the work necessary to make a really good regiment; the constant drill, the regular studies and recitations of the officers, the habit of unhesitation obedience of orders, to be obtained only by slow growth. These, ours has had. Even last winter, daily recitations, in two classes, who conducted by the Colonel and Lt. Colonel, instead of allowing idleness. The result is, a regiment whose main idea is, *duty*.

As to the character of the recent retreat, I see nothing to change in what I wrote you. We have since learned that the rebels were astonished and infuriated at the escape. They suffered greatly. Over seventy graves have been counted of men of one southern regiment, the one, I think, which suffered terribly from the sudden fire of the brave Connecticut 5th. The stand of our own regiment near Newtown, we have learned, puzzled the enemy. When they afterwards learned from prisoners that only one regiment did it, they were surprised, and ashamed that it had checked their march.

The *World's*[141] account, by the way, which I see extensively copied, has two items rather queer; one day it says that our regiment went through Winchester with colors flying and drums beating; another, that the second, after firing one volley, broke, ran through Winchester and could not be rallied for two miles. Both statements are untrue. There was no drum beat. And on the other hand, they never broke; nor was there a moment when the regiment was not perfectly in the hand of the commander. We did not even take the double-quick step, except twice when ordered, once in turning a street corner, and once when passing five or six burning buildings in a narrow street where the heat was insupportable. The disjointed items of a youngster who says he slept through the conflict below Winchester, comfortably in a bed at a hotel, are, however, scarcely worth alluding to, but for the fact that some Boston papers copy them.

This experience has had one evident effect on our regiment, to create the happiest feeling between officers and privates. The coolness of our officers, their indifference to danger, and their constant care of their men, have won respect and affection; and officers feel the same towards the men who did all that men could do. It had been enviously said that officers like ours, young men more than two thirds of whom were graduates of some college (two of West Point,) and reared in comparative luxury, would neither endure hardships nor manifest bravery. The reverse precisely is true. The great difficulty with all, was to keep them out of useless danger. In the action at Winchester, those who had any breakfast, ate it unconcernedly. Some, not actively engaged, went to sleep. One servant, even passed along with food, in the midst of a fire of grape. One officer there had a forcible appeal from Brother Trask, in the shape of a bullet from the storm, which knocked his pipe out of his mouth, and so spoilt his smoke.[142]

---

141 The *New York World* was a New York newspaper that started in 1860 under its publisher, Manton Marble. A voice for the Democratic party, The *World* got in trouble with the Lincoln Administration for printing forged calls for 500,000 volunteers in 1864. *The World* relied heavily on soldier's letters for civil war news since it didn't have the funds to pay for news staff. The *World* found its niche under its next publisher, Joseph Pulitzer who employed, among others, the first female investigative journalist, Nellie Bly. Hudson; *Journalism in the United States*.
142 The Reverend George Trask (1798 – 1875) was a graduate of Bowdoin (1826) and Andover Theological Seminary (1829). From his pulpit in Fitchburg, Massachusetts, Trask was particularly known for his anti-Tobacco sermons and as a founding member of the Anti-Tobacco

The regiment remained at Williamsport, with its Brigade until June 10. The other brigade of our corps had left some days earlier. On that day it crossed the river, and bivouacked near Falling Water. The next day it went to and camped at Bunker Hill. The following day it passed through Winchester, where Gen. Banks was, and Gen. Sigel, whose forces had, a week earlier, come up from Harper's Ferry, and camped six miles south, at the exact spot where our regiment had its successful brush with the cavalry. That place we left on Wednesday last, and we are here, a few miles north of Front Royal.

Much of this march was over ground traversed last July, and so had its peculiar interest. Some of its features, however, struck us as peculiar. The conciliatory policy is extreme. A guard from the Brigade was stationed at every house, and no person, officer or man, was allowed even to rob the inhabitants of well-water; fortunately we met brooks occasionally. The General of the corps has just issued an assuring proclamation to the farmers, to the effect that if they gather their crops, nobody shall touch them, unless Government wants them, in which case their value shall be paid. Considering that it is hard to find a Union man this side of Martinsburg, this method of making war by merely furnishing an excellent market to the secessionists, is eminently forgiving. Winchester, with its villainous spawn of hell for inhabitants, is most carefully protected. Houses from which it is capable of clearest proof citizens fired on our soldiers, are unharmed. The dwellers in that town are unharmed. I would not favor any indiscriminate pillage, but the policy which makes it for the interest of men to be rebels is queer. A rebel, he is protected by both Union and Secesh soldiers. A Union man, he is protected by Union, but terribly maltreated by Secesh; therefore – be Secesh. Still, if that is the policy of Government, doubtless there are sound reasons for it. In the meantime I have reason to know that rebel citizens laugh at us, and believe that we do not dare to be justly severe. Some cases of protection would make people stare.

We have had some changes. Our noble Colonel Gordon has been made a Brigadier. He deserved it. Recommended by Congressional delegates last summer, a written protest from a high official in Massachusetts, an enemy from personal disagreements, prevented the appointment. It could not be helped now. Petty

---

League. He used quite a bit of slavery imagery as a metaphor for tobacco addiction. Andover Theological Seminary; *General Catalogue*.

spite was baffled, and one of the best officers in service the country gains. Last Sunday morning the new General addressed a few words to the regiment by way of parting. He could hardly command himself; and when Col. Andrews, who most worthily succeeds, replied, the men testified their regard as only soldiers can, towards one who had been the soul of the regiment and their partner in all its hardships.

Then, Major Dwight had returned before this on parole. His safety had at last been assured. He came back, on his way to Washington. As he neared the camp, "The Major! The Major!" burst from man voices. Over the line the whole regiment burst in a mass. They surrounded him, grasped his hands, his coat, hurried him along, the happy Major almost overwhelmed in their joy. They forgot all about the field-officer; they only remembered that he had been one of his kindest friends for a year, and in action, brave as a hero, cool as a veteran. When it was found, too, that while a prisoner he had buried our dead, and brought back the names of our wounded, and told just how each man was hurt, and what were his prospects, it was "just like the Major," – such cheers were never heard before.

These, and other changes, will necessitate promotions. The second lieutenancy first falling vacant will probably be filled by a sergeant recommended for gallant conduct at Winchester. We shall still have a most efficient set, and if we can get into Gen. Gordon's Brigade, the Regiment will be happy.

As to the general situation you know better where Jackson is than any here except the leaders.

The valley in which we are runs from Pennsylvania, southwest. It is bounded by the Blue Ridge on the east, and the Alleghanies on the west. Two principal places of entrance from Maryland are Harper's Ferry and Williamsport. The valley is tolerably open until we reach Strasburg, where, in the center begins a separate chain – the Massanutten range, which splits the valley for just fifty miles, where, near Harrisonburg, it abruptly ends. Now at the head of the western division stands Strasburg; at the head of the eastern, Front Royal. When Jackson came northward, it was by the eastern side of the Massanutten, Gen. Banks' force not being sufficient to guard either side. Middletown, a few miles north of both Strasburg and

Front Royal, seems the strong point from which to support both places. This is now occupied. Gen. Fremont holds Strasburg, and some distances below; and we are part of the force occupying Front Royal.

These measures seem as if preventative rather than aggressive, but they can easily become the latter. The difficulty here seems this: parts of, or the whole of, *three* army corps, have lately been occupying the valley, each responsible only to Washington. It is a puzzle why all the troops in this limited area should not be in *one* command. Gen. Fremont's department and that of Gen. Banks are separated by only *a line in the road* for fifty miles. If this whole artificial cutting up of territory were done away, and if all the forces this side the Blue Ridge were given to one General, would there not be greater efficient? In fact, ever since Gen. McClellan was limited to his narrow area, and three other independent departments made in Virginia, matters have worked badly. The army would rejoice to hear that the war in Virginia was under one General, and he McClellan.

For myself, I had enough to do in the hospital at Winchester. Several buildings are occupied for this purpose. Our wounded are at the "Union House" hospital, under charge of our own Dr. Leland, formerly of Milford. He has had only one surgeon with him, and a hundred and seventy patients; but everything is neat, the care is admirable, and the men quite cheerful. The surgeon has a great heart, and equal skill, and has the warmest regard from all our men. There is a post chaplain at Winchester, but he has several buildings to visit, including those with the rebel sick. It is very noticeable how the Winchester women send their delicacies to the rebel quarters, few to the Union. Still, our men do not lack. It was a great privilege to go into the hospital, though it was a six-mile ride, and meet our own men of the Second. Take good care of them friends, when they go home, as they will, to recruit. They deserve it.

I am not surprised that many persons are discountenancing stories of rebel insolence and barbarity, because it is hard to believe human nature sunk so low. One thing is true; the wounded collected into hospitals were well treated. Whether the fact that they must and did leave a large number of their own to our care, had any effect, I do not know. I am satisfied that no shots were *knowingly* fired into actual hospitals. But aside from these, there is no reason to qualify any statements which I have seen of rebel barbarity. This race is not fully civilized yet. For ignorance and stupidity, I could tell you facts I never would have believed but for seeing them. And I tell you again, until slavery is broken, and until a new race is introduced to a very great extent, there will be no true peace. Senator Sumner never uttered more true words than those in his speech "The Barbarism of Slavery."[143]

A. H. Q.

---

[143] Charles Sumner, Senior Senator from Massachusetts gave his "Barbarism of Slavery" speech in June of 1860 in support of the Kansas admission to the Union as a free state. This was his first speech since he returned to the Senate a year previous following the 1856 beating he received in the Senate at the hands of Rep. Preston Brookes of South Carolina. In the speech, Sumner shows the economic stifling that is the result of slavery and a slave-based economy.

July 25, 1862

On the Road, Rappahanock Co., Va.,
July 9, 1862

Last Saturday evening, we as we looked at the red, sunset sky, we said, "it will be hot, to-morrow." Why we felt special interest in the expected weather was, because we were to march to-morrow. The tidings had come of reverses at Richmond. We knew that there were consternation at Washington. A large force must be interposed between the loyal and rebel capitals. With sorrowful hearts we learned what long ago, able and wise military men had foreboded, difficulties to Gen. McClellan by reason of the jealousies which had first cut up his Virginia command into absurd geographical districts, and then had left the modest, brave, faithful, soldier, with inadequate forces. Yet nobody felt discouraged. Nobody doubted but that Gen. McClellan would do all that man could do; for the army believes in "Georgie," and detests the political gamesters at Washington. The army knows *who* are jealous of him, and *why*; and wonders that the indignation of an outraged people does not *demand* the removal of men in whom all confidence was lost long ago.

It *was* hot, Sunday. Reveillé was beat at the usual hour. All was made ready to move. Another brigade had gone in the night, whose rumbling wagons we could hear when we were foolish enough to lie awake. The morning hours wore on. At eleven o'clock we heard "route step forward!" The sun was blazing hot, when we started, and grew hotter and hotter. A few miles on was the Shenandoah, the junction of its north fork and main stream. There we waited under a hill, on a exposed plain, where the very leaves hung stupefied. Hours passed before the indolent wagon trains in front moved out of the way, and then we moved again. We crossed the temporary bridge built at the junction of the rivers; passed over the site of Col. Kenley's contest, where relics still lie in profusion, but which we left untouched, having long since got tired of carrying loads of old iron; went through the rather pretty little town of Front Royal, which is well shaded, a mile or so from the railroad to which a branch runs; and camped a mile or so south of the town. No sooner had the regiment reached its ground, than men fell utterly exhausted, and passed under the surgeon's care. The march had not been long, but horrible for heat. On it, we wondered, why as our destination was said to be Warrenton, government did not transport the troops by railroad, in one day, rather than break them down by a four day's march under a Virginia July sun. We also wondered why we might not have had our Sunday in quiet, and, starting at, say five o'clock in the afternoon, made the same distance by eight o'clock. Soldiers may "wonder," but they cannot help themselves. However, many of us had no scruples at taking a cooling bath that evening in a brawling brook near by, and having followed the Apostle's directions as to "pure water" and a "clean conscience," slept very well.[144]

And, on Monday, at three o'clock, reveille awakened us. At six o'clock we were in the road, towards the Blue Ridge. It was a lovely morning; and truthful, for it promised another hot day, and was right about it. It was an eventful anniversary, too. For, one year ago that day, we left Camp Andrew, in West Roxbury; and left Boston; and left wives, children and friends. Some wives, some children are to be seen no more; and some of that number of brave men, have sealed their patriotic contract with their blood.

Four miles, or may be, five, from Front Royal, is Chester Gap, a break in the summit of the Blue Ridge. The ascent is gentle; the scenery beautiful. The heat was severe, but when at last we reached the summit of the road, and began to descend, the breeze swept over us gently and cooled the heated men. We were descending the Ridge, and I doubt if there was one there who did not rejoice that at last we were out of that hated Virginia valley, into which our evil fortune had sent us one year ago, and where our energies had been uselessly spent for that time. We were in Eastern Virginia, at last.

Twelve miles that day before eleven o'clock. Then we rested in a beautiful wood, and towards night pitched our tents. By and by a delightful shower came

---

144 New Testament; *Epistle to the Hebrews 10:22.*

up, so that when next morning we marched on, the ground was delightfully firm. We were rear-guard that next day, and so were troubled by the long wagon trains. Troubles easily borne; for this section is prolific in cherries, and as we halted for hours, the men luxuriated in cherries; they eat cherries among the branches; they picked cherries and eat under the shade as they marched. Providence evidently made these cherries ripen for our march.

But, five miles on the road we halted. We camped. Orders came, based on the facts that anxiety for Gen. McClellan was over, and that sufficient forces were at Warrenton. What to do with our two Brigades, nobody seemed to know, and we are waiting till somebody finds out. As usual, we are a kind of encumbrance, placed nobody knows why; and what to do with us, I think always puzzles the authorities. But we wait. Nothing is given us to do. Our brethren at Richmond, we would gladly help. Our own comparative uselessness we lament. But if our Government desires us to "spend the summer in the country" we can do so; tough a little preferring, if our wishes were consulted, some sea-side spot. For instance, Nahant is cooler; or the line of he Lowell and Lawrence Railroad, ought not there to be a force sufficient to defend it? Or say at Tewskbury, which, if my memory serves me, is quite warm.

Barring our wishes, however, clearly the country needs men. The call for three hundred thousand surprises nobody here. It will take half that number to fill up existing regiments. The Second left Boston with 1040 men. Now it cannot bring into the field, of fighting men, over 400. A hundred and thirty of the loss is due to Winchester. Of the remainder, quite a number have been discharged; not a few died. And then, a small multitude is detailed everywhere. Of officers, Lieut. Col. Dwight is a paroled prisoner. Surgeon Leland is acting Medical Director of the Division. Four captains are off on various orders: five first lieutenants, and four second lieutenants, some are aids to Generals; one is on signal service; some are recruiting. Send back our men who are wasted in our other employments; employ "civil" nurses at Frederick; restore to a fighting position the many, officers and men, who are engaged in the trucking business (here called Quartermaster's department,) and the provision trade, (here called Commissary's department,) and hire some good truckmen and pork dealers from Boston, infinitely better fitted than West Point graduates; cut down the hosts of men wasted on staff employ, as witness the late enormous list thrown out by Gen. Fremont's being "relieved" of command; and then the terrible deficiencies of our 600,000 men would melt away one half.

But after that were done, (which never will be,) the country needs more soldiers. It has a right to demand them. After God, it has the first claim. When at home a few days last January, I could see no diminution in the street throngs; no want of men in business. *Here*, it is rare to find an able-bodied man; ask for one, and regularly you are answered "he is in the army." In the army to support the most infernal institution the world ever saw, and to overthrow the best government the world ever saw, while in Massachusetts there are multitudes who criticize and carp at the noble McClellan, as though they knew all about war, but never lift a hand. You whose families *must* have your services at home, there are enough without you. But you whose only trouble is your dislike at leaving them, -- your fellow-men have left wives and children, with sore hearts too; can you? You who are sick, stay at home; but you whose faces are white and forms slender only because you need air and activity, come, and grow stalwart. You whose highest work is to sell ribbons and laces, bonnets and slippers, -- leave that to *women; be men*; a musket is more honorable than a yardstick; a hard hand is better than flabby fingers; an honest tan is a better color than tallow. A soldier is a *man*.

Influential men at home ought to set the example. *They* can fill up the army in a week. Let them throw their wealth, their ability, their persons to this cause, and hosts of followers would fall in. If they have wealth, that excuses nobody from serving his country. If they *can* live at ease, that is no reason why they *should* live in ease.

And you, brother ministers, whose work is not, and ought not be, to fight, -- you whose hearts are in this cause, and who would gladly be in it yourselves, -- will *you* not use your powerful influence to fill up our armies? Tell the people what this war is for. Tell them it is a war holier than ever were crusades. Show them what the country needs. Explain what patriotism is. Convince your young men that the patriot *must* not refuse this call. Make them understand what few do understand, the exigencies of the Age; that this is the war of Civilization against Barbarism, Light against Darkness, Right against Wrong; that now is the culmination of the Heathenism of two centuries; that that Heathenism is indeed earnest. The ministry of Christ have a trust in their hands which this generation never equaled before, never will again. Thank God, I know they are TRUE.

A.H.Q.

Near Warrenton, Va., July 16, 1862.

Your letter came a day or two ago. You say you have had none from me since one I wrote concerning the "retreat" of May 24 – 25. You inquire whether I have ceased writing. "Ceased writing!" when I have written as often, at least, as once a fortnight! Long ago the *Congregationalist* ceased its welcome visits. I waited in patience. Little did I know the sad truth; how all my brilliant thoughts, my statesmanic disquistions, my beautiful descriptions – had all gone, through the Post-Office tunnel, into some paper-mill. The world can never know what it has last. It is a hopeless loss: should they come to light, alas for their freshness. A good brother of my acquaintance had a bottle of champagne sent him by a General. The excellent brother thanked the donor, and stated to him that he never drank, but would keep this bottle to use a little from time to time in case of sickness. He learned his mistake. In case my letters turn up, -- they are too long uncorked; they are flat forever.

I do not know what I wrote. I never read my letters in print, much less keep copies. But by way of recapitulation as to peregrinations of our Regiment, -- the Second (in its Brigade) left Williamsport, Md., June 10, and crossed the river, to the inspiring music of "Carry me back to old Virginia, to old Virginia's shore;" bivouacked that night near Falling Waters; passed through Martinsburgh to Bunker Hill, and there camped; next day marched to and through Winchester in close order; camped that night at Bartonsville, a flourishing town of three houses, -- the scene of a brisk little fight of the Second in May, -- about seven miles south of Winchester; remained there until June 18, when we moved to a spot about four miles north of Front Royal, where we had the capital fortune to get back, as Brigadier, our own Massachusetts soldier, Gen. Gordon. Sunday, July 6, we were ordered on; one night we camped a mile south of Front Royal; one night snug by a pretty, locust-shaded little village called Flint Hill; two nights near Gaines' Cross Roads; here we pitched our tents late Friday night; and here we wait for orders.

All along the roads are great wheat fields, into which no sickle will enter. Crops sufficient to feed all New England are to be lost for want of laborers. Owners have gone to war, and blacks have run away as the army moved. The strength of the rebel army is in slave labor. Able-bodied men can be spared to fight wherever the black laborers remain. The North has made a great mistake in supposing that slavery is an element of weakness at the South, in time of war. Practically, the reverse is true. It need not be so. It ought not to be so. Had we given the slaves to understand that they are *free*, the crops now gathering would never have been food for rebel armies.

While waiting, we are amid a large army. Brigadier-Generals are plenty. Regiments are on every hand. The 12th and 13th Mass. are again our neighbors, and we revive old friendships with great comfort. Our baggage is cut down; one valise to an officer. Our tents are partly taken away; the officers crowd into a diminished number, and the privates have, or are to have, "shelter" tents.[145] Ten days' rations are to be kept on hand, and each regiment to be ready to move any time, rations and all, at an hour's notice. Gen. Pope's address to his army implies work.[146] For myself, I am better fitted for a march than I was a week ago, when I had lost my horse! He turned up, at last, in the 5th New York horse-thieves, (known *officially* as cavalry.) Gen. Gordon lost a horse of his; it was found in, and with great difficulty (ending in the arrest of a captain) procured from, the 5th New York horse-thieves. Our adjutant lost two horses; both were discovered – in the 5th New York horse-thieves.[147]

Everybody hopes we are to move towards Richmond. Whether it were wise, we cannot judge. We have confidence in the Union Generals. What little esteem we ever had for the civilians who manage the war, was long since lost. Let them manage their politics; but let soldiers plan campaigns, -- is the universal feeling.

---

145 Shelter tents are designed to that each soldier carries one half of the tent and they are buttoned together through an overlapping seam. Each tent covered two men. Volo and Volo; *Daily Life in Civil War America.*

146 John Pope (1822 – 1892) was a graduate of West Point (1842) and served in the Mexican-American war as well as on the frontier. Just prior to the Civil War, Pope surveyed southern routes for the Transcontinental Railroad. Pope began the war as a Brigadier General in the Western Theater where his early successes brought him to the attention of the Lincoln Administration. Encouraged to come East, Pope took command of the Army of the Potomac after McClellan's failure on the Peninsula. Pope's message to his new troops in Virginia unfavorably compared the Eastern troops to the Western troops. Pope's failure at the Second Battle of Bull Run in August of 1862 found him posted back to Missouri shortly thereafter. Warner; *Generals in Blue*

147 The 5th New York Cavalry was organized in July of 1861 by Colonel Othniel De Forrest. Originally entitled the "Ira Harris Cavalry" after the Senator from New York, it left the state in November of 1861. The regiment participated in Cedar Mountain, Groveton and the Second Battle of Bull Run and it was heavily engaged at Gettysburg. The regiment remained in the east through the end of the war, particularly serving in the Shenandoah Valley under General Sheridan. "5th New York Cavalry Regiment;" *Unit History Project;*

To the citizen-leaders at Washington are due the wails in thousands of households; to them, the prolonging of the war; to them, the waster of untold millions of money; to them the imminent danger of foreign intervention; all accomplished when men in civil life determined to dictate to educated soldiers what they, as soldiers, must do; when they thwarted the best plans; refused the leading General the forces he asked as indispensable; tried to balance the jealousies of parties by giving each General an inadequate independent command. I tell you, the execrations of the army upon the authors of our disasters are deep and endless. And while not dismayed, yet we are saddened upon hearing now that no change is to be made. Unless a *practical* change is made, I insist that the South *cannot* be conquered.

There are differences of opinion in the army, as to the slavery question. Some want emancipation proclaimed. Some practical and effectual emancipation without proclamations: some, to leave slavery as it was before the war. The drifting is towards emancipation, mainly to the second position. In that, I rather coincide, though I want the thing *done* at any rate, as necessary for the country. But all love their country first and best. If we can accomplish emancipation, it would be a glorious deed for our country. If not now, yet the old Flag must triumph. And then, eternal attack on slavery. But, to emancipate is the way to succeed; and therefore the Government needs a policy, needs firmness, needs energy.

The more I see, the more I believe in the feasibility of emancipation. The difficulties in the way are not unconquerable; I mean, as to adjusting the elements of the new state of society caused thereby. The only obstacle is in the masters, who have so long made men work without wages, that, like all tyrants, they cannot bear to go to work for an *honest* living. The slaves could be freed, and remain on the soil. Compulsory colonization seems to me a perfect humbug, -- unless you colonize the masters, the real encumbrances. To remove the industrious portion of the community is foolish. France tried that when it banished thousands of Protestant artizans. Let us not commit the same folly. Suppose Massachusetts were to expel from its borders its day-laborers, its working farmers, its shoemakers, its blacksmiths, -- where would the wealth of Massachusetts be? The blacks are the workmen, -- peasant laborers generally, but often mechanics. They do not wish to leave their native land. Why should they? What *right* have we to expel them? Is there race not a native of the soil? No more is ours. You who weep over "Evangeline," wherein have *we* a right to imitate the conduct of the arrant humbug-nation of Europe?[148]

Of course, in freeing the slaves, there would be trouble. They are unfit for liberty in some respects. But who made them so? What right have the masters – the criminals, to plead their own crime as an excuse for perpetuating that crime? Whatever troubles would ensue, are the penalty of transgression, the price of reform. When our surgeon sets a broken leg, there is pain in the operation; there is subsequent inflammation in the very process of healing; there is, for a time, helplessness; but then there comes health and power; and in spite of, and at the cost of, pain and fever, it was better to have the leg set. Society here has both legs broken; better set them.

Better set them, because it is *right*. I thank God that I can stand, untrammeled, on the simple basis of *right*. I doubt all politicians who dodge the question of *right*. Your Fourth of July oration is powerful, but I cannot see that it touches one point, viz., that the legality it argues for is iniquitous. Every man has a *right* to freedom, save in crime. Every man who deprives another of that freedom is a robber. Every law which sanctions that robbery is wicked. In conversing with Virginians, there is one argument which they cannot answer: *every man has a right to his liberty.* On secession, or nullification, or republican party, or compromise, they will twist and dodge; but from that simple principle there is no escape. "I believe," I have told many of them, "in just what your own constitution of Virginia says, adopted in the last century, reenacted by Convention in December, 1861, when in its preamble it declares that "all men are created free and equal, and possessed of rights of which they cannot divest themselves or their posterity." That is the platform. It is astonishing how simple one's duty becomes, when he gets at this fundamental principle, and means to adhere to it.

You will see that Congress, by recent legislation has materially reduced the pay of chaplains, and possibly you will be curious to know its result. It is hard telling yet. There are two things involved; one is, the pay as to be established, is about the same as that of a second lieutenant of infantry, showing the estimation in which chaplaincies are held by the governing power. Moreover, second lieutenants are men who

---

148 "Evangeline" is an epic poem by Henry Wadsworth Longfellow that proved to be his best-selling work in his lifetime. The story follows a young woman as she searches for her true love Gabriel after the two were torn asunder by the removal of the Acadians by the British. Evangeline becomes a Sister of Mercy in Philadelphia and finally finds Gabriel in the hospital, ill from an outbreak of disease. Gabriel dies in her arms.

have been at no expense in training for their position; chaplains have spent thousands of dollars in acquiring education. Second lieutenants are usually very young men; chaplains are necessarily men of considerable experience. Second Lieutenants are unmarried; chaplains have families forty-nine times out of fifty. The other thing to be considered is, that while some chaplains will receive more than in any of their settlements, very many are already making comparative pecuniary sacrifice. The expenses of a campaign are very large. I judge from a year's experience that the pay newly established is inadequate, and must speedily send home all except the poorer class, who never had a parish of any size, and wealthy men, who can afford to stay. As to your correspondent, he loves this service; but he has a wife and child to support; he cannot do it long on the pay now offered; but he will stay, economizing as much as possible, until the necessity, plainly to be foreseen, drives him home. He laments that Congress thinks no more of chaplaincies; but he does no wonder at it. The entire annual saving to the government may possibly amount to $225,000.[149]

But wherever our country wants us, she should have us. And unless this rebellion is soon crushed, we shall have war enough. Our country will then need all its sons. Never should I have any temptation to be more intimately connected with a soldier's life than now, unless foreign powers intervened. Then I should feel that any place was glory. To be one of an army to humble and cripple forever that hypocritical, arrogant, incarnation of selfishness, that Pecksniff of nations,[150] England, the tyrant in Ireland, the barbarian in India, the hereditary ally of despots, haughty to the weak, fawning on the strong, "whose end is destruction, whose God is their belly, and whose glory is in their shame" – *that* would make ancestral fire burn in my veins; *That* I should recognize as a duty to the civilization of the century and to the voice of God. It would be a *holy* war.

A. H. Q.

---

149 In July of 1862 the United States Congress cut Chaplain's pay from $145.50 per month to $100 per month and they went from 3 rations to 2 rations a day, plus forage for a horse. Hospital Chaplains received the same pay but were paid $25 per month for renting quarters (finding his own meals) in place of rations and forage. This happened at the same time that they were dismissing Regimental bands in an effort to "economize" on the war. Brinsfield; *Faith in the Fight.*

150 "Pecksniff" refers to Seth Pecksniff, a character in Charles Dickens' novel Martin Chuzzlewit. As Quint intimates, Seth Pecksniff is insincere and a hypocrite.

August 1, 1862

Letter from the Army.
Near Washington, Rappahannock Co., Va.,
July 24th, 1862

It is rather curious to reckon over the various titles and commanders of the corps in which, for one year, we have served. We have been in the Army of the Valley, the Army of the Shenandoah, the Army of the Potomac, the Army of Virginia; we "change the place, yet keep the pain." General Patterson has commanded one Division, Gen. Banks alone, Gen. Banks under Gen. McClellan, Gen. Banks alone again, Gen. Pope, and now if rumor be true, Gen. Halleck[151] over Gen. Pope. For brigadiers we have had Generals Abercrombie, Williams, Hamilton, Greene,[152] and

---

151 Henry Wager Halleck (1815 – 1872) was the senior commander of the U.S. Army in the Western Theater at the beginning of the war. Halleck attended West Point (1839) and early on in his career wrote a report on United States Coastal Defenses. During the Mexican-American war, Halleck was stationed in California and through his experience there became involved in California's admission to the Union, including becoming one of the authors of the State Constitution. Halleck was placed in charge of the Department of Missouri at the outset of the war, but McClellan's failure and Halleck's success at administration convinced President Lincoln that Halleck could be useful in Washington to prod the lower-ranked Generals. Halleck wasn't particularly successful as "General-in-Chief" but proved an able "Chief of Staff" to Grant when Grant took over that role. Warner; *Generals in Blue*
152 George Sears Greene (1801 – 1899) attended West Point (1823) and graduated 2nd in his class. Greene chose to accept a commission with the 3rd US Artillery, though he spent a few years teaching at the academy where Robert E. Lee was one of his students. After 13 years of service duty, Greene resigned his commission in 1836 and became a civil engineer. At the outbreak of the Civil War, Greene was over 60 years old and had been out of the army for 25 years,

Gordon, varying backwards and forwards until one tenure of each would not last a month. As we have been kept in a limited locality, and formed part of but one army, the simplicity and straightforwardness of public management is pleasingly illustrated.

Now, matters seem to have come to a stop. The army and the country pauses to consider. Richmond will not fall this week. The rebellion will not end the week after. What is the look of things?

After more than a year's fighting, after untold expenditure of treasure and blood, we seem no nearer the end than when we commenced. The forebodings long entertained by experienced men have been realized. A year ago, and repeatedly since, high, very high authority predicted to me just this state of things. The predictions were based upon the way public matters were managed, and upon the misunderstood energies and resources of the South.

Yet there are some hopeful matters with us.

One is, the union of the forces in Upper Virginia under one general. It has long been waited for. The evils of the opposite course have been most painfully felt on the ground. While the people have been amused with pompous headings in the dailies about some little skirmish, they did not know that our strength has been frittered away, our resources wasted. Who should tell it? Who could venture to speak in view of the stringent rules against communicating "information?" Now, the troops are under one head. Of Gen. Pope himself, the country knows. His deeds declare what he is. The recent inaugural (so to call it,) did not favorably impress the soldiery; but the subsequent orders are received with delight. They indicate a vigor and policy which have long been waited for. Baggage, well called *impedimenta* by the Romans, has been reduced. Wagons are in order. A hundred and fifty rounds of ammunition per man are kept with the regiment. And all are quietly and courageously waiting to second him in what the general may do with the Army of Virginia.

---

still, Governor Morgan of New York gave him a commission as Colonel of the 60th Regiment in January of 1862. While General Greene led his men in stubborn defenses and aggressive attacks, his greatest success was the defense of Culp's Hill on the 2nd day of Gettysburg. Greene went with his brigade to join Sherman's army near Chattanooga and on the march to Atlanta, Savannah and the Carolinas. Warner; *Generals in Blue*

There is sense, also, in the appointment of General Halleck (if it be true) as general-in-chief. Not merely that it is General Halleck, but that it is a general-in-chief; and also that it is one whom we may hope will not be interfered with. A soldier is to plan our campaigns; let civilians in office attend to their civil duties. What could be more proper? The contrary has cost the country enough woe. Thank God for this symptom of reason in high quarters. Why a republic has been considered incapable of carrying on wars with success, is evidently because the political leaders cannot willingly keep their fingers out of military affairs. Rome, in time of peril, committed its powers to a dictator, charging him to see that the republic met with no harm. The universal demand of our people for unity and efficiency, have virtually done the same thing. They should now demand that the head of the armies be not interfered with. Wielding the vast resources of the North, and eminently qualified, he cannot fail. The civil authorities can settle political questions; the military must rule the armies. If this be not done, I see no successful issue to this war; nor do men infinitely better qualified to judge. Now, we may hope that Gen. Pope, in Upper Virginia, will have more men and a place. We may hope that Gen. McClellan, the noble soldier who has with true greatness kept all his grievances to himself, will have what he needs.

The new indications as to the vigor with which all proper warlike measures are to be pushed, are hopeful signs. Government has been very slow to be in earnest. It has long been a matter of astonishment that the importance of the occasion has not been recognized. The south is in earnest. It takes what property it wants. It impresses its citizens. It scourges Union men. We play with the rebellion. We treat Union and rebel alike. We have kept negroes at work to support their masters in the rebel army. We have guarded rebels' straw stacks while our men slept on the ground. We have used the labor of negroes with hesitation and apology. That is, we formerly did. Now, we shall take rebel property. We should receive, organize, arm if advantageous, our black allies. We could make the south tremble by the statement, "your slaves shall be free, and they shall help conquer you." I have seen the effect a suggestion of such a policy makes on rebels. It angers them, but it terrifies them. Of all the Union generals, they consider McClellan the most of a military man; the man they are most afraid of is *Fremont*. They *dread* him. In the rebel army at Winchester, there were plenty of black soldiers, *actual soldiers*, as many will testify. Why should not *we* use such?

But there are reasons which account for the indecision of government. One is, the stupefying air of Washington. It benumbs one. It is hard, there, for anybody to realize the condition of the country, immersed in petty details and surrounded by corruption. But another is, the people have not spoken in a clear and decisive tone. A noisy demagogue editor makes as much noise as a true patriot. "Conservative" patriots are afraid to venture on anything out of the old track. Even old Massachusetts presents a divided front in the councils of the nation, and its delegates have been seen congratulated after speeches, by the remnant of traitors there. How then, can the President see what the people want? If the administration could but rise above even such considerations, and ask "what does God want," then the pillar of fire by night, and the cloud by day, would go before us in our war of escaped from our slavery to southern despots. But, is the old Bay State to be misrepresented forever? Is it to re-send to congress shaky politicians or open misrepresentatives? If you want more of your sons slaughtered, choose again such men at the next election; but if you want to conquer, give us a clean delegation.

Congress, at its last session, has, on the whole done well. It has voted men and supplies. It has pledged the country. It has made and urged stringent and energetic measures. Of course, whatever Congress should do, *we* are bound to respect it; for that pleasant literature, the Articles of War say, "Any officer or soldier who shall use contemptuous or disrespectful language against the ..... Congress of the United States, ... shall be cashiered, or otherwise punished, as a court-martial shall direct." But apart from the respect thus secured, I really think that congress has done well in its late session. Yet, there is a feeling of relief that it has adjourned. Nobody knew what it would do. Now it has done its work well and gone home, we are glad. They leave power enough in the President's hands. They authorize the calling out of men, the equipment of armies. So soon, therefore, as our armies are filled, the rebellion must falter.

So soon as our armies are filled. When will that be? The dark spot in our horizon is at home. The fact is evident that men come in slowly. The worse fact is evident, the more disgraceful one, that large bounties are offered to secure enlistment! We read your papers with amazement. Glowing meetings are held in this and that town. Great speakers are called out to address the people. The honorable and reverends speak; the rich offer money. Is this needed?

Is it possible that Massachusetts has fallen to this? Must its sons be bribed to fight for their country, in a war in which all are agreed? Have our fellow citizens sunk to such cowardice that they must be *bought* for a hundred dollars? Talk not, after this, of the Hessians, who sold themselves in the war of the Revolution. Is patriotism so precarious as to need the weight of a hundred dollars?

Is it true that the authorities have themselves lost self-respect to such an extent as to *offer* these bribes? Has not the country a *right* to the service of every able-bodied man? And as it has that right, why should not the manly course be taken? Call for the men on just the pay as thirty thousand men of Massachusetts have already gone for. There is the power to do this; is there not the courage?

The argument seems to be that it would be a confession of weakness to draft. Is it any less so, besides the disgrace, to *bribe*? The subterfuge is too apparent. Your great gatherings, and your hundred dollar bribe are confessions that simple volunteering is ended. That there are not fifteen thousand men ready to go if needed, cannot be true. Many a man who hesitates would be willing to submit to the draft. The conscription is the true method. I believe in it because it is *democratic*. The conscription, which will take rich and poor alike, high and low, and so guarded that the rich man's money will no secure his immunity. The idea is preposterous that only certain social classes ought to fight. *Men* fight, not your dollars. I know no man too good to fight for his country. It *was* a noble sight, when six hundred thousand men rushed to arms. It *is* a disgraceful sight, when recruiting officers buy men at a hundred dollars apiece.

The emotions of the army to a great extent I know.

The soldiers are disgusted with the able-bodied speech makers. Why do not they, at the close of their speeches, say, "*I* go for one." Their country, *they* love it dearly; at a safe distance.

The soldiers feel a sense of injustice in this matter of bounties. "We," they say, "came in time of doubt. We have borne the hardships and dangers of work, and bullets. These new men have had all the comforts of home for that year; and now, they are to be rewarded with a hundred dollars apiece! And we, so far as we have property, are to be taxed to pay for this!"

The soldiers feel that this whole business is fostered by many men who wish to secure themselves. They will not volunteer; they might be drafted; if drafted, it would be disgraceful to secure a substitute. They talk loud; they vote bounties; but *they* will stay at home, buying and selling and getting gain.

The soldiers see the prodigality and reckless waste of this system. Towns vie with towns in proffers States rival states. Is Massachusetts so affluent that it wants to throw away fifteen hundred thousand dollars before it puts a gun in a man's hand, or a pair of shoes on his feet, or a piece of bread I his mouth? Are taxes so light, are expenses so small, that this bagatelle of a million and a half is of no consequences? If so, offer the soldiers already in the field the three millions they deserve.

It is humiliating. It must be that Massachusetts is not aware of the imminent dangers of the occasion. It may not know that Gen. McClellan cannot stir without new aid; that the army of Virginia is confronted by heavy forces, which may be hurled upon it any week; that – I dare not say how many – thousands are the sole and anxious defense of the Potomac? And instead of ordering a conscription, a hundred dollar bounty, and huge speeches are gathering driblets. An active, wise, unscrupulous foe is threatening, with great forces, even the North itself; the North refuses to take the only manly course to fill up its exhausted armies.

Your paraphernalia of recruiting is an abomination; your bribes are disgraceful. There is a cheap, simple, fair way. Call together your able-bodied men. Select by lot the requisite number. Take care of their families while they are gone; or, better, draw first only from unmarried men. If the people will not submit to this, a republic is a failure. If the administration is afraid to risk its popularity, the administration is a nuisance.

A. H. Q.

August 8, 1862

Letter from the Army.
Near Washington, Rappahannock Co., Va.
July 30, 1862

How we came here was by road from Warrenton, across Carter's Creek just above its junction with Hedgeman's River, and then across the river itself, over a temporary bridge, (very temporary – a freshet started it towards the sea two days afterwards,) on whose bank we camped that night, July 20, in a beautiful thunder storm; then, next day, through Amissville, a forlorn, deserted village, to Gaines' Cross Roads (so called because no roads cross there,) and turning westward, traveled, in another thunder storm, to a steep hill side, where we made a stay quite long for this pilgrim life. It rained when we camped, and rained next day. Sunday morning it did not rain, and we had public worship, but it rained in the afternoon.

    A beautiful view was visible from that camp. Broad fields, broken now and then by woods, were bounded only by sharply outlined hills, wooded almost to their tops. The little village of Washington lay nestling under the shadows of the Blue Ridge, with white houses gleaming out of the dark green foliage, and a church or two visible, a third of a mile away. Even in rainy days it was pleasant to watch the riotous clouds on the mountain sides. I was sorry I went into Washington, one day. Centered in green meadows, watered by a tree-fringed brook, overshadowed by mountains, -- with dirt contends with whitewash, nasty streets lead no where, three mean taverns intimated the ancient character of the place, in fact, it images Southern chivalry; fair to view at a distance; a sham when inspected.

I hate shams. And so I was glad when we left the hill side, as we did to move a mile or two, for military purposes, last Thursday. It was irritating to sit in our lofty camp, say at sunset, and look down to the village, so quiet, so fair to view, and yet feel "you are a dirty sham." I appreciated the sensations of the little girl, when she learned that her pretty doll was filled with sawdust. Not for this, however, did we move. War does not care for scenery.

Why we came here was to occupy a more appropriate position for the purposes of the campaign, than we did at Warrenton. Indeed, I have heard it stated that some mistake sent us down there at all. Gen. Banks' whole corps is here or hereabouts, barring one brigade which is at or near Culpepper. Somebody else is at Sperryville, six miles southwest of this. Somebody at Luray, not far westward of that. Somebody at Warrington. And so forth, and so on. All are under command of Gen. Pope, whom we should be glad to see. I am told that he has lately moved his headquarters from Washington, D. C., to Warrenton. Our forces are within supporting distances of each other, from the Potomac to the Blue Ridge; while in the valley, just over the Ridge, troops hold Winchester, rather shakingly, and the railroad to Harper's Ferry.

Yet I see no prospect of immediate activity. True, the troops are kept in readiness, but so they ought always to be. Should the rebels dash up this way, there would be work. Should they conclude to try the valley again, perhaps there would be work. The crops there are well worth their efforts. And I do not see why they may not be gathering them in the vicinity of Harrisonburg. But that any movement is to be made toward Richmond, does not appear. Gen. Pope, however, keeps the rebels well irritated below. We want troops to accomplish much.

The new orders of the General are well received. Every one feels that we have played at war. War is to destroy, not protect an enemy. Some Union people in the valley told us, and always told us, that our cause was weakening. If "we are coming, Father Abraham, three hundred thousand more," it is a comfort that it is intended now to fight. The orders requiring the inhabitants behind our lines to take the oath of allegiance, or else travel southward, is exceedingly disliked by rebels. But this is just what has been long needed. I am satisfied that, were the people sure the rebel armies would not return, they would almost all take the required oath without objection. This country was unanimous for secession; but terror made it so. And genuine secephers will submit without feeling any loss of honor, so soon as their cause becomes hopeless by the defeat of their main armies. Curiously enough, the people were told the secession was the only way to prevent "war," and were fools enough to believe it. They *are* an ignorant set. Passing through quite a village in the Valley, we found the people troubled as to the instruments of our band; they had never seen any; they imagined them some terribly destructive kind of fire-arms; "yes, ma'am," replied on to the questioner, *this is the belt-teezer*, to fire grape at short distances, and is awfully powerful!" The wondering people gazed in dismay.

We have public worship quite regularly. Rarely, this spring and summer, have bad weather or movements prevented. Our Colonel is very exact about it, and where that is the case, few interruptions are necessary. Last Sabbath *you* would have enjoyed our meeting-house better than yours. Ours was an open, yet shady and beautiful wood, just above a rapid brook; yours was a hot, confined, four-walled building. Your cushioned seats are not equal to our grassy sod. Nor your miserable penitentiary of a wooden box, to be compared with our level sward, for a pulpit. Some in your house went to sleep; ours do not, (they might get a couple of hours of "attention" if they did). It is humanizing, in war, to have the Sabbath, however inadequately observed, and public worship – the text, the old tunes – so like home. Yet there was a lack – no wives, no bright-eyed children, nothing but armed men. Such as the worship is, it is growing less in the army. Many regiments are without chaplains now. These officers are leaving quite rapidly. Several have tendered resignations within three weeks, and I think many others intend to do so soon. Then batteries have no chaplains. I had a funeral service in one last Saturday; a youth of twenty years, whose name I knew not, whose home I had not heard of, whom I had never seen; but the tears stood in the eyes of the officer who came to ask me to officiate, as he said, "he was a good boy, and the only child of a widow." The whole force of the battery went to the grave, and sight at them would cure, I hope so, at least, the officials who want to leave our Sabbaths unnoticed, our sick without religious comforters, our dead buried like beasts.

One of our own number, too, was buried on Sunday. Two miles from camp his company, officers and men, carried him to the village graveyard, overgrown with weeds and neglected. Other dead were there, newly buried. Ours was reverently placed in their line, and a plain board tells where the stranger lies. These scenes have never lost their first sadness.

Last week, I wrote somewhat plainly, I believe, as to the bounties offered for enlistments. I hope that letter went safely. Most of the dailies now arriving try to conceal the real results of the plan in vogue, but it is easy to see through the deception. Recruiting is a failure. In spite of "eloquent remarks" and "soul-stirring resolutions," in spite of bounties ranging up to $150. per man, recruiting is a failure. I am glad of it. The army is glad of it. Not glad that men do not volunteer, but glad that the bribe is ineffective. The army feels ashamed of such methods; indignant at their injustice; astonished at their recklessness. If the 15,000 had come forth spontaneously, well. But everybody knew that could not be. The adventurous had gone already. Thousands upon thousands remain; equally courageous, and who are willing to go if actually called upon, but who do not care to volunteer. A draft would have brought out the best material in the state, and have organized a splendid soldiery. You have tried bribes, and in that very thing confessed your weakness. The slowness of enlistment, even with the bounty, shows what anybody might have seen, and what many did see, that the draft is unnecessary. Foreign powers will say that the war is growing unpopular. Had an instant draft been ordered, there would have been no room for the allegation. To read, at this distance, the accounts of war-meetings, with their imported enthusiasm, and their impotent results, humiliates every son of Massachusetts. Its regiments have covered their state with glory; its politicians are doing their best to disgrace it. Stop the foolish, wasteful, useless humbug; give us the conscription!

A.H.Q.

August 22, 1862

Letter from the Army.
Hazel River, Culpepper Co., Va.
August 8, 1862

With some trepidation did I write you my notions, and those of our soldiers, against the bounties you are wasting, and in favor of draft. With pleasure did I see, before my letter appeared, that the same ideas were running though the community. The readiness of our people to meet every exigency as it has arisen, is indeed wonderful. It suits me, for I have always believed that the sober sense of the People is the best reliance for any government. Their instincts, their conduct in all times of rational thought, are apt to be right. No reign of privileged classes for me. The present aspect of affairs justifies this faith. Rising superior to party when this war broke out, they rallied around the flag. Depressed by Bull Run, yet they sent their hundreds of thousands into the field. They demanded to be taxed. They yielded to the policy which returned Mason and his fellow scoundrel. Now, after their disappointment with the governmental leading for a year, yet they reply, draft us; take six hundred thousand more, and with the generous offering of a free people, crush this rebellion.

But I tell you one thing. *Believe it.* That six hundred thousand men will be *needed.* No matter by what leak – not by Representative Diven's speech – believe this; that foreign interference is *very* near.[153] If we do not succeed soon, then *that* is

---

153 Alexander Samuel Diven (1809 – 1896) was a Republican Congressman from New York, serving also of the Lt. Col., and Col. of the 107th New York Infantry. Diven had, with Secretary

the plea. If we are likely to succeed, then *that* is the real reason. I rejoice to believe that such interference will rouse every man, woman, and child. I would like leave of absence then, to say to my patient people at home, "go every man, into the field; fight to the last soldier; let your country be a howling wilderness again, as your forefathers found it when they fled from English tyranny, if need be, in opposing the same infamous power." Read how England conquered, and has treated Ireland, (I have some *Irish* blood in my veins, thank God,) how it stole realm after realm in India; how France stole Algiers, how Austria stole Venetia, and betrayed Hungary, how the three Eastern powers divided Poland; and then see these, or any of these interfering with us, not for stealing, but because we are determined to crush a brood of pestilent traitors; France, with cry of liberty, England, the villainous hypocrite – to interfere against freedom and for slavery. But we should need make no desert; we could raise an army of a million of blacks, to take care of the South, and dive every foreign soldier into the sea.

We have moved again. We left Washington, Va., on Wednesday, and had a hot time of it for twelve miles. Sperryville, through which we passed, is as shabby as the rest of the Virginia villages. Woodville is little better. But the free fields and woods, and Hazel river, with hardly a house in sight – these are God's work, and shiftless Virginians cannot spoil them. Here we came yesterday – under a burning sun.

Seward's permission he said, told representatives of foreign nations that the rebellion would "soon be crushed," in order to prevent foreign intervention. However, as the war dragged into 1862, Diven stated publicly that the only way to prevent "imminent foreign intervention" would be to recruit or conscript 300,000 men immediately. "Diven on the War," *New York Tribune*.

Here is Gen. Banks' corps; and Gen. Pope's eadquarters. Gen. Sigel remains as yet at Sperryville.[154] And eastward is Gen. McDowell.[155] Gen. Burnside is – somewhere.[156]

---

154 General Franz Sigel (1824 – 1902) was a German-born military officer who participated in the German revolution of 1848. Sigel's troops were routed and Sigel sought refuge in Switzerland, England and finally the United States. Becoming a professor at the German-American Institute in St. Louis and a director of the St. Louis Public Schools. At the outbreak of the war, Sigel was commissioned Colonel of the 3rd Missouri Infantry. Though his early war efforts proved ineffectual, his popularity with the German community made Sigel a good candidate to be made Brigadier General. Unfortunately, Sigel proved unable to live up to his position as a Corps commander and as the war progressed, Sigel found himself more and more on the sidelines. Warner; *Generals in Blue*

155 General Irvin McDowell (1818 – 1885) was a graduate of West Point (1838) where one of his classmates was Pierre Gustav Toutant Beauregard, his future adversary at the First Battle of Bull Run. McDowell was an aide to General John Wool during the Mexican-American War and had a close personal friendship with General Winfield Scott. McDowell led the Army of Northeastern Virginia in the First Battle of Bull Run and following his defeat, McClellan made him commander of I Corps and was placed in defense of Washington. When General Pope took command of the Army, McDowell was given III Corps at the Second Battle of Bull Run. Following that defeat, McDowell spent two years without a command until he was given command of the Department of the Pacific. Warner; *Generals in Blue*

156 General Ambrose Everett Burnside (1824 – 1881) was a native of Indiana and a graduate of West Point (1847). Burnside did garrison duty at the end of the Mexican-American war but spent most of his pre-Civil War career on the plains, where he was wounded in the neck by an Apache arrow. Burnside resigned from the Army in 1853, and began a firearms company that produced a carbine that bore his name. The loss of a major government contract, the burning down of his factory and a failed bid for political office, drove Burnside to seek employment with the Illinois Central Railroad where he worked for the future General McClellan. At the outbreak of the war Burnside was commissioned Colonel of the 1st Rhode Island Volunteers, a 90-day regiment. Following the mustering out of the 1st Rhode Island, Burnside was made a brigadier General and commanded the North Carolina Expeditionary Force with whom he made a successful amphibious assault on the North Carolina sea coast. Following his expedition, Burnside was made Major General and given command of IX Corps. Burnside twice turned down the command of the Army of the Potomac, but following on McClellan's failure at Antietam, Lincoln ordered Burnside to take command. Burnside decided to assault the town of Fredericksburg which led to one of the Union armies worst defeats with assault after assault upon strong Confederate defenses on Marye's Heights. Lincoln removed him from command but would not accept his complete resignation sending him instead to command Eastern Tennessee. Burnside was sent back to command IX Corps for the Overland campaign of 1864. Because of his failure at the Battle of the Crater, Burnside was sent on leave by General Grant and not recalled to duty during the remainder of the war. After the war Burnside managed some political success being elected Governor and Senator of Rhode Island. Warner; *Generals in Blue*

What nonsense the papers publish about Gen. Pope's advance. Little reconnoissances, or vexing expeditions are introduced with huge headings, as though an army was in action. These little affairs keep the enemy alert, and inspire confidence, but have no more to do with success, than the tuning of violins with the orchestral performance. The army of Virginia has moved southward by degrees, but some time will be likely to elapse before a steady and resistless movement on the enemy takes place. That time will pass; and then, with well digested plans, this army will press forward to victory. But sell your dailies by the big headings, in the meantime; but "sell" the people too. If "a hearty laugh helpeth digestion, and serves to sweep the cobwebs out of the brain," the Sanitary Commission could do no better work than forward a steady supply of such trash as the Baltimore – I won't say what – and other thundering-headed columns. By-and-by, there will be something to say.

The army is delighted with the indications of energy at Washington. Items creep down to us of low degree, which indicate more than is printed. Not of plans, for we know little enough of them; and the writers who wisely pretend to keep silent, because their revelations of plans might hurt the cause, are self-conceited liars. But as Marryatt[157] says in one of his books, that sealed orders to war vessels were nonsensical, inasmuch as the supplies taken on board indicated to what quarter of the globe it was going – so the preparations of government often show what is in the wind – a good illustration, by the way, for a sermon; for the supplies and clothing spiritually which any person is taking in *this* world, indicates where he is going in the *next*.

One good effect of recent orders is in the fact that negroes are being taken for teamsters, laborers, &c., thus returning able-bodied soldiers to their regiments. In this way, we are recruiting as fast as you seem to be. The negroes (some as white as we are,) are delighted to get away. I could narrate some cases of cruelty, from whose repetition they are glad to be released; but what is the use? It is enough to say they were *slaves*. Our men are glad too, that they have no more hay-stacks,

---

157 Frederick Marryatt (1792 – 1848) was a British Naval Officer and author, his most famous work being *Mr. Midshipman Easy*. Marryatt also invented a flag code that became the basis for the International Code. His father being a large plantation owner in the West Indies, Marryatt also wrote a book called *The New Union Club*, illustrated by George Cruikshank (of Punch Magazine fame) that was a satire against abolitionism. Patten; *George Cruikshank's Life and Times, and Art: 1792 – 1835*.

pig-sties, and chicken-coops to guard. What an outrage it was, ever to put our noble soldiery to such mean employment. Not that I believe in private depredations; but I do believe in taking everything wanted for public uses, or our soldiers' comfort, by orderly methods.

I see in some Northern papers a statement that the soldiers have now become satisfied that the policy of the Democratic party was right. If this means that the soldiers have become at all enamored of slavery, it is, so far as this army is concerned, totally false. There has been a very general change the other way; not to "Republicanism" particularly; but to a clear idea that the sooner slavery is ended, the better. Stout Breckinridge Democrats "forage" for negroes, just as coolly as anybody else; because it weakens the enemy. As to leaving the slaves of Union men, -- there is not one Union citizen in a thousand, and the one does not care a copper for slavery. As to the "Constitution," there is no such thing in our part of Virginia; no courts, no judges, no constables; only some very respectable armies, with some sturdy Generals, who try cases very rapidly, and decide very summarily.

Talking of Generals – one General is very much liked, General Banks. Were he in danger, there are regiments who would defend him to the last man. Regiments detached from his command, have used their utmost endeavors to be returned. I do not think he would leave undone anything in his power for the good of his men. Certainly I know, that his respect for all religious efforts is practically very great. The telegraph stated that, last Sunday, after a review of the whole corps, the General and his staff left the field, and that then prayer was offered by the chaplain of the Second, and church music performed by the band. The fact was, that a review had been ordered before Gen. Pope; and that Gen. Banks, finding it to be on the Sabbath, requested the chaplain of the Second to conduct a religious service before the whole corps; and Gen. Banks himself arranged his corps for the service, ordered up a caisson for a pulpit, and joined reverently in worship. (Gen. Pope had left, however.) The chaplain in charge pressed into service his brother Winslow of Great Barrington, then chaplain of the Connecticut Fifth, to make the address, which he did in a way all who know his enthusiasm, will understand. It was a peculiar service; a whole army corps for congregation; a caisson for pulpit; bands for organ; and a group of hardy Generals by one's side. Barring the fact that it was preceded by review, it was a pleasant service. God should be honored infinitely more than many of our leaders do honor him. And it is pleasant to find a man like our Major General throwing his public influence, as he always does, on the side of religious duties. No chaplain meets obstacles from *him*; no hospital but shall have religious helpers, if he can accomplish it. And similarly are we favored in our Brigade, by another Massachusetts General, always present at public worship, and always giving his influence for its due observance. So, too, with our own excellent and soldierly commander. I am often pained by seeing statements made against chaplains. Religious newspapers, from best of motives, and jealous for God's honor, have uttered remarks very disparaging. Some of these profess to be based on actual examination. I doubt not the truth of some reports. But I do wish to vindicate the honor of many. In more than thirteen months' service – with a commission which, as to date, would make me nearly the senior in the whole volunteer service – I have met many chaplains, Congregationalists, Baptists, Methodists, Episcopalians, Presbyterians. My circle has been limited, it is true. But so far as it extends, I have not known an immoral chaplain, or one who did not seem to have a right spirit. True, not all succeed; some may lack the tact necessary to keep them confined to their own department. But as to example, or intention – with natural human imperfections, of course – so far as this corps is concerned, I wish you would mentally make an exception. I recall the names of men whom I personally know, from Massachusetts; of our own denomination – Dr. Cleaveland of Lowell,[158] Winslow of

---

158 John Payne Cleaveland (1799 – 1873) was a graduate of Bowdoin College (1821) and his early years were spent in teaching and further theological studies. He was first ordained the pastor of the Tabarnacle Church in Salem, but his pastoral duties took him to congregations in Detroit and Cincinnati, Ohio. Cleaveland came back East in 1844, he served a seven-year post at the Beneficent Church in Providence, The First Church in Northampton and the Appleton Street Church in Lowell, Mass. In January of 1862 he was commissioned Chaplain of the 30th Massachusetts Infantry and traveled with them to New Orleans. After five months, however, Cleaveland resigned his commission. Pioneer Society of the State of Michigan; *Pioneer Collections*.

Barrington, Carver of Raynham,[159] Clark of Swampscott,[160] James of Worcester,[161] and E. L. Clark of Boston,[162] all well known by years in the ministry, save the last named, ordained only last year, but whose enthusiasm and ability will by-and-by make a noble mark. Add to these, Gaylord of Boston,[163] from the Universalists,

---

159 Robert Carver (1810 – 1863) was a graduate of Yale (1833) and of Andover Theological Seminary (1836). As with many 19th-century ministers, Carver was posted in congregations from Pittston, Maine to Lancaster, Wisconsin and several congregations in Massachusetts where he also served a term as a State Legislator. He was commissioned Chaplain of the 7th Massachusetts in 1861, though he resigned about a year later due to illness. He returned to his wife and died about a month later. Andover Theological Seminary; *General Catalogue*.

160 Jonas Bowen Clarke (1816 – 1894) graduated from Dartmouth College (1839) and studied divinity at East Windsor Theological Institute (1842). The Reverend Clarke was ordained pastor of the East Granby, Massachusetts Congregational Church in 1842. Clarke served congregations in Lynn and Swampscott before being commissioned Chaplain of the 23rd Massachusetts Infantry in October of 1861. Clarke spent most of the war working with the Sanitary Commission in the transportation of wounded men and supplies back and forth to North Carolina. Hartford Theological Seminary; *The Hartford Seminary Record*; Brinsfield; *Faith in the Fight*.

161 Horace James (1818-1875) Attended Phillips Andover, Yale University (1840) and Yale Theological Seminary (1842). James was first ordained in Wrentham, Massachusetts in 1843 and from there moved to the Old South Church in Worcester. He was commissioned Chaplain in the 25th Massachusetts in 1861 and served with them until 1864 when he was commissioned a Captain and Asst. Quartermaster of U.S. Volunteers and made Superintendent of Freedmen in Newbern, North Carolina. After the war, he took over his father's proprietorship and editorial duties of the *Congregationalist*. "Horace James;" *The Bulletin of Yale University*.

162 Edward Lord Clark (1838 – 1910) was a graduate of Brown University (1858) and Andover Theological Seminary (1863). He was commissioned chaplain to the 12th Massachusetts in June of 1861 and resigned in June of 1862. Following the war Clark was pastor to the First Church in North Bridgewater, the Presbyterian Church of the Puritans in New York and the Central Congregational Church in Boston. Clark was an amateur Egyptologist and wrote several works on Ancient Egypt as well as an expert wood carver. Andover Theological Seminary; *General Catalogue*.

163 Noah Murray Gaylord, see n.8

Scandlin of Grafton,[164] from the Unitarian, Cromack,[165] from the Methodists, all laborious, warm-hearted, good men. I reckon up only, and all personal acquaintances, and I ask you to consider whether these men are likely to cast any dishonor on the ministry?

But I could tell you of Generals, whose outrageous profanity is an insult to decency. While one General has said, not only to me, but to another General, "this country has forgotten God; and no country that forgets God can prosper!" – others challenge the wrath of God upon us. I tell you too, that if the public could *see* men, not as they are in the newspapers – but face to face, the gasconade of some would speedily collapse. Things cannot be known as they are – now. But when this war is over, how many reputations a sensible soldiery will overturn!

Before sending this rambling letter, let me say how much pleased I was by Gail Hamilton's[166] (charming writer that is) puncture of certain religious advertising dodges. There is another line, too, where that pen could be employed for the same purpose. For instance, the advertisements which prefix some army heading. I read in a Boston paper a heading, "Gen. Butler's whole army capture." And it is

---

164 William George Scandlin (1828 – 1871) was an English born son of an Irish mariner. Following a youthful and brief career at sea, he settled first in Boston and then in Pennsylvania where he entered the Meadville Theological School. Following the death of his first wife he moved back to Boston and preached at the Hanover Street Mission before accepting a call to minister at the First Congregational Church in Grafton. He was commissioned a chaplain in the 15th Massachusetts in the spring of 1861 and he resigned his commission in August of 1862. Following his mustering out, Scandlin served as an agent of the Sanitary Commission and the American Unitarian Association, in which capacity he was taken prisoner by Confederate soldiers just outside Gettysburg and held for three months at Libby Prison. "William George Scandlin;" *Meadville Theological School Quarterly Bulletin*

165 Joseph Chapman Cromack (1812 – 1900) was educated at Wesleyan Academy and licensed to preach in 1835. Cromack was commissioned Chaplain of the 19th Massachusetts in August of 1861. He resigned that commission in November of 1861 and took a Chaplain's Commission with the 22nd Massachusetts Infantry. He resigned from the army in March of 1862. Adjutant General of Massachusetts; *Massachusetts Soldiers, Sailors, and Marines in the Civil War*; also; Hurd; *History of Essex County, Massachusetts*.

166 Gail Hamilton was the pen name of Mary Abigail Dodge (1833 – 1896). Hamilton was a regular contributor to the *Congregationalist*, as well as its companion periodical *Scholar and Schoolmate*. Hamilton wrote numerous columns, opinion pieces, instructional lessons, and essays about rural New England life. Fetterley; *Provisions: A Reader from 19th-Century American Women*.

followed by a puff of an eating house. The miserable scoundrel who will so trifle with the holiest feelings of our national struggle, should be kicked out of Boston; and every man who will patronize such a cur, ought to choke with the first mouthful. Another, urging certain pills on the soldiers, tells them that the surgeons in the army are incompetent. The villain, who tried thus to trouble the multitudes who must entrust their friends to these surgeons, ought to have to swallow a box of his stuff for every letter in every word of his miserable lie. Why will newspapers, for the sake of a little money, give such fellows space?
    A. H. Q.

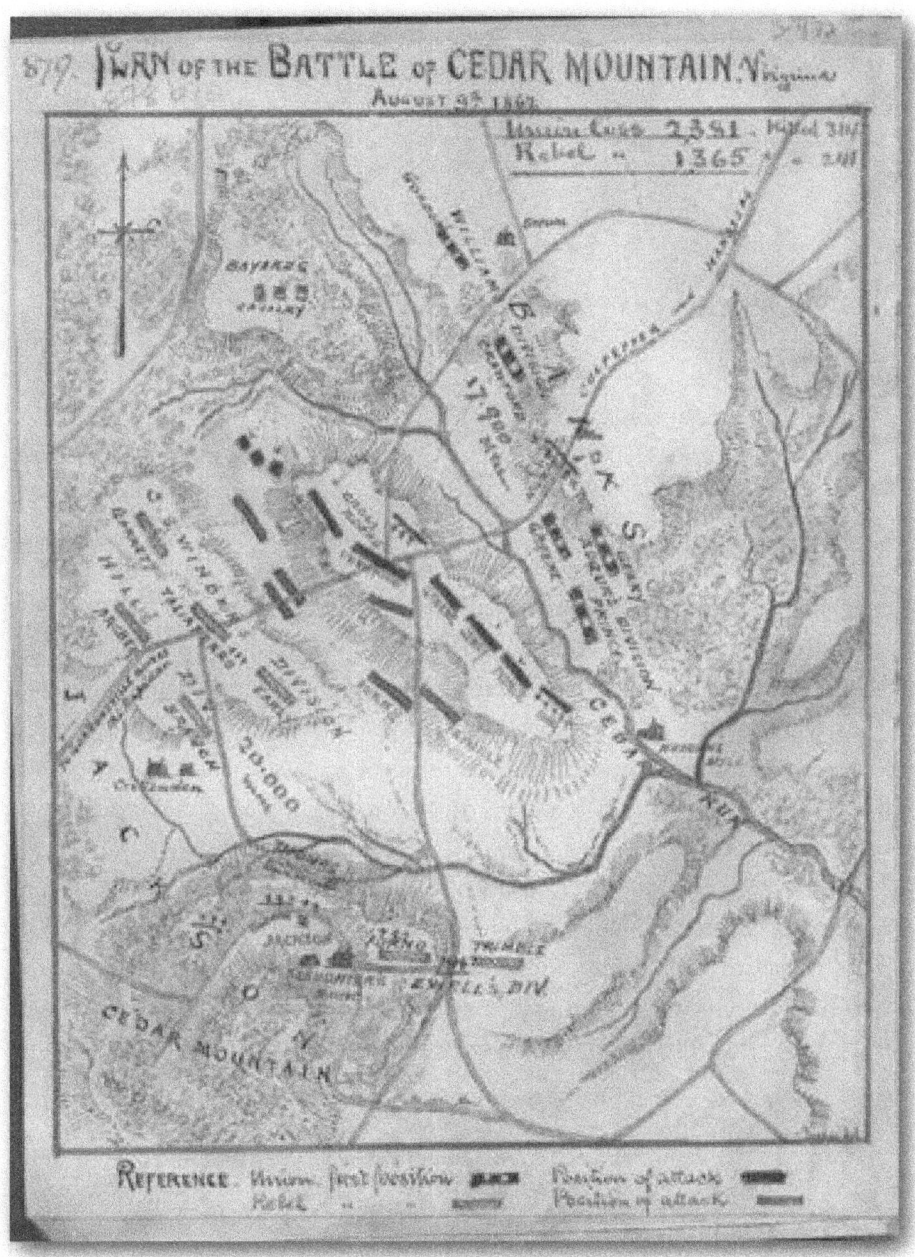

Image courtesy of the Library of Congress, Maps Division.

August 22, 1862

The Battle of Cedar Mountain.
Culpepper, Va., Aug. 13, 1862

I have never felt so sadly in writing you as I do today. Last night we went into camp for the first time since the recent battle. How touchingly our emptied tents reminded us of our loss! Our beloved Major wounded and a prisoner. Our excellent Surgeon wounded. Of seven captains who went into action, four gallant men dead, two prisoners, of whom one is wounded. Of eleven lieutenants, one killed, four wounded, and one wounded and a prisoner. And lying in a soldier's grave, or shattered by bullets, one in every four of our men, as noble a group of soldiers as every graced a country's name.

Last Wednesday we left Little Washington. Friday night, at 12 o'clock, we bivouacked by Culpepper. Next morning, after varying orders, we were moved six miles, hastily, to support Gen. Crawford,[167] known to be threatened by the enemy, who, having hastily crossed the Rapidan with his advance, was hurrying up his main body. That army, if I may rely on the statement of a rebel Colonel whom I met on

---

[167] Samuel Wylie Crawford (1829 – 1892) was the surgeon attached to Fort Sumter at the time of the Confederate bombardment in 1861. After Sumter's surrender, Crawford accepted a Major's commission in the 13th U.S. Infantry. Promoted to Brigadier General in April of 1863, Crawford led a brigade in the Valley Campaign but didn't engage enemy troops until the Battle of Cedar Mountain. Crawford was wounded at the Battle of Antietam following which Crawford took command of the Pennsylvania Reserves. Crawford saw further action and Gettysburg and the Overland Campaign of 1864 and was present at General Lee's surrender at Appomattox. Crawford retired from the army in 1873. Warner; *Generals in Blue*

Monday, consisted of three divisions, Jackson's, Ewell's[168] and Hill's,[169] -- numbering forty-five thousand men. Gen. Pope's army consists, as you know, of the commands of Gen. McDowell, Gen. Banks, and Gen. Sigel. Why these were not concentrated is known only to those in power. As it was, Gen. Banks was thrown forward; Gen. Sigel was still at Sperryville, or perhaps on the road, and Gen. McDowell was too far to help – no, we passed one brigade at least less than three miles from the battle ground, which had lain there since four A.M., waiting for orders, and which lay there till we were done fighting, -- while an inadequate force was opposed to the enemy, as usual.

Losing one man that day by sun-stroke, at 12 M. we reached the position assigned us, the extreme right, which was slightly bent from the enemy, -- and were stationed on a hight important to be held. A mile and a half due south, or very nearly so, is Cedar Mountain, in front of which, and round its sides, lay the

---

168 Richard Stoddert Ewell (1817 – 1872) was a graduate of West Point (1840) and first served in the 1st U.S. Dragoons, providing escorts for wagon trains along the Santa Fe and Oregon Trails. Ewell served with distinction in the Mexican-American War following which he helped to explore and map the Southwest Territory where he was wounded by Apache Indians. Ewell resigned his commission in the U.S. Army in May of 1861 and accepted a command with the Virginia Provisional Army as a Colonel in the cavalry. Ewell quickly rose to the rank of Major General under General "Stonewall" Jackson where Ewell proved more than an able match against Union General Banks. Ewell lost a leg at the Battle of Groveton but recovered it time to assume command of the Confederate II Corps, leaderless since the loss of General Jackson at the battle of Chancellorsville. Ewell's failure to capture Culp's Hill at Gettysburg has led to much discussion among historians, but he retained command of his corps until assigned to the defense of Richmond in May of 1864. Ewell was captured as he and his forces retreated from Richmond at Sayler's Creek and he spent three months as a prisoner of war at Fort Warren in Boston. Warner; *Generals in Gray*.

169 Ambrose Powell Hill, Jr. (1825 – 1865) was a native of Virginia and a graduate of West Point (1847) who saw service in the Mexican-American war and the Seminole wars. Hill worked on the U.S. Coastal Survey from 1855 – 1860 during which time he became engaged to the Ellen Marcy who later broke the engagement and married General George B. McClellan. Hill resigned his commission in March of 1861 and following the secession of Virginia, Hill accepted a commission as Colonel of the 13th Virginia Infantry. Hill's "Light Division" participated in the Peninsula Campaign, but a disagreement between General Hill and General James Longstreet saw Hill ordered to the Shenandoah Valley. Hill became commander of III Corps after the death of General Jackson, and they participated in every campaign right up through Petersburg in 1865. Just seven days before Lee's surrender at Appomattox, Hill was shot and killed by a Union soldier. Warner; *Generals in Gray*.

rebel forces, -- troops being entrenched westward, however, holding as their left a wooded eminence, but the bulk of their army running southwest, back of their right. Part way up the mountain they had posted artillery also. On the side of the mountain was Jackson himself, and from that eminence could see all our movements, as I have who had crept off the battle-field said that the rebels had left most of our wounded there. It was a statement hard to be believed – it was barbarous – but it was true. A party was immediately and cordially detailed by our Colonel, at the suggestion of our General, it being rumored that the rebel pickets had been drawn off. Lieut. Abbott commanded it. We went three miles, but half a mile from the field, Gen. Sigel refused to allow the risk of losing the party. It was midnight, and we slept by our outer pickets. Early in the morning we went. Telegrams say that the rebels "asked leave to bury their dead!" Asked leave? They had held the ground for thirty-six hours, and I saw not one rebel corpse. It chanced to me to be in advance, and I had the indescribable happiness of being the first to tell to the wounded men still there that help was at hand. As we came to each they cried for joy. They put their arms around our necks. Our strong men, who had fought well and now came back for their comrades, cried with joy too. Though the rebels had been guilty of the barbarity of not taking to hospital our severely wounded men, and of not informing us of the fact, though the field was in their possession – while we always treat both sides alike – yet rebel soldiers had been kind. They had built shelters of boughs; had brought water, and sometimes biscuit, and apples. But all the dead, and many of the wounded, had been stripped of everything valuable, even to outer clothing.

We removed our wounded. We buried our dead. Our dead! The pride of Massachusetts! There lay Capt. Abbott; just before the regiment moved into action we were in conversation; he was ordered to advance with his company as skirmishers, and I noticed then the clear, ringing, brave voice with which he said, "fall in, men!" And Capt. Williams the frank, straightforward, courageous man. And Capt. Goodwin,[170] who had left an ambulance to go to the field, and who, as I had

---

170 Richard Chapman Goodwin (1833 - 1862) was a graduate of Boston Latin School and Harvard (1854). Goodwin went into business after college, serving for a few years in Europe. In May of 1861, Goodwin was commissioned Captain in the 2nd Massachusetts Regiment. Goodwin was killed at Cedar Mountain. Quint; *The Record of the Second Massachusetts*; and,

asked him, "Are you strong enough to go?" had answered with a smile, "I *cannot* stay, when my men go!" and buckled on his sword. And Capt. Cary, lying there as though asleep, falling with a miniature on his breast – a true, brave man. And all around, the men, the noble men so uselessly slaughtered. My heart was full. How long, O Lord, how long, before these men, slaughtered by infernal ambition, be avenged? Come, Lord, and tarry not!

Southern men were about us. I went to the rebel lines, for we heard there that it was now truce. I met colonels and a general. They were courteous and kind, and far from exultant. On learning that I was a chaplain, the general showed the greatest regard for an office which some Union generals treat with contempt; so did one of our generals, who late in the day found me the only one on the field except enlisted men.

But it took till far into midday to bury our dead. Those of the Second (and we identified most) are in ten graves, near together; and I had trees around them marked deeply, each with three cuts, that if any one should ever wish to know where these men of the Second lay, the spot should be identified for their holy pilgrimage.

As soldier hands were laying our brave men in their graves, and we were covering them first with green leaves, my eye was attracted by a leaf which with others, had evidently been in the hands of some man. And my glance fell first on these words:

"Seeing then that all these things shall be dissolved, what manner of persons ought ye to be in all holy conversation and godliness.

"Looking for and hasting unto the coming of the day of God, wherein the heavens being on fire shall be dissolved, and the elements shall melt with fervent heat.

"Nevertheless we, according to his promise, look for new heavens and a new earth, wherein dwelleth righteousness."

We left our dead. But the leaf I reverently folded and carefully keep; and I will leave it to my child and tell her to honor the dead of the brave, gallant, Second Massachusetts, whom her father loved.

A. H. Q.

Adjutant General of Massachusetts; *Massachusetts Soldiers, Sailors and Marines in the Civil War.*

September 12, 1862

Letter from the Army.
On the Road to Somewhere, Sept. 3, 1862.

To somewhere; but where to?

My last letter forwarded told about the Cedar Mountain battle. My next was stopped by orders which prohibited all mails from leaving, expelled reporters, and denied the use of the telegraph. Instead, therefore, of reliable information, the people have had unfounded rumors, lying statements and gross deceptions. They have learned however, the general fact that the army which was recently on the Rapidan was soon on the Rappahannock, next at Bull Run, and now, doubtless, near, or in the fortifications in front of Washington; that, day after day, the thunder of artillery has been the music of our armies, while hard marches and hunger have taxed our strength, and pitched battles have drawn the blood of the gallant soldiers of the Union. But they learned this only by the gradual sifting of the statements it was impossible to confine.

Of many of the recent movements, and of the recent battles, I know little from personal participation. Our corps was not called upon in the battles of last week. Why, we do not know; who does? But a part I saw; and of the general bearing of events it is easy to learn. And, in the army, we are constantly saying, "what is the use of lying?" Things transpiring under our very eyes, are so grossly misstated that we become skeptical as to *all* accounts. I am reminded of a map of the battle ground of the 9th of August, which appeared in the New York -------; I made the top north; I made it east; I made it south; I made it west; but not the least resemblance could

I trace. Such are many accounts of affairs – until the public press – which may God preserve free as the refuge of our liberties – examines and sifts.

Cedar Mountain a victory! One brigade almost annihilated; another losing one third of its strength; all badly suffering; our forces driven from the field; the ground occupied by the enemy for two days, and then left at their pleasure; our dead buried, and our wounded brought off at the sufferance of the enemy thirty-six hours after the fight; what a glorious victory!"

Then these successive states of affairs appear. First, the movements between the Rapidan and the Rappahannock, ending in our retreating over the latter river; secondly, the various operations on that line, ending in Jackson's appearance at Manassas, in our rear. Thirdly, the various maneuvers and fightings by which we and the enemy reverse positions, he establishing his line of communication with the south, and we with the north, following which are the battles of Friday and Saturday last. Fourthly, the attempt or appearance of attempt to turn our right while we still held Centerville, and the necessary falling back, to the line of the fortifications. In all this, that we were tolerably clearly outmaneuvered, and partially defeated, is evident, though the relative size of the armies may have rendered any other result impossible.

First, Gen. Pope appeared bent on a vigorous pursuit of Jackson. He advanced to the Rapidan. He threatened battle. Jackson had retired thither after the battle of the 9th, and is reinforced. On the day that Jackson awaits the attack, Gen. Pope – the 19th of August – suddenly withdraws. He had been sending all his supplies and trains to the rear. They were all safe, and rapidly and in perfect order, the various columns move northward to the Rappahannock, cross it before Jackson can harass the army, and accomplish most successfully a skillful movement. Our forces were not sufficient to hazard a battle at the Rapidan, but were enough to engage attention, while Gen. McClellan accomplished his withdrawal from the Peninsula. That object attained, Gen. Pope retires, to unite with Gen. McClellan.

Our own regiment – by way of parenthesis – on the Sunday after the battle of the 9th of August, was moved to a wood about two miles and a half from the battle ground, where we bivouacked two nights. On Tuesday we returned to our camping ground, just outside of Culpepper on the north, where our wagons had been left, and where our tents were then pitched. It was a sad evening, because so many tents were empty. But there we stayed until Monday, when, in the afternoon, tents were struck, and wagons despatched to the Rappahannock. We remained until midnight finding rest as we could under rather unfavorable circumstances; then moved a mile or so, and built fires, and slept somewhat till day; then, after various vexatious delays, moved several rods; then waited for orders and got them, and moved several rods more; and by fits and starts moved along, vexed by somebody's trains, several miles; then cut the trains dead, and marched on to the north side of the Rappahannock river, at the crossing of the railway to Culpepper; there we bivouacked – our wagons still ten miles onward. Then, the enemy having soon followed, the Rappahannock river is the scene of operations. The day after our arrival, about noon, we hear rapid firing, and soon see on the plain across, the movements of cavalry and skirmishers. So for day after day the cannon gives the morning reveille, and up and down the river we move. At first our right is Gen. Sigel; our center, Gen. McDowell; our left, Gen. Banks. But each corps is moveable, and Gen. Reno[171] is added. The enemy felt our lines at all points. Every ford for miles was tested in turn. August 21, our corps moved down the river a mile. The next day up the river five or six, where brisk cannonading was going on, and a union battery driven off. The next morning, Cothren's gallant battery of ten pounders, which our brigade supported, silenced and shattered *two* batteries of twelve pounders, and we could see dead and wounded carried off, while Cothren's loss was one man wounded, one caisson demolished, one horse struck. That day up the river again, and a damp bivouac; the next day the whole move up, passing a terrific fire from the opposite enemy near Sulphur Springs, -- his shot crashing through the woods for several hours, but nearly silenced, with little loss to us, none to the Second. Next day down the river, and next day, and so on, until our corps was near Bealeton.

---

171 Jesse Lee Reno (1823 – 1862) graduated from West Point (1846) and while there was a close personal friend of Confederate "Stonewall" Jackson. Reno was brevetted twice during his service in the Mexican-American war and was seriously wounded at the Battle of Chapultepec. Prior to the Civil War, Reno served in several posts both on the Western frontier and in the Washington area. Reno was appointed Brigadier General in the fall of 1861 and commanded a brigade on Burnside's expedition to North Carolina, after which he and his Brigade were transferred to the Army of the Potomac. Reno was killed by a Rebel sharpshooter at the Battle of South Mountain. Warner; *Generals in Blue*

Accounts tell how the enemy was repulsed at all points on the river. I could not see that he ever made an attack in great force at all. He kept the line alive, but for three days, he was visibly sending his columns up the river, infantry in long lines, and artillery. Where was he going? Amusing our army below, he was steadily crossing somewhere above, and suddenly we awoke to find that, on Friday night, the 22d, his cavalry had dashed through Warrenton, pushed on to Catlett's, burnt Gen. Pope's baggage, (sparing Gen. McDowell's;) that a little later his columns had occupied Manassas Junction, where they burnt supplies and property worth hundreds upon hundreds of thousands; that he held Thoroughfare Gap through which his forces had poured, tidings which two blacks had brought; that he was in our rear, our communication with Washington cut off, our junction with the Peninsula army incomplete.

Then our front was changed. Jackson was "in a trap." On Wednesday, Aug. 27, Warrenton was evacuated by the Union troops. Gen. Banks remaining near Bealeton. The army moved to Gainesville, -- Gen. Sigel toward Manassas, -- and a portion of Gen. McDowell's corps toward Thoroughfare Gap, to prevent a junction between reinforcements and Jackson. An action took place there, from which our troops "withdrew." On Thursday night Gen. McDowell was on the Centerville road, looking northward – where I saw it, being sent thitherward with sick. Friday morning commenced the battle. Of that I know nothing personally, leaving Gainesville early with Gen. Rickett's division,[172] which was moving towards Manassas. That day's fighting undoubtedly resulted favorably to us. But on Saturday heavy reinforcements reached Jackson. He had skillfully changed position till a junction could not be prevented. On Saturday we were defeated. Not pursued, but still defeated,

---

172 James Brewerton Ricketts (1817 – 1887) was a graduate of West Point (1839) and commanded a battery at the First Battle of Bull Run where he was shot four times and taken prisoner by the Confederate army. Exchanged in January of 1862, Ricketts was promoted to Brigadier General and assigned to General McDowell's Corps. He was wounded again at Sharpsburg where his horse was killed and fell on top of him. During his recuperation, Rickett's was assigned to the court-martial of General Fitz John Porter. Ricketts returned to command of a division of VI Corps during the Overland Campaign. While in command of a corps during Sheridan's Shenandoah Valley campaign, Ricketts was wounded again by a bullet through the chest. Ricketts returned to duty a few days before General Lee's surrender at Appomattox. Warner; *Generals in Blue*

and with great loss. It was Gen. McDowell's which gave way. Then our lines fell back to Centerville, and held a strong position.

In the meantime Gen. Banks was near Bristow Station, four miles below Manassas Junction. Valuable stores were there. Gen. Hooker[173] had driven the enemy away from the junction. The stores were being rapidly removed. But during Friday, during Saturday, the corps was not summoned to the field. All day Friday we impatiently heard the steady fire. Saturday night found us still between Bristow and Manassas Junction. Sunday morning we were suddenly ordered to burn stores, burn heavy baggage, and make a forced march by a long detour. Our direct communication with the army was sundered. So past the flames of long lines of burning cars, past exploding ammunition, we hastened to Brentsville, forded the rapidly rising Occoquan creek, and by noon had safely come into junction with the main army. It was well done. Gen. Banks did it.

Centerville was a strong position, but it could be turned too easily. So backward to Fairfax; backward still. Fighting here, fighting there. Immense lines of ambulances loaded with wounded. Laid upon the ground for transportation to come, they covered acres. How they cursed one man!

Sunday night there was a rumor that Gen. McClellan was to command. How it thrilled the army! How it electrified the soldiers! I should not have believed the enthusiasm had I not seen it in passing through two corps. I saw some of his own

---

173 Joseph Hooker (1814 – 1879) was a graduate of West Point (1837) and through his pre-Mexican-American war service rose to the rank of first Lieutenant. Hooker served in both Zachary Taylor and Winfield Scott's Mexican campaigns and through meritorious service won brevets up through the rank of Lieutenant Colonel. Hooker served in the Pacific Division until 1853 when he resigned his command to become a California farmer. In August of 1862, Hooker was commissioned a Brigadier General of Volunteers and was given command of a Division of Heintzelman's III Corps, eventually rising to command I Corps. In Burnside's attack at Fredericksburg, Hooker commanded the Center Grand Division. Hooker headed a list of officers that Burnside wished to have removed because of Hooker's open criticism of Burnside following Fredericksburg. Instead, Hooker took Burnside's place as commander of the Army of the Potomac. Hooker's own attempt at taking Richmond by way of Chancellorsville was thwarted by Stonewall Jackson's sudden attack on the right of Hooker's army and the Army of the Potomac was forced to retreat again. Hooker was shortly replaced by General Meade, but Hooker was sent with XI and XII Corps to Tennessee after the Union defeat at the Battle of Chickamauga. When Sherman promoted O. O. Howard to command the Army of the Tennessee, Hooker asked to be relieved of his command. Hooker retired from the service as a Major General in 1868. Warner; *Generals in Blue*

soldiers. Said one to me, "If Gen. McClellan should say to his old soldiers, 'Boys, who will go back to the Peninsula and try it again?' *every one* would say, '*I will*, general!'" Always believing in Gen. McClellan, yet I was astonished to see the spirit with which that rumor was welcomed.

That disasters have come is undeniable. That anxieties must prevail for some time is clear. But we have a great army. We have courageous soldiers. Reinforcements are rapidly coming. The great North is not defeated. Every day of delay will strengthen us. While McClellan remained on the peninsula, the enemy dared not send away a too heavy force. The order for his return freed the hostile army, and therefore we have to meet it. But be not discouraged. The army is not, though several features of affairs hopeless of remedy, do depress it. But so far it has not been broken; it has fought splendidly, and retired because driven, but to prevent flanking in force. No pursuit of a routed force has taken place whatever.

But Jackson skillfully passed the river above us. He threw himself boldly in our rear. Supposed to be trapped, he yet held his own, and so maneuvered as to secure his line of reinforcements. He destroyed immense stores. He has changed our positions until he has an untroubled rear and a clear road from Richmond. He has transferred the war to the vicinity of Washington. He has made us the defenders. Put himself in the aggressive.

A. H. Q.

September 19, 1862

Letter from Chaplain Quint.
Maryland, Sept. 10, 1862.

I wrote a somewhat general account of the recent events. Before you received it, I am asked for "personal observations." This request presumed that our regiment was in some of the battles, which was not correct. Nevertheless I will follow my own line of travel as to what I saw. I *had* seen a rebel general, whose prayers, as pitted against outrageous profanity, I was more afraid of than of twenty thousand men.

While we were moving up and down the Rappahannock, where the enemy were amusing our General by little attacks along the line, I saw rebel columns on the opposite side of the river, moving northward. Where they were going, nobody knew. Where they were to strike, who took the trouble to find out? But they struck in our rear, destroyed millions' worth of property, cut off our lines of communication, reinforced their moderate army, and defeated the army of Virginia.

I saw there, on the Rappahannock, soldiers faint with hunger; considering whether to eat a biscuit, or save it until morning; glad to receive the remnants of meat which some others had to spare; roasting green corn, not as a luxury, but to satisfy hunger. This was in an army whose General had, in his first order, ridiculed having "bases of supplies."[174]

I saw, on eventful and disastrous days, a whole corps lying idle within sound of the battle.

---

174 This is a reference to General Pope's first address to his Army of the Potomac when he took command.

I saw millions of dollars' worth of property destroyed, all of which could have been saved, had the General not laughed at "lines of retreat."

I saw the order which prohibited all mails from leaving, all use of telegraph except by the General and excluded all newspaper reporters.

More particularly and personally, when news came that Jackson was between us and Washington, we were near Sulphur Springs. It was immediately thought that the enemy had rashly exposed themselves to capture, and movements appear to have been made with the view of accomplishing that result.

Our corps was sent toward Bealeton, on the railroad, and took no part in subsequent activities, beyond marchings.

It was on the 23d of August that we heard this, but I do not learn that any marked movements were made until the next Wednesday the 27th. On the 26th, while we were on the road toward Bealeton, I was sent to Washington in charge of a sick man, a member of Gen. Gordon's staff, with the hope of sending him through to Washington. Reaching there about noon, I found hospitals full of sick men. They were in churches mainly, but in the afternoon were placed in cars and started for Washington. They were brought back that night, the road not having been repaired. My own charge I concluded to put into a house in Warrenton.

But the next day it was determined to evacuate Warrenton. The sick were again put into cars, to be sent as far as the road could allow. Gen. Sigel and Gen. McDowell were in town. Gen. Sigel started early in the day, Gen. McDowell toward night. Unable to return to my regiment on account of unsafe roads, indeed, ignorant of its position, and without transportation for the sick man, I concluded to join friends and keep with a column. So, finding the brigade (in Gen. McDowell's corps,) which held the 12th and 13th Mass., being cordially received and furnished with an ambulance for my friend, I left Warrenton with the corps about 5 P.M. It moved through New Baltimore toward Gainesville, on the Centerville road. It was a weary march. The road was rocky, the numberless streams (of course bridgeless) seem to run lengthwise of the road, and it was dark. The column gradually wasted away, until about 1 A.M., when a halt and bivouac was ordered.

Of that wearisome march I have a marked recollection, because it was the last time I saw Col. Fletcher Webster, as kind hearted a man as ever lived, and a brave officer.[175] We rode side and side much of the way. The remnant of the night I lay near him, and we slept soundly, though he had only (as I did) a rubber blanket, and overcoat, and it rained a part of the night. He shared with me his breakfast – which he ate without grumbling, though it was only coffee (with sugar) and hard biscuit. He seemed to me on that march rather thoughtful, though by no means sad, and playfully endorsed me, as I had been received into their care with my sick, as their "acting chaplain." He was a noble-hearted man; God hallow his memory.

In the morning, providentially, I met two wagons of our own (one an ambulance) loaded with supplies, but unable to reach the regiment. One wagon-master, one ward-master, a driver, and three soldiers as wagon-guard, were of the party, and gladly did I greet it. We kept with the Brigade until it turned off, about two miles back of Gainesville, to go to Thoroughfare Gap, with the hope of checking the advance of the rebels through that entrance. They had there a fight that afternoon with partial success, and retired to near Gainesville that night – which I did not learn till next day.

After that Brigade turned off, I continued with Gen. McDowell's corps to Gainesville – a railway station – with two or three houses. The corps went on the road to Manassas a few miles – the same road by which Gen. Sigel, I was told, had gone in the forenoon. Here our small party halted, built a fire, and cooked its dinner – in the midst of immense wagon trains, cavalry pickets, straggling soldiers, enough to make several regiments, and opposite a house whose hospital flag showed its use. An hour or two afterwards we tried the Manassas road, in the presumption

---

175 Daniel Fletcher Webster (1813 – 1862) was the son of Daniel Webster the Senator from Massachusetts and renowned orator. Webster was a graduate of Boston Latin School and Harvard College (1833) and served as Chief Clerk of the State Department during the time his father was Secretary of State. Webster sailed to China with Robert Bennett Forbes and worked with Caleb Cushing as the secretary of the legation in Canton China. Just prior to the outbreak of war, Webster was a customs surveyor in the Port of Boston. When war erupted between the North and South, Webster raised the 12th Massachusetts which in a very short time raised a regimental fund of over $30,000. Webster was killed at the Second Battle of Bull Run and his body was captured by the Confederacy. The Confederate Army sent his body to Washington where it was embalmed and shipped by rail and it lay in state in Faneuil Hall before being buried in the family cemetery in Marshfield, Massachusetts. Davis; *Bench and Bar of the Commonwealth of Massachusetts*; and, "Strange Story of the Burial of Col. Webster;" *Idaho Register*.

that Gen. Banks would be moving thither, to strengthen our then right; but a few miles on, before we had emerged from Gen. McDowell's regiments, we learned that the road was unsafe for so small a force as four guns and two pistols. We could hear, also, vigorous firing in that direction. So remaining awhile quiet, we watched events. Gen. McDowell himself was on a hill near, to the right of the road to Centerville, studying a map, and sweeping the country with his glass. Soon and suddenly, his regiments began to move, and steadily poured toward and on the Centerville road. Curiosity led to an investigation, and discovered that he took position on a beautiful ridge across the road a mile or so, looking northward, and about three miles from Gainesville. Here a very pretty little fight took place. The enemy attacked but our men repulsed them with great ease. This was Thursday about sunset. A little earlier we had been told that Banks was at Thoroughfare Gap – just the other end of the line from his real position. I knew better, of course.

Moving back a mile or two, our little party camped. That is, it turned into an open grove by the roadside, unharnessed, and unsaddled, and fed horses, cooked supper and went to bed; that is, wrapped "the drapery of our couch" about us, viz.; blankets, and laid down under the trees. Just opposite was a party of cavalry in charge of rebel prisoners. I visited the party, and talked with the prisoners, a very good-natured set of men. One was a South Carolinian, of good education. Pardon me, patriot, if I, for the memory of others of that state, helped him to something better than the confederate paper which was all he had for his captivity.

That night we could hear the rumbling of artillery wheels, apparently moving westward, though there was no firing. Where they went, or how our army changed its front, I cannot yet understand. But in the morning I found Gen. Rickett's division already on the road from Gainesville to Bristow, south of Manassas Junction. We followed, and, seven or eight miles on, found Gen. Banks' corps.

That day, Friday, we heard – all day long – the sound of the battle. Impatiently we waited – in vain. It is said that ten thousand men more would have given the country the victory. Why, then was Gen. Banks' corps kept idle?

At night, just after tattoo, came orders for our brigade to go out on picket. So we did, moving about two miles, to near Broad Run, where we lay down by the side of a graveyard. No alarm took place, whatever. The next day, the corps began to move northward, by Manassas, saving one brigade, which remained to see to the removal of long trains of supplies, as well as of sick and wounded. About noon we crossed Broad Run ourselves, moved on a mile, and then returned and took up our position on the north side of that stream; and here, before dark, came back Gen. Banks' corps, with tidings that Gen. Pope had gained a great victory. But while we were cooking our suppers, the battle was raging – that Saturday evening – which proved so disastrous to our arms; and our corps was left uncalled for.

Next morning we had sudden orders: "Burn all baggage but two ambulances. Move instantly." At seven we started, but saved one little train. The corps was said to be cut off, and we must hasten to Occoquan Creek before the pouring rain should render it unfordable. A half mile on the road we crossed the railway; on it were scores of loaded cars, wrapped in flames. The melancholy and useless loss of property to be paid for by the hard toil of our citizens, accompanied by occasional explosions of ammunition, the drenching rain, and the exigency of the march, made it a spectacle I never desire to see repeated.

Passing through Brentsville, fording Occoquan Creek, never stopping for five hours – at last we saw the railway again, near Bull Run, with the road open to Centerville – a virtual junction. Of the real exigency I knew nothing. But under the orders which he received, the promptness with which Gen. Banks moved, the steadiness of his march, (with our Second leading) and the perfect order of his movements, are characteristics of a man whom Massachusetts delights to honor.

At the railroad I was again sent forward with sick, in the hope, finally to be accomplished, of finding an open road to Washington. We went on by the rebel corduroy roads of last winter to Centerville. This new observation of the rebel position only strengthened my old conviction that an attack on the rebel stronghold last winter would have been madness.

At Centerville, on the hights, were immense forces. It was difficult to conceive how they could have been worsted the day before; but all whom I questioned as to events, had no lack of confidence in the soldiery; they attributed the whole ill success to two men.

I had no time to delay. Already I saw signs of backward movement, and to be entangled in trains would have been unpleasant. Besides, I heard orders which evidently contemplated movement. I had but just started, when Providence favored me with a sudden meeting which delighted me. It was with my friend Mr. John A.

Fowle,[176] the excellent chairman of the executive committee of the association in Washington for the relief of Massachusetts soldiers. He had procured a government ambulance, loaded it with supplies, and, with his brother and – I will not say whom else – worked for twenty-four hours among the wounded, binding up hurts, comforting and relieving the helpless.[177] I have seen him in hospitals in Washington, too, and know his faithfulness. The widow and the fatherless bless him! Of him I procured supplies; joined a long, long train of ambulances; reached Fairfax Court House, and was then ordered to Fairfax Station.

The sight there cannot be described. The floors of cars and roofs were covered. Acres of ground were strewn with the wounded men. Train after train had gone. Yet still the ambulances came on, on. Camping there, the shriek of the steam-whistle broke the hours of that Sabbath night, and morning showed loaded trains still. I did not see any chaplains there, but I think there were some; indeed, I know there were next day. The wounded were as well cared for as possible, lying upon hay, and attended by surgeons. The most disconsolate men were divers government clerks, who had come out to assist, and who were distressed beyond measure because they could not return to Washington in cars, every inch of which was needed for the wounded. "I came out by invitation of the Secretary of War!" pompously remarked one. "Well," said the sentry, "we don't know that individual here." "But where *shall* I stay to-night?" asked the clerk. "Just where you please," said the sentry. I advised him to sleep on some hay, if he wished to sleep. He was horrified. He wanted to know, with a triumphant air, if *I* had ever slept out of doors. I rather

---

176 John Allen Fowle (1826 - 1916) was born in Boston and studied under the great American historian, George Bancroft, at Northampton Academy. At the outbreak of war, Fowle joined the Massachusetts Coast Guard being formed by Robert Bennett Forbes. Through Captain Forbes' influence Fowle received an appointment to the Navy Department in Washington where he also engaged in philanthropic work. Fowle became chairman of the Navy Association for the Relief of Soldiers, in which effort he was accompanied by his future wife Elida Barker Rumsey, and also founded the Soldiers' Free Library in Judiciary Square. They were famed for giving concerts throughout the hospitals in Washington the money from which they put towards the operation of their library. He and Eliza were married in March of 1863 in the Hall of Representatives, and Rev. Alonzo Quint performed the ceremony. "John Allen Fowle;" *Biographical Sketches*.
177 Probably George Washington Fowle (1821 - 1913) who was a bookbinder and printer in Woburn, Massachusetts. These brothers had been in business together for a while before the Civil War.

thought I *had*. Had I ever slept when it *rained*? (It was sprinkling just enough to make it pleasant.) I intimated to him that he was a great baby, to fuss that way, with acres of wounded men lying around him, and gave him up. Perhaps I ought not to despise him; I suppose I was just a fool once.

The wounded bore their sufferings manfully. But they did execrate one man. But here, as well as at Fairfax Court House, the rumor spread that McClellan was in command! The enthusiasm was delightful. To me especially, who have, as my letters testify, always believed in that noble man, their hearty joy was pleasant. I still believe as before, that with McClellan in command, we should not be now defending Washington. So the army believes. I have been inquiring of myself when and how I got my liking for him. And I remember that this personal kind of feeling began when I saw him for a moment only at Charlestown, Va., last February. He seemed to me a man born to command, and I felt then that he was one whom I could follow to the world's end.

Monday morning I went back to Fairfax Court House, and direct to Alexandria. Still the long trains of ambulances were on the road. The eye wearied, the heart grew faint, in seeing them. I was appealed to for water, as I had some. Now every ambulance of the kind there used has two kegs for water. I examined and found that in the long train moving a score of miles, there was not one drop of water in the kegs! I am happy to say that in our division such a fact would court martial somebody!

The army was now in retreat. I saw no disorder. There was no panic whatever. And, within the fortification line, I rejoined my own Second.

Of present movements it is not right to speak. Enough, that our forces are large. New troops swarm in. Energy and skill are evident. Disaster may still come, for we have thrown away the greatest opportunities. But all that large armies, under Generals whom the men believe in, can do, will be done.

A. H. Q.

September 26, 1862

Letter from Chaplain Quint
Below Boonsboro', Md., Sept. 16.
Sunrise!

After the long, dark hours, light began to dawn when the patriot-soldier, McClellan, was restored to command of the army which demanded him.

The dispirited soldiery, depressed by knowing that they were steadily outgeneraled, without confidence in leaders, immediately became enthusiastic. The man whom they always loved and respected inspired them.

Yesterday, while we were on the road in several parallel columns, McClellan rode through. Without orders, out of the enthusiasm of their hearts, sprang deafening cheers. The sound rolled up from regiment after regiment, brigade after brigade, until the scores of thousands repaid their leader for the temporary trials he had undergone.

We are, for once, in pursuit of the enemy. His invasion of the free North is hurled back. He took his own time, chose his own positions, occupied hills of wonderful capacity for defense, but northern valor forced his fastnesses, and drove him flying.

On the 4th of September our own corps left Virginia for the third time. We crossed at Georgetown, soberly. That day we camped a mile or two above Tenallytown. The next day we moved to a brook a mile and a half above Rockville, where, attached to Gen. Sumner's[178] corps, we formed in line of battle. Gen. Sumner's force on the right, ours the center, and Gen. Couch on the left.[179] The enemy appeared to threaten on our road with 30,000 men, while the remainder of his force was moving toward Frederick, which he soon occupied. Gen. Burnside came up on our right still further off, and on the 9th – it appearing that the enemy had moved his whole force toward Frederick. We began our march thitherward, Gen. Burnside in advance. Our corps bivouacked at Middlebrook that night; near Damascus next night; still nearer Damascus the next; half a mile from Ijamsville, on the Baltimore and Ohio Railway the next; and Saturday night, we were less than a mile out of Frederick.

---

178 Edwin Vose Sumner (1797 - 1863) was commissioned directly into the army from Boston, Massachusetts in 1819. Sumner had risen to the rank of Major in the U.S. Dragoons by the time of the Mexican-American war. During that conflict, in which he served with distinction, he was brevetted Lt. Colonel and Colonel while in the field. Sumner became a full Colonel in the U.S. Army at the head of the 1st Cavalry in 1855. Sumner was appointed a Brigadier-General in the Army in 1861, just prior to the outbreak of hostilities. He commanded II Corps and McClellan cited him for his bravery and gallantry during the Peninsula Campaign. Sumner was criticized for his corps' performance at Sharpsburg but at Fredericksburg Sumner commanded the Left Grand Division. Upon Joseph Hooker becoming commander of the Army of the Potomac, Sumner tendered his resignation. His son-in-law Armistead Lindsay Long served as an Aide-de-camp of General Robert E. Lee and later commanded the artillery for Richard Ewell's II Corps. Warner; *Generals in Blue*

179 Darius Nash Couch (1822 -) was a native of New York and a member of the class of 1846 at West Point along with Gen. George B. McClellan and Confederate General Thomas J. Jackson. Upon graduation Couch served as a lieutenant of artillery and was brevetted for bravery at several engagements during the Mexican-American war. In 1853 and 1854, Couch was under employment of the Smithsonian Institution in an expedition to California during which Couch discovered a new bird and a new toad which both bear his name. Following his marriage to Mary Ann Crocker, whose family were well known copper manufacturer's in Taunton, MA, Couch joined the family firm. At the outbreak of the Civil War, Couch raised and was commissioned Colonel of the 7th Massachusetts Infantry. The regiment performed well at the First Battle of Bull Run and when McClellan was made commander of the Army of the Potomac, Couch's fortunes rose also. Although illnesses, contracted during service in Mexico, plagued him his entire service, Couch turned in a steady and solid performance as a Brigade, Division and Corps commander. Couch's open criticism of General Joseph Hooker led to the acceptance of Couch's resignation, although Couch would once again be called upon to lead a division in the XXIII Army Corps during the battle of Nashville and throughout the Carolina campaign. Couch's association with McClellan would hinder his post-war political career, depriving him of several offices, including Governor of Massachusetts. Warner; *Generals in Blue*

Gen. Burnside had entered Frederick the evening before, with no action save a slight cavalry skirmish in the main street – the enemy having evacuated the place the day before. I revisited old friends in Frederick Saturday afternoon, and had good opportunities to learn a few facts derived from high rebel sources. They had over 90,000 men in that army, with 160 pieces of artillery.[180] They admitted that McClellan had worsted them in every one of the "seven days' fight" on the Peninsula, but left Richmond with perfect confidence in their ability to beat Gen. Pope. Had he still been in command, they said they would have conducted their campaign differently in Maryland – standing a fight at Monocacy. But Gen. McClellan's appointment made them more cautious, and they fell back to an immensely strong position west of Frederick. In Frederick they conducted themselves peaceably. Purchasing everything they could make useful, they paid in confederate money, by which some secessionists there suffered nicely. It was a favorite amusement to tie the American flag to their horses' tails, whereby they made plenty of Unionists out of the lukewarm or secessionists. In their main design they were terribly disappointed. Not only baffled in their purpose of invasion – but they found Maryland a Union state. Their pompous proclamation fell dead. A few hundreds were all the recruits they obtained in Maryland, where letters had assured them they would find a general uprising of the people. They left Frederick, cursing it as a Union city. When I remembered the almost supremacy of secessionism there last winter, I was delighted to witness the change. Our forces were welcomed with tumultuous cheers. The city swarmed with American flags. Frederick is a loyal town, and confirmed in its loyalty by its disgust with the secession soldiery – the leaders educated and iron-willed, the privates usually the poorest of "poor white trash."

We had hoped to rest on Sunday. But at 8 A.M., we were put in the road – a road we were on for *sixteen-hours*. Long halts, but in tiresome places, and not for rest; road obstructed by trains and artillery; immense bodies of troops two or three abreast; by-roads, across fields, wading brooks – up to and over the Catoctin range of hills four miles west of Frederick. Here the rebels had made a stand, on a ridge

---

180 Modern scholarship estimates the Army of Northern Virginia at about 60,000 soldiers though at Antietam only about 40,000 would be engaged. The Confederate army also had 246 pieces of artillery. Ballard; *Battle of Antietam*.

capable of great defense. But, on Saturday, Gen. Burnside had attacked them, carried their position, and drove them beyond the river at Middletown Valley, where they burned a bridge.

The view from this ridge is delightful. The Middletown Valley is wonderfully fertile, and its whole breadth of nine miles is covered with beautiful fields or green forests. Had it only a broad river like the Connecticut at Mt. Holyoke, or a lake, the scenery would be unsurpassed for quiet loveliness.

But we heard the sound or artillery all day, and we pressed on. The march was a singular one, bearing north, south, east, west – by road, through fields. At sunset the flashes of guns on the opposite range, the Blue Ridge, and the black puffs hovering in the air, marked the site of guns. Our object seemed to be to reach the slope by night. The general in command found a good place for supper, and we went on, directly across the country a while; through cornfields, the tops of whose products one could not reach standing in the stirrups, through brooks, and at last wading a river; resting in damp air and on damp ground; found at last, at 10 P.M., by an orderly of the General's hunting for us; going on until midnight, and at last, of camping, in lack of higher orders, by direction of our Brigadier; exasperated, tired, some of us supperless as well as dinnerless; having marched over *twenty* miles to reach *eleven* in distance; wondering whether it pays to break soldiers down without need.

We were to go into position at 3 A.M., as support to Gen. Sturgis.[181] But at 3 A. M. the enemy were gone. Some of us visited the field.

---

181 Samuel Davis Sturgis (1822 – 1889) was a graduate of the United States Military Academy at West Point (1846). Sturgis served in the Mexican-American war with the 1st U.S. Dragoons and was captured and made prisoner of war while scouting the area around Buena Vista. By the time the Civil War broke out, Sturgis had served on the frontier in several campaigns against several tribes of Western Indians. Sturgis was with the 1st U.S. Cavalry at the Battle of Wilson's Creek and following the death of General Lyons took command of the Union Forces in the west. Sturgis was sent east prior to the 2nd Battle of Bull Run and succeeded to the command of the 2nd Division, IX Corps at the battles of South Mountain, Antietam and Fredericksburg. In March of 1863, Sturgis went west with his Division to serve in the Army of the Tennessee, but his troops were routed by Nathan Bedford Forrest resulted in his being transferred to other stations. Sturgis remained with the U.S. army after the end of the Civil War, at one time commanding the 7th U.S. Cavalry with George A. Custer as his Lt. Colonel. Warner; *Generals in Blue*

The position they had held should have been impregnable. Imagine a range of lofty mountains, with here and there a winding road through "gaps" themselves elevated, the ground often rocky, with plenty of wood, and commanding every approach for miles. At their own pleasure they planted their batteries, and placed their infantry, having all the forces needed, and occupying a succession of crests as you ascend the hills. This was the line which Gen. Sumner, Gen. Burnside, and Gen. Hooker attacked.

From crest after crest, the enemy were driven, up to the last. When night came on, the enemy held the highest land on our right, our troops having driven them back from two positions, and lying within a few rods of them. In the center, the hight itself was taken. They were well sheltered behind the crest of a slope and walls and fences, yet Gen. Burnside's troops had pressed up, driven their batteries, slaughtered their infantry, and held the ground. On our left, Gen. Hooker had succeeded equally well.

In the center, the rebel dead, in their strongest position, lay actually heaped one on another – almost all shot through the head as they rose to aim. Near by was a secluded road where they had evidently cared for their wounded; I rode half a mile, and found relics of their hospital work the whole distance. Our loss was very slight in comparison.

The enemy began to retreat as soon as night covered their movements; all night they moved, pressing to the Potomac, and at daylight our forces were in rapid pursuit. The enemy not only left their dead, but frequently we find along the road their wounded, abandoned to our mercy. In Frederick, indeed, they left six hundred sick men, paroling a hundred and fifty of ours, sick there in hospital.

I believe that the campaign is now to be active. The enemy will, I think, succeed in getting most of his stores and men across the river, but we shall follow and a battle there is probable. The men are confident of success. They feel now that the army is one, instead of detached pieces as heretofore. It would be a little remarkable, if the vicinity of Centerville should witness another battle.

For ourselves, we have a new general. Gen. Mansfield[182] takes Gen. Banks' place. I may be pardoned for referring to our late commander again, although I

---

182 Joseph King Fenno Mansfield (1803 - 1862) was a graduate of West Point (1822) and spent the twenty-five years or so before the Mexican-American war engaged in building

have before repeatedly told you how brave and fearless, as well as discreet, he was as a soldier, and how much he was respected by his command. The poorest soldier had a friend in Gen. Banks. Modest, keeping all grievances to himself, obedient to his orders, he has won great respect in the army. Had his opinion been listened to, the now famous "Banks' retreat" would not have been needed, -- though then the SECOND would not have had so good an opportunity to exhibit the discipline and valor of its noble men.

I had known our commander earlier. Holding a state educational position during the whole of his service as Governor of Massachusetts as well as before and after, I had occasion officially to know the judgment, integrity, and firmness with which he acted in the Board of which he was chairman, in regard to most important interests, pecuniary and others; and often to see in his general administration, how firmly he adhered to the good of the state, regardless of mere partizanship. And now, while no longer under his command, I can say that the same qualifications he applied to his military position. Yet he is more. I speak with reasons, in saying that he is a sagacious statesman. His predictions have been fulfilled, his opinions gradually adopted.

As a chaplain, I know that Gen. Banks has always been on the side of right. Every chaplain has had all opportunities for usefulness which the General could give. For that, I owe him the people owe him, a debt of gratitude.

A. H. Q.

---

fortifications along the Southern coast. During the Mexican war, Mansfield worked on the staff of General Zachary Taylor as chief engineer as well as a brief stint of field command. For his efforts in the Mexican-American war, Mansfield was brevetted Colonel of the U.S. Army. At the outbreak of the Civil War Mansfield was commissioned a brigadier general and assigned to the defense of Washington. General McClellan ordered Mansfield to command of XII Corps. At the Battle of Sharpsburg, Mansfield personally led his corps to the assistance of General Hooker's Corps and he was shot and killed. Warner; *Generals in Blue*

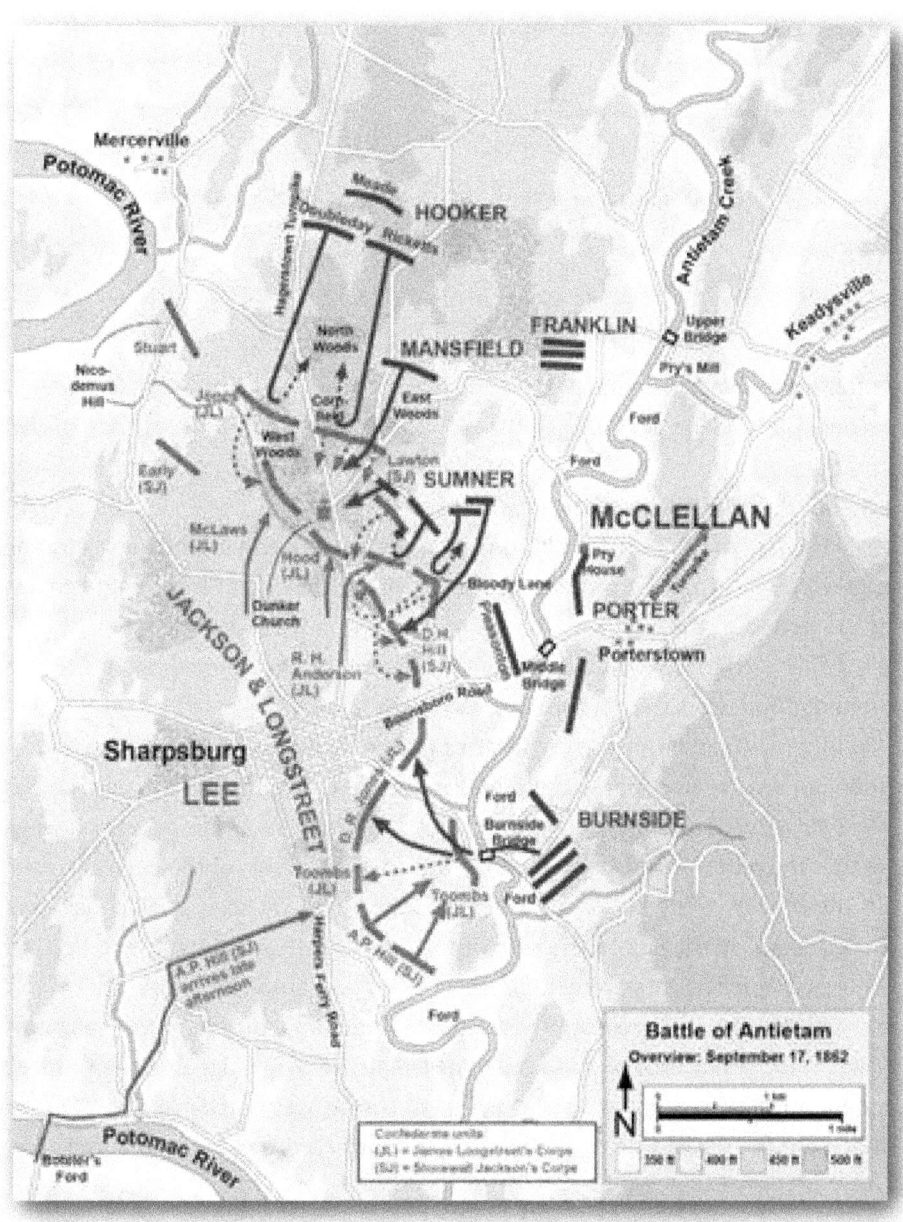

Map by Hal Jespersen, www.cwmaps.com

October 10, 1862

Letter from Chaplain Quint.
Frederick, Md., Sept. 20, 1862

I cannot describe the battle of Antietam Creek.

I heard – the thunder of cannon all day long; the horrible whirr of shells; the musketry which sometimes became a mere roar; the cheers of success; the groans of the wounded; the whisper of the dying.

I saw – the smoke of a battle-line of five miles; the fierce flashing fire; the wounded and dead; the advance, the waver, the recovery.

But what it then meant, or what our commander was trying to do, who – confined to near one spot – could tell? So far as I could imagine the next day, as I examined a county map, it seemed as if it was wanted to drive back each wing, so that the rebels would be shut within a kind of peninsula of the Potomac river. Of the history of the battle, no other account I have yet seen at all equals that by "Carleton" in the *Boston Journal*, with whose inferences I sometimes differ, but whose comprehensive statement of facts has no peer among reporters.[183]

On the Sunday preceding the battle of Antietam (Ant*ee*tam, the neighbors call it without any exception, to my knowledge) the Blue Ridge had been carried by our forces, excepting one point, which, of course, was untenable alone. During that night the rebels evacuated the ridge, and hurried to and through Boonsboro',

---

[183] Charles Carleton Coffin (1823 – 1896) was a well-known Civil War journalist whose reports from the seat of war to the *Boston Journal* gained wide notoriety. After the war Coffin wrote a series of books based on his Civil War columns and experiences. Griffis; *Charles Carleton Coffin*.

towards the river. Our forces rapidly followed. It was generally reported by the inhabitants that the enemy were crossing, and undoubtedly a portion had. Monday evening our corps found itself south of Boonsboro' a few miles, where it bivouacked. On Tuesday morning no orders came until about 9 o'clock, when we made ready to move. Gen. Mansfield soon rode up, saying, "You are going immediately into battle," a declaration received with as much coolness as if he had said, "you are going to dinner." He was mistaken; we were moved about a mile and a half only, where we came suddenly in view of large forces. On the crest of the hills were posted batteries for a mile or more. Down the slopes were drawn up long lines of battle, first and second. Just below were still other forces. And off to the right was a dense mass in reserve – perhaps the most impressive sight I ever witnessed – black, motionless, silent, but like a silent thunder cloud in its threatening. We took our place as reserve. No battle ensued that day. For two or three hours a smart cannonade only enlivened the scene. Movements were, however, steadily going on. A whole corps was sent to the left. Other forces placed in the center. From the front, nothing could be seen but a gun or two, and a few skirmishers; the rebels lay behind the slopes as ours.

At night we lay down there. But about half past ten came quiet, low orders to be ready to move. Then, orders to move. On the road – in the darkness – crossing river, woods, fields – in a light rain – at half past two we were in a field new to us, but destined to be better known; for within musket range were the rebel forces occupying one of the hillocks of Antietam.

A little past five we were awakened by artillery. That broke the last slumbers of thousands. Looking about us we saw our thousands upon thousands destined to be the right wing; for our corps, in the night, had traversed more than half our line. Without breakfast, our column was formed. Silently the forces moved into position; no drum, no bugle, nothing but the word of command, and the dull roar of the batteries. Our whole corps moved by brigades, in column by divisions, dark and heavy spots on the field. A little distance, and the order is to halt. The men of ours begin to make their coffee, but before it is drinkable, the corps moves up to support Gen. Hooker.

Gen. Hooker had our right. All the morning, he kept up a gallant contest, while we could hear little from the left. He drove the enemy at first, but then commenced what seemed to me the enemy's object all day – to mass their forces heavily against our right. Gen. Hooker's gallant force was inadequate, and our corps was ordered into action. Nobly did it respond to the order. Backward fell the enemy before the tremendous fire of Gen. Mansfield's corps; and Gen. Hooker's men were relieved. But as the hours rolled on, still the fierce conflict at just that point went on. Reserves went in, and still the fury of the fight was unchecked. It was after hours of fighting, that the last regiment in reserve there went in – the last – and as it seemed to have no effect, the anxiety was intense. The line was forced back; was it in retreat? No; it had but left a position untenable, as affairs then were, but it stood like iron. Soon Gen. Summer's corps came on. How reviving was the sight! Up they came in mass, then deployed into line, and amidst the cheers of our almost exhausted corps, they rushed into the conflict; the gained and lost ground was again regained, and the effort to turn our right was defeated.

By and by, there was a lull in the iron storm. Soon after 1 P.M., there was almost entire cessation; but after a little while, the cannonading was more intense than ever. I wondered what woke it to such life; I found afterwards that it was because MCCLELLAN was there. Wherever he was, at any critical point on that eventful day, the fury of conflict was tremendous. Cheers always awaited him, and the very weapons themselves seemed to recognize the presence of the beloved General.

It was not until sunset that the guns sullenly and gradually ceased firing. Then the sky was red with conflagrations. The houses, the barns, the gardens, were full of wounded men. We did not know the general result; we knew that their left, our right had forced back; but of our left we knew nothing.

On this day, our troops fought as never before. A rebel officer, wounded, and a prisoner, to whom I ministered in his turn, said to me, "I was in all the seven days' battles on the Peninsula, and your men never fought as they do to-day." Indeed, our men have acquired that "vindictiveness" essential in war. And in all the fighting, our own regiment and our own brigade kept its name unsullied. Our own SECOND, which has never retreated an inch without orders, lost a quarter of all its force in action; it had more than twenty new bullet holes in its already scarred flag, (the one given it by the historian Motley;)[184] it captured a rebel standard; and its

---

184 John Lothrop Motley (1814 – 1877) was a graduate of Boston Latin School and Harvard College (1831), following which he spent a year in Göttingen where he formed a lifelong friendship with Otto von Bismarck. In 1841, Motley joined the legation at St. Petersburg, Russia

fire, under the skillful management of its commander, (an educated soldier,) told with visible and terrible havoc in the ranks of the enemy. The brigade, under our Massachusetts General Gordon, behaved well. The two new regiments, the 107th New York,[185] and the 13th New Jersey,[186] did themselves honor. The latter broke once, but its Colonel rallied the men, gave them a word or two of address, and led them into action, where they honored themselves greatly. Gen. Gordon himself – in daring, skill, and experience, equaled by few, led his brigade like himself. Gen. Mansfield's early wound, with that of Gen. Crawford, put him in command of the division. Gen. Gordon's aid, Hon. C. R. Train,[187] was in the hottest of the fight. This gentleman had left the comforts of home – though a member of Congress – to take the moderate position of an aid-de-camp, where he found his services needed. He plunged at once into the hardships of veterans of a year's experience, and bore

---

as secretary. Motley was a regular contributor to various publications, including the North American Review. His most famous work *The Rise of the Dutch Republic*, was written during his stay in the Netherlands and Brussels. Arriving back in Massachusetts in April of 1861, J. L. Motley wrote several defenses of the Union cause to newspapers, notably the London times. Motley was asked on short notice to officially present the flag to the Regiment on Wednesday, June 30, 1861 at Camp Andrew, West Roxbury. Shortly after delivering the flag to the Second Massachusetts, Motley was appointed United States minister to the Austrian Empire. "Obituary – John Lothrop Motley;" *Boston Journal*; and, Quint; *Record of the Second Massachusetts*.

185 107th New York Infantry was organized in August of 1862 in upstate New York under Colonel Robert B. Van Valkenburgh. The regiment fought its first battle at Antietam but didn't see any much action at Gettysburg. Ordered to Tennessee with the remainder of 12th Corps, the 107th took part in the Atlanta and Carolina campaigns right through Averysborough and Bentonville. The regiment was mustered out in June of 1865 suffering a total of 222 deaths in the regiment. "107th Infantry Regiment;" *Unit History Project*.

186 13th New Jersey was recruited in July of 1862 for three years under Colonel Ezra Carman and was assigned to the Army of the Potomac's XII Corps. The regiment remained with XII Corps through all its wanderings from Chancellorsville, Gettysburg, Atlanta, the Carolinas and was mustered out in June of 1865. Adjutant General of New Jersey; *Record of Officers and Men of New Jersey in the Civil War*.

187 Charles Russell Train (1817 – 1885) graduate from Brown University (1837) and studied law at Harvard University. Train was elected a Representative to the General Court of Massachusetts, served as a district attorney and declined an appointment to the U.S. Supreme Court. He was elected a Congressman for two terms and served as a volunteer aide-de-camp to Generals Gordon and McClellan. After the war, Train served as a State Representative and as Attorney General of Massachusetts. New England Historic and Genealogical Society; *Memorial Biographies*.

them well. And in this battle, his first experience under fire, like a true and brave man, he deserved well of his country.

From the excitement of the battle-field to the hospitals in the rear, is a sad change. From the earliest of the fight, the wounded are removed. Often two, four, six, and sometimes ten men, armed men, were sent with one wounded man; and the worst was that some of the surgeons retained these well men as assistants, by which maneuver thousands of armed soldiers were kept out of the fight, most of them doing nothing at all. It was an outrage, a usurpation, on the part of the surgeons. On the field itself was some care. Dr. L. R. Stone, an assistant surgeon, was a perfect hero; regardless of bullets, in the hottest fire, he kept coolly on his work, -- while near, Dr. Kendall of the 12th was killed.[188] The nearest hospital, that of our own corps, was necessarily in range of the enemy's shell, which every now and then fell around and beyond. Near by were five other hospitals, all for one wing. Here were generals and privates brought together. Gen. Mansfield I saw dying, and a few feet off, an unknown private; Gen. Hartsuff[189] badly wounded, and by his side a throng of others now on the same level. There is no distinction as to what body or soul needs then.

Our own regiment helped fill these hospitals. Our gallant dead, they are remembered with all the other gallant Massachusetts dead. But one we lost, -- hard to replace, -- our brilliant, brave, generous, kind-hearted Lieut. Colonel, Wilder Dwight, shot mortally, but living two days; who had unhurt galloped up and down with the captured rebel flag, amid the cheers of our men, and afterwards hit while in comparative security; a young man of wonderful promise at home; cheerful, resigned, ready to die, -- his only wish ungratified being to see his father and mother; strong

---

188 Albert Asaph Kendall (1828 – 1862) was a graduate of the Medical College of New York and a resident physician and surgeon in Newton Lower Falls. He was commissioned Assistant Surgeon of the Twelfth Massachusetts Infantry in 1861. Cook; *History of the Twelfth Massachusetts Volunteers*

189 George Lucas Hartsuff (1830 - 1874) was a native of New York and a graduate of West Point (1852). After graduation he was assigned to the 4th U. S. Artillery and saw service in Texas and Florida. In one skirmish with the Seminoles Hartsuff was severely wounded. In 1861 and 1862 Hartsuff served on the staff of General Rosecrans and in April of 1862 was commissioned a Brigadier General. Hartsuff was severely wounded at Sharpsburg and spent many months recovering during which time he was promoted to the rank of Major General. Once he recovered, Hartsuff commanded the XXIII Corps for seven months when his wounds forced him to rest. In March of 1865, Hartsuff took command of the army on Bermuda Hundred during the siege of Petersburg. Hartsuff remained with the army until 1871 when he retired from the army. Warner; *Generals in Blue*

in faith and trust; hard is it to part with *him*. While lying in the garden, moved only on a stretcher, he sent our own surgeon to relieve the wounded lying all around unattended to by the surgeons busy cutting off limbs of men even death-struck; and again and again sent water provided for him, to the poor fellows calling for it. Yet he was not free from brutal insolence. While waiting there into the night for an ambulance into which to place Col. Dwight for shelter only, (as he could not bear its motion) some men of ours, detached for that purpose, were waiting to help, while all was quiet save the groans of sufferers covering the ground, a harsh voice insisted on turning out all our men. I found a pompous little surgeon angry and furious. I informed him why the men were there, assured him of their perfectly good behavior, and requested permission for them to remain, as we were momentarily expecting the ambulance. It was all in vain. Col. Dwight himself was treated most harshly, although of higher rank than the brute himself, and although I told the surgeon that it was a man mortally wounded. He ordered the guard to turn them out at the point of the bayonet, and to prevent their return even to move Col. Dwight, -- refusing to tell his rank, and even his name, until I obtained it of another party. The men *were driven away while actually giving water* to wounded sufferers who had been calling in vain for help. I assured the brute that I would take care his conduct was made known, and I have already sent charges against him – knowing, from several opportunities to see that day, that he is, from brutality, pomposity, and harshness, utterly unfit to be in charge of wounded men, and from gross disrespect to an officer higher in rank, unfit to be in the army. That the medical department needs reorganization, I can attest; and of its merits and demerits I mean to write some day. This fellow's name is said to be "King," – a medical director in Gen. Reynold's corps, Penn. Reserves, -- too good troops to have such a fellow among them.[190]

Jamaica Plain, Mass., Oct. 7, 1862[191]

[To the above unfinished letter I cannot add anything; not strong enough yet. A.H.Q.]

---

190 James B. King (1818 - 1880) of Pittsburg and was appointed Brigade Surgeon of the First Brigade in Pennsylvania Reserves. In 1862, King resigned his commission to accept the post of Surgeon General of Pennsylvania. After the war King was elected President of the Medical Society of Pennsylvania in 1866. *History of Pittsburgh and Environs*.

191 This letter was written from home as Quint had accompanied the body of his friend and comrade Wilder Dwight home for burial.

November 21, 1862

Letter from Chaplain Quint.
Near Sharpsburg, Md., Nov. 13, 1862.

Weeks have passed by since I wrote you. I do not remember how many, but I hope somebody has missed my pen. I know that my last letter was written just after the awful day of Antietam, by the dying bed of a heroic soldier, dying in Christian peace, the memory of whose friendship is forever sacred to me. Its postscript was added at home from a sick bed, -- in nervous prostration and malarious fever which the Rappahannock campaign had originated, and which the sudden return to a different climate developed. Then, as strength was gained, there were the meetings with wounded of our Regiment; with convalescents whose highest comfort was to drop in to our recruiting office; with some not seen since Cedar Mountain, whose grasp of hand was accompanied only by starting tears as we remembered the gallant dead of the mournful day. Alas for the weeping hearts which write the history of this war! Friends told me I had grown ten years older; it is not hard fare or hard marches; it is such lives as those of the Valley, of Cedar Mountain, of the Rappahannock, and of Antietam, with their sick, their maimed, their dead, that deepen the lines on one's face ten years in one. And what then is the growing old of the childless, the widows and orphans?

You said in one issue that various persons thought that Chaplain James and myself wrote too cheerlessly. Ask that noble chaplain and dear friend of mine why, and he will tell you from his sick bed, what I would say in restored health, -- that we always wrote as encouragingly as we *could*. There is, first, the wearing upon personal sympathies. There is, or was, next, the knowledge to be uttered only delicately, of useless and needless disasters, of a lack of vigor where vigor was essential, and of opportunities wasted, of time, means, and men thrown away, with a lack of confidence in – I will not say what, who could write exultingly? I *will* tell you, that many a man in this army, in high stations and low, has for months believed this war to be utterly hopeless except as to the mere question of boundaries, and that men high, very high in civil life, have privately admitted the same opinion; and this, *not* from the strength of the South, nor from any inability in the nation to restore its authority over every spot in its domain. Not that there is the least hesitation as to fighting on, but that there is a desire to fight usefully. The same spirit which I supposed to be at the bottom of the recent elections exists in the army, though I doubt whether it would have expressed itself in the same way by vote *now*, but which *will* do so whenever the war is over. I am speaking now from a tolerably wide knowledge, not from speculation, nor from my own purpose.

Nor do I feel that the war is hopeless. I believe, on the contrary, that it never promised as well as now. We have a magnificent army. It is well led. It is brave. There is much loss yet to be had, but we can succeed. A winter campaign will destroy, by death or disability, one half of our numbers, but if the country wishes success at that cost, success can be had. I say this notwithstanding two facts which look, to one or another unpromising.

These two are, first, the result of the recent elections. I do feel confident that while there are some double-dyed traitors in the successful party, the great mass is truly loyal. They have voted against the administration, because they had no confidence in the energy of the administration. They meant to rebuke it, and they did rebuke it. But I am more mistaken than ever before if that party as a whole does not demand a vigorous prosecution of the war.[192]

The second is the removal of Gen. McClellan. Of course, the intimations that the army would not fight under anybody else, are perfectly foolish. Our men fight

---

192 In the midterm elections of 1862 the Republicans lost 22 seats in Congress and the Democrats picked up 28 seats, however, the Republicans still managed to retain control of the House of Representatives, while their control of the Senate actually increased by three seats. The Republicans also lost a number of gubernatorial elections, most importantly, the state of New York. Heidler, Heidler, and Coles; "The Election of 1862;"

for their *country*, not for a *man*. I cannot answer for any other corps than ours, but in ours, there is a feeling of deep sadness at the loss of our beloved, trusted leader. I have hardly yet seen the man who does not mourn over it, although ready to give his successor all their help. Indeed, the new commander is personally liked. I remember the cheers with which he was greeted the morning after the battle of South Mountain, after entirely passing the line, stopped to shake hands with a wounded soldier hobbling along on crutches. But we remember how Gen. McClellan reinspired the shattered, despondent troops, and by the magic of his name and presence made the invincible army which, against superior forces (I say what is true,) saved the North at Antietam; who restored the wavering fight of the right wing whose falling back I witnessed; who infused life wherever he went; who ordered an advance which he stopped at the urgent request of corps commanders; who would not throw his brave men into a hasty advance and a winter campaign without suitable clothing. The soldiers remember these things; a few hundred thousand men will remember these things; a few hundred thousand men will remember them in some future exercise of their civil rights. But, in the mean time, they will follow the directions of their leader; they will give all their powers to his successor; they will imitate the glorious patience, the heroic patriotism of their late General, who loves his country too well to make his personal position any cause for weakening that country's power. Do I "believe in McClellan yet?" Most heartily *I do*. He was virtually deprived of command before; necessity recalled him, to save the cause. He is deprived of command again; but the end is not yet.

Holding such views I have been grieved in reading most virulent attacks on Gen .McClellan even in a religious paper. His conduct is a proper subject for fair criticism, such as I have seen in your own paper, while I disagree with your conclusions; but the bitter, malignant, personal attacks, such as I have read, against a general actually in command, were certainly unsuited to the columns of a religious paper. I have seen such reiterated week after week. I have seen what I know, personally, to be actual falsehoods, put forth in a spirit which should exclude such a paper from every Christian home.

But now the army advances. I regret, on some accounts, that I cannot chronicle its movements; but we have no anxious longing to re-travel either the east or west side of the Blue Ridge. Our own corps is guarding the Potomac line, which is necessary, as the enemy hold the Virginia valley, and Maryland is therefore exposed to sudden raids. Harper's Ferry is thus to be defended, and the river lined, up I do not know how far. When I left our regiment two days after the battle of Antietam, it was just moving. It went to Brownville that night, having passed through Solomon's Gap, and slept in the road. On Saturday it crossed the mountain of Maryland Hights, and after occupying a spot on the side for a few hours, went up to the signal station where it bivouacked. Sunday afternoon it went down the east side of the mountain to Pleasant Valley; on Tuesday, it moved to the old camping ground of a year ago. There it was, until Wednesday, October 30, when it moved hither, and now finds itself within a few miles of its position during the battle of Antietam.

Gen. Gordon has charge of a long stretch of river. That is, all the fords are guarded carefully. Our own position is at the main ford hereabouts, which extends for a mile up and down the river. It takes nearly a third of our regiment at once to do picket duty. Gen. Gordon's care is most active. He knows every part of the line himself for some thirty miles. We are in Gen. Morell's[193] division.

The excitement of a battle is sublime. But I am not earnest to see many more for our regiment. I mourned very dolefully in your columns last summer because we were likely to see no active service. Then immediately came Banks' retreat with the Second as rear guard, and a battle at Winchester. Then, Cedar Mountain. Then Antietam. The regiment has made its name honored. It is now ready for onward movement, having gone up from less than two hundred to six hundred men fit for duty. But battles – a sunset finds too many gaps in the line. Such officers as Abbott, Cary, Goodwin, Williams, Perkins, Dwight – dead. And now we are sad at the loss of another, Major Savage,[194] who died in Virginia, of wounds received at Cedar Mountain. An honorable, brave soldier; refined, gentle, warm-hearted, and

---

193 George Webb Morrell (1815 - 1883) graduated from West Point (1835) but resigned his commission after only two years. After a brief stint in the railroad business, Morrell went into law which he did until the outbreak of the Civil War. In 1861, Morrell was commissioned a Colonel on the staff of the New York Adjutant General and later in the defenses of Washington. In August of 1861, Morrell was commissioned a Brigadier of Volunteers and commanded a brigade of V Corps. In May of 1862 Morrell was given command of Division and was promoted to Major General in July of 1862. The court martial of General Fitz John Porter also ended Morrell's field career. He served in a few administrative posts before being mustered out of service in December of 1864. Warner; *Generals in Blue*

194 See note 101.

one of the purest-minded men I ever know; an only son, whose parents may God bless! Nobody knew James Savage but to respect and love him.

And such men in the ranks. I miss too long a list to be written out, though they deserve it, and some day shall have it in permanent form. Men like one of Co. A, one of my Christian brethren, dying after just time enough to say, "Lord, receive my spirit!" Or like one dying day before yesterday, a warm-hearted Christian; but lately returned from a captivity of weary months, long ago freed from the captivity of sin, now released from the captivity of the body, into the glorious enjoyments of the children of God – of perfectly consistent Christian example always, meeting death in peace.

Brave men. Patriots. Long is the list. But many brave men are left in the Second yet. A new commander we must have, for Col. Andrews, our brave and skillful soldier, is made a Brigadier, and gone with Gen. Banks. Thus we have furnished *two* Generals from our Regiment. Wilder Dwight would be our commander, but he is dead; James Savage, but he is dead; Edward G. Abbott, but he is dead. And so Samuel M. Quincy,[195] now at home, wounded while fighting bravely, is next. Richard Cary would be Lieut. Colonel, but he is dead. And William Cogswell is next. Richard C. Goodwin would be Major, but he is dead. And Charles R. Mudge[196] is

---

195 Samuel Miller Quincy (1833 - 1887) was a graduate of Harvard (1852) and admitted to the practice of law in 1855. Quincy was a State Representative for Ward 4, Boston, and was commissioned as captain in May of 1861. Quincy was wounded at Cedar Mountain and taken prisoner and kept at Libby Prisoner, Richmond. Quincy was paroled in October of 1862, and didn't return to duty until March of 1863 at which time he returned as Colonel of the regiment. Quincy resigned the colonelcy on 2 June 1863. Four months later, Quincy accepted an appointment as Lt. Colonel of the 73d U.S. Colored Troops and inspector of troops on the staff of General Andrews at Port Hudson. Quincy rose to be Colonel of the 81st of the U.S.C.T. and mustered out in January of 1866. Quint; *The Record of the Second Massachusetts*; and, Adjutant General of Massachusetts; *Massachusetts Soldiers, Sailors and Marines in the Civil War*.

196 Charles Redington Mudge (1839 – 1863) was a graduate of Harvard (1860) and upon the outbreak of war, raised a company of men from Lynn and Swampscott into which company he was commissioned 1st Lieutenant. By July of 1861, Mudge was commissioned captain and wounded in the leg at the First Battle of Winchester. He was commissioned Major in November of 1863 and Lt. Colonel in June of 1863. Mudge commanded the regiment at Gettysburg which occurred between Col. Quincy's resignation and the return of Col. Cogswell from his wounds. Mudge was killed on the 2nd's attack across the meadow near Spangler's Spring, in Gettysburg. Quint; *The Record of the Second Massachusetts*; and, Adjutant General of Massachusetts; *Massachusetts Soldiers, Sailors and Marines in the Civil War*.

next, who was the *junior captain* when we left camp Andrew. Such are the changes since July 8, 1861.

A. H. Q.

P.S. On returning, I found various letters of inquiry from friends of soldiers. The failure to receive answers, the writers will attribute to my forced absence. Most of them have been answered by others; the balance I have replied to. I wish the writers would not apologize for "troubling me; it is a chaplain's business to link home and camp together. This hint I give to the large number of friends of our Regiment who read your excellent paper.

A. H. Q.

December 5, 1862

Letter from Chaplain Quint
Near Sharpsburg, Md., Nov. 21, 1862

We have little share in the great movement on which hang the destinies of the campaign; but we watch with intense eagerness. With all the affection borne to our late General, God bless him, everybody feels, as that chief himself teaches us to feel, the warmest interest in the progress of his successor. It seems, indeed, as if the critical period of the war were now. With success before January, we ensure the masses to determined measures; we dispirit the rebels. With defeat, we create a party ready to recognize the South; we encourage the rebels; we give opportunity for foreign meddling. With undecided results, we ensure a disgraceful compromise, worse than separation. Without success in this war, the North crumbles to pieces. National life is suspended on present issues. Often have I thought, in such anxieties, of the remark an honored soldier uttered to me, "this nation has forgotten God!" But no. There are too many praying men and women to allow us to believe so fatal a statement. But does the nation have an adequate conception of the things at stake? When a policy measure was adopted in this war, that soldier referred to, said, "I never felt so sadly but once; that was when my child died." National destruction is a worse personal loss than loss of children; worse than death itself.

But we follow the army with our hopes. We watch its progress, since its change of base, over the very line which Gen. McClellan had adopted for Gen. McDowell's army, when under his command, with which Gen. Banks and Gen. Fremont were to cooperating. Generals Banks and Fremont were peremptorily ordered back, and the day before an intended attack on Jackson, who was so situated near Harrisonburg, that his annihilation was morally certain. Gen McClellan was left without cooperation. Now, the ravings of the editorial fools who abused McClellan for not advancing by way of Manassas, are shown to be absurd, by the abandonment of that line, and the selection of the very one for which Gen. McClellan had destined a large army. If, now, we had the means to advance on Richmond, by the other route also, that from the sea, success would be certain. You have your opinions of McClellan; I have mine. I could reply to your editorials most easily, though, perhaps, not convincingly. With the rank and file, with the great bulk of the officers of the army, I believe in McClellan. When you read official documents, I beg you to remember that no man in the army has the right to deny or rebut a statement; that Gen. McClellan utters not a word; and that the men who have fought under him and know him, reverence, love, and believe in him now as before; and because they love McClellan, will fight enthusiastically under his successor. Print this, and I will have no more to say of Gen. McClellan, until he is recalled to command, or – until the next Presidential election.

The work of our regiment is picket duty. We are in front of a ford, of which the water is but knee deep for a mile. The enemy still hold the valley. If Jackson went southward, it was only in a parallel line with our army on the east of the Blue Ridge, and he returned. Whether he remains, is doubtful, as Gen. Lee will need him. But the enemy are still opposite us, though rarely showing themselves. A few days ago, a man who went over for his family, was stopped by a rebel party just as they were embarking. One man took to the water, was wounded, and finally killed. Two days ago, the deepening twilight brought into view, at least a mile of camp fires, which were speedily extinguished. Yesterday, we heard cannonading half the day, apparently from supposed reconnaissance from Harper's Ferry. The ease with which a rebel party could make a raid into Maryland, keeps here a large force; besides the possibility, now growing less, that Jackson might seek to divert troops, by a sudden threatening this way, as he succeeded in doing, when he forced Gen. Banks to retreat from Strasburg. The river is not yet raised to any noticeable degree, by the light rains of this week; but we have not yet heard from the mountain regions. It is *their* waters which swell the Potomac.

Our own regiment maintains its morale, notwithstanding the loss of its Colonel, Andrews, to gain of Gen. Banks; a modest, unpretending, but wonderfully skilled and energetic soldier, is our late colonel. He is a graduate of West Point, whose pupils prove altogether the best soldiers. I have been some-what surprised to see jealousies fostered at home against educated soldiers. I have seen a good many of the graduates of our military schools, and from observation, I have acquired the highest confidence in them. That they often feel superior to mere militia officers, is doubtless true; they are superior. That many volunteers feel distressed because they recognize their own comparative inferiority, is true; they ought to feel distressed. Educated soldiers are as much superior to one beginning without any training, as an educated physician is to one who begins practice utterly ignorant of medicine. The latter may learn by years of experiment; so may the raw soldier. But each sacrifices life to do it. I could instance slaughters which no educated soldier would ever have allowed to occur; they were the cost of teaching raw men. I could point to a brigade uselessly sacrificed; and to our own, saved in similar circumstances, by having a soldier for a commander.

A curious paragraph about our regiment has gone the rounds, viz.: that "the color-bearer of the Second Massachusetts regiment" – when, at the battle of Antietam, his regiment showed signs of giving way – "rushed fearlessly forward, and, jumping over a fence, led the regiment into the lines of the enemy. Of course, the charge of the 'gallant Second' was successful."

Now "of course, the charge of the 'gallant Second' was successful." But the Second never for a moment showed signs of giving way, on that fiery day, nor any other day. The Second never yet fell back an inch without orders. As to leading the regiment, our brave Col. Andrews did that.

The public press, just now, are speaking of the great number of deserters from the army; and government has issued stringent orders, I believe. The evil is by no means magnified. In battles too, there are many who go to the van. I saw, at least, *thousands* at Antietam. Even when men carried off the wounded – which was not their business, surgeons kept them from returning; I saw it. But is there not a reason why men do not fear to desert? I know of a case where a man deserted, and was afterwards apprehended in citizen's clothing, a salesman in a store in New Hampshire. He escaped after being taken, but was recaptured. He was tried and convicted. The sentence was entirely remitted, because the powers that were could not see sufficient evidence of the crime of desertion! He was returned to his regiment, and again deserted, before being put to duty, and was not heard of again.

Another matter of public puffing of somebody, is the new system of Ambulance Corps. All ambulances are being taken away from the regiments, and put under charge of one brigade officer. When the sick are to be moved, the surgeon sends a written requisition for ambulances. The new plan has some merits; in one place, viz.: the field of battle. But for regiments as such, it is exceedingly unpleasant. For instance, on leaving a recent camp, ambulances were wanted to transport the sick. The ambulances were not four miles off. On sending for them, they were not to be found. Again, suppose at this point, the enemy came suddenly, and in such force that it were madness to remain. There would be no time to send a requisition for ambulances. The sick, in such a case, must be left to the enemy. Or, suppose a regiment is ordered suddenly to move ten miles on a dangerous service. It has no time to get ambulances. Such occasions I have seen repeatedly, when, having ambulances, there was no difficulty. It is hard for soldiers to feel, going on such a service, that if wounded, there is no way to remove them. The old system, of having all ambulances with regiments had evils; but it is just as bad – worse – to give them none. The true system would be to give a limited number to each regiment, say four or five, and have a general ambulance corps besides, for emergencies.

In this connection, our excellent surgeon, worn down by the arduous duties of the Rappahannock and Maryland campaign, and wounded at Cedar Mountain, has resigned. With enlarged experiences and returning strength, he will be an acquisition to Milford. Dr. Stone, who behaved so nobly at Antietam, is promoted to the position, and Dr. Heath, a well-known physician from Stoneham, remains.

While on this point, I want to say something about surgeons. The medical department is sometimes severely criticized; like all general criticisms, sometimes unjustly. Many of the surgeons are gentlemen, soldiers, and men of skill. Many are neither. I have seen such a medical director as the brute of a fellow I told you of at Antietam, now placed in a higher position, I believe, a disgrace to the service. And, on the other hand, such a man as Medical Director Chappel, an ornament to the corps.[197] I have seen surgeons work night and day; and I have seen some sleeping

---

197 Artemus Chapel (1824 - 1868) was a graduate of the College of Physicians and Surgeons. Following graduation he moved from New York to Nebraska. Chapel was commissioned a Brigade Surgeon of Volunteers in 1862 and rose to become Medical Director of Gen. William's division. Chapel continued in that post until he became Surgeon in charge of the General Hospital, West's Buildings in Baltimore, Maryland in 1864. College of Physicians and Surgeons;

all night, after a very short but destructive battle, while wounded men were suffering for want of their care. As a whole, the *better* volunteer surgeons are more able than most of those of the regular army that I have seen. The appointments from Massachusetts have been made with great judgment. I wish I could say the same of all the states.

The greatest reform that could take place in the medical department, I am satisfied after long thought, would be to deprive surgeons of all military rank, and take off their shoulder straps and gold lace. Leave them enough distinctive dress to show their occupation, but none of a soldier's uniform. The system works well with chaplains; is an army surgeon any more of a soldier than a chaplain? It is true, indeed, that some chaplains wear shoulder-straps, wreath on the cap, and gold cord, and now and then sport a sword; but no sensible one does. To do so is in violation of orders, and such men are laughed at. So are those who give them swords, as I remember some silly Sunday school did a new Massachusetts chaplain the other day.[198] But – a chaplain is none the less respected for having no shoulder-straps. Nor would a surgeon be. The effect of this aping the soldier is, that many men who were unassuming doctors at home, begin to swell when they get on a uniform. They think they must be dictatorial. The poor soldier who comes to sick-call is only a private, and the officer gets to be pompous and harsh, until there are cases where sick men rather suffer than be brow-beat. The uniformed surgeons often prefer to be taken for soldiers than doctors; they put the U. S. on the cap instead of the M. S. (medical staff) which the regulations prescribe. In Washington, many of them (and some in the field) call each other *Major*, (their courtesy rank). Contract surgeons, mere hired doctors, at Washington, have put on uniforms. Of course, a multitude are more sensible than all this; such it would not hurt to lose their shoulder-straps. And a multitude more need to lose their feathers, and be taught that they are doctors, their sick men are patients. Such a change will never take place. But a good many persons in the army believe it ought to take place.

Catalogue of the Alumni, Officers and Fellows; and, "Medical Department;" *The United States Service Magazine*

198 From the *Salem Register* of October 9, 1862 we learn that the Reverend William F. Snow, who had yet to graduate from the Andover Theological Seminary, was presented "a beautiful sword and belt as a token of the love and esteem of friends in the Sunday School and church."

Before closing, let me allude to the matter of gratuitous supplies. Many presents sent to soldiers are worse than useless. What a soldier needs, is what government gives him, as to clothing, only a supply of better flannels and stockings. Now indiscriminate giving is useless. First, know what a soldier lacks, before sending anything. Our own regiment is partially, and sometimes entirely, supplied with under clothing, by a systematic method of donation. This works well. It saves the soldier's money, and gives better articles. Such a systematic method is good. The Sanitary Commission's attempt to make themselves the medium of *all* donations, is absurd, although that would be better than indiscriminate presents. Whenever persons can supply, and keep supplied a regiment, let them do it.

So as to donations of reading matter. If anybody has money for such purposes, for a particular regiment, -- well, I want to say more on this matter than there is room for this week.

A. H. Q.

December 5, 1862

Letter from Chaplain Quint.
Camp near Sharpsburg, Md.,
Nov. 28, 1862

Matters continue tolerably "quiet along the upper Potomac." There is reason to suppose that the ubiquitous Jackson has left the valley himself, to assist in the defense of Richmond or Fredericksburg. But reconnoisances [sic] discover quite a large rebel force somewhere near Berryville, which is about ten miles from Charlestown. That force is said to be under command of one of the Hills. It is rather difficult to account for the fear of Jackson. He has one quality, suddenness and rapidity, of high excellence. But in actual fight, he has never shown any particular generalship. He was foiled last winter by Gen. Lander. With forces quite even, he was beaten by acting Brig. Gen. Kimball in the first Winchester battle.[199] With an overwhelming force, he fell upon Gen. Banks in May, and utterly failed of his pur-

---

199 Nathan Kimball (1822 – 1880) was a native of Indiana and after graduating from college he studied medicine until the beginning of the Mexican-American war. During that conflict, Kimball served as a Captain of the 2nd Indiana Volunteers. Kimball continued with practicing medicine until the outbreak of the Civil War when he was commissioned Colonel of the 14th Indiana. At the battle of Kernstown, Kimball had temporary command of his brigade and for his success at that battle, was commissioned a Brigadier General in April of 1862. At Antietam, his brigade lost over six hundred men, while Kimball was severely wounded at the Battle of Fredericksburg. After he recovered, Kimball led a division of XVI corps at the siege of Vicksburg, and participated in the battle of Atlanta. Following the war, Kimball served as Indiana State Treasurer and in 1873 was appointed surveyor general of the Utah Territory. Warner; *Generals in Blue*

pose – an army only one-seventh as large, holding him at bay for three hours. In the return movement, he fled before Gen. Fremont. The last battles at Manassas were under Gen. Lee, not Jackson.

I wrote you last week of a murder – mere murder – committed on a man trying to get a family out of Virginia. The men were actually enticed over by the apparent distress of some women, purporting to be refugees; went over on an errand of mercy; fell into the power of the guerilla captain Burke,[200] for whose apprehension a reward was once offered.

The appendix to the affair, is a very pretty operation of our own commander, Capt. Cogswell, with sixty men. Ordered to cross in the night, he moved off about 9 P.M., and by making a cautious, and rather circuitous march, entered Shepardstown after midnight. The houses wanted were easily found, and surrounded. In one of them was Capt. Burke and five of his gang. The Captain was dressed and armed, and the horses of the party stood saddled. As it proved, Burke was to have started on one of his plundering expeditions in about an hour. As ours were preparing to enter, a man suddenly sprang from a door and attempted to escape. Capt. Cogswell ordered him twice or more times to surrender, and then told two men to fire. A ball entered the heart of the rebel, who, on examination was found to be Capt. Burke himself. The other five were captured, and their horses, arms, and important papers brought away. The expedition was a perfect success, and Union men in Virginia will breathe free now this miscreant is gone.

Capt. Cogswell, with the same men and some cavalry, was sent again the day following, in broad daylight. They crossed and occupied the town before the people had any suspicion of the approach. They arrested the man they wished for, paroled three officers and twenty privates in hospital, took some arms and returned in perfect safety. The rebels in that neighborhood express no very kind feeling towards the Second Massachusetts. They vow vengeance; but our means of defense at the river are such that our men would hail a brush for amusement. The

---

200 Redmond Burke (ca. 1810 - 1862) was a stone-worker on the C & O Canal and had lived in the Harper's Ferry area since about 1850. A die-hard secessionist, Burke initially served in Co. B of the 1st Virginia Cavalry before being assigned as an aid-de-camp in General J.E.B. Stuart's headquarters. In 1862, Burke was commissioned Captain and led a team of guerilas who kept watch on the flanks of the Union army. Trout; *They Followed the Plume*.

perfect success of the "surprise parties" within thirty hours is due to the reliable character of the Second.

On that night while our men were descending the valley, another man, in our hospital, was entering the valley – the valley of the shadow of death. From his bedside I heard the tread of our men. As they were crossing the river, he was crossing the river – the final river. As they landed, he died. They were victorious. Trust in God that he was.

Yesterday was Thanksgiving day. The weather was lovely. The air was mild. In sight of the river, almost hearing its ripple, (we do hear it at night as we lay awake, and our men hear it as they pace its shore all through the darkness,) we had our public services; our old New England singing; our prayers. How many of us kept home in mind all day! How many at home were praying for us! The preacher told them that what was a crime at home, was a crime here; what they would be ashamed of in their homes, they should be ashamed of here; what they would not do at home with their good mother's knowledge, they should not do here; what they had been taught of truth at home, was truth here.

Then the men had their quoits and ball. Some tried the speed of their horses. All – I hope – had their good dinner; the turkeys, the geese, the chickens, the plum puddings, were many. Our hospital inmates all had such peculiar luxuries as would not injure them. The officers dined together; and as at home, members of families return to their old hearthstones on Thanksgiving day, so yesterday there came back to us all the officers in our vicinity who had gone from us into other commands – back to the good old Second Massachusetts, God bless it, whose men have been tried in the furnace of fire, and stood by one another like true comrades. Among officers and men were many who had felt the bullet, and a multitude more who had had them in their garments. Many were not there. It was like the vacant chairs in a household – to think of the departed heroes.

In the morning we had visitors. They were ladies, part of whom had come from Chambersburg, Pa., thirty-five miles off, to bring some gifts for our hospital; some home bread, fruits, butter, jelly, pillows, and other needed articles. "Verily, verily, I say unto you, they have their reward."

In the midst of the merriment in the evening, a sick man was dying. Some relatives were by his bed; so was a good man whom I found bending over him, and commending him to God. Soon he passed away. "I wanted to go home before I died," said he, "but I hope I am going to a better home." These were his last audible words. "Home." How every sick man's heart grows sicker, because he wants to be at home. It is the hardest part of a soldier's life. But, when the surgeons are anxious to send a man home, in cases where home would save his life, it takes so long to prevail upon higher officials somewhere to sign the papers, that the favorable time often passes. But the home above is always ready.

But now for another subject. I have repeatedly thought how fortunate the *Congregationalist* is in some of its writers. The weekly summary of war news I read as altogether the best prepared, most comprehensive, and most exhaustive of any published. "Spectator" at Washington, is unapproachable. I think I know who he is. But the article of the "Watchtower" series, on the President's Proclamation, is the richest in thought, and the clearest in method of anything I have read on that subject.

I have said nothing by letter yet on that Proclamation. I preferred to wait. At home, I did not hesitate to praise it, in the solitary half day I had strength enough to occupy my own pulpit; nor to denounce the infamous utterances of an infernal press, whose great comfort was that slavery would be preserved whether the Union was restored or broken.

I have taken some pains to see the effect of the Proclamation upon the army.[201] A few, very few are distressed about it. They love slavery. They admit, upon questioning, that they deem servitude the proper condition of the "inferior" race. But the number is incomparably less than a year ago. One year has brought about an immense change of opinion as to the character of slavery, and the civilization of slaveholder.

Many like the Proclamation on the grounds of decided opposition to all slavery. They receive it as a matter of justice.

The great bulk of the army, however, look at it only in the light of a military measure, and feel no excited interest in it whatever. They regard it as perfectly within the power of the President as Commander-in-chief of the armies, while most would dissent from his right to issue such a decree as a civil magistrate. As a military measure, they believe it proper and needful. But it is no new thing in

---

201 Quint refers to The Emancipation Proclamation, the preliminary version of which President Lincoln had released in September of 1862.

practice. We have been freeing the slaves in a rebellious state these nine months. We never think of returning a fugitive. A slavehunter would be kicked out of our lines. Contrabands are everywhere, in public service and in private; and are treated as other men are. The Proclamation only enlarges what we have been doing this long while; and therefore creates far less talk than it does at home.

The army, moreover, is in a different state of discipline from what it was at the beginning of the war. When it has what Gov. Andrew felicitously called a "collection of town meetings," such a measure might have made great trouble. Now, the army is under control. It understands its duty to be obedience. Its work is to fight, and not discuss; hence it gives such a measure much less consideration than it would once.[202]

Again, we have become accustomed to seizure of blacks on the other side. When Jackson came to Winchester last May, he seized all blacks, free and slave, except some belonging to rebels there. When he went southward he swept the country clear, carrying many freemen into slavery. When the rebel army captured Harper's Ferry, it seized all blacks, and they are still in the hands of the men-stealers Southward. Nor do we forget that the blacks who drove the ambulances when the wounded were gathered in under a flag of truce after the late Manassas battles, were seized and carried away. Southerners steal negroes whenever they have an opportunity; steal them to make them slaves. Are we to regard their slave property as sacred?

Nor can we distinguish between seizing slave property as property and seizing wheat. Whatever the rebels have that we want, government takes. We are not worshippers of slavery, and we can see no more harm in taking slave property than the products of slave labor. It is all one. If the constitution gives no right to touch the wheat the slaves raise. If the right is a military one to take wheat, we cannot see

---

[202] Governor John Albion Andrew (1818 – 1867) made the remarks at a dinner for the Twentieth Massachusetts held in New York in September of 1861. From his speech, Andrew remarked "We went down to Bull Run, as I had the honor to remark in conversation this morning to some gentlemen around me, an aggregation of town meetings. Wheresoever we march again, we march – an army disciplined, drilled, and thoroughly equipped and ably commanded, the men knowing who their commanders are." In essence, Governor Andrew acknowledged the truth behind the opinions of the professional soldiers who disliked the idea of fighting beside militia troops who elected their own officers. Heidler, Heidler, Coles; "John Albion Andrew."

why it is not the same to take slaves. Those who can find nothing of such a power in the constitution, remind us of the man who said "as to liquor, give me whisky-punch; for there is not a single word in the Bible against whisky-punch!"

Nor do we relish the statements which come to us from Richmond, how the rebels everywhere impress slaves to build fortifications. Have we got to encounter those fortifications? Have northern fathers and mothers to believe that the work which slaughters their sons, is a labor not to be meddled with? *We do not see it so.*

I have been told by a rebel officer, a prisoner that slavery doubles the number of men they can keep in the field. I believed him. I saw, one day, as noble a regiment as ever was raised, go into action full of genuine men. The best blood of Massachusetts was there. Two days after I buried its dead. Shorn of one third of its numbers was the regiment. Lying on the field were the pride of their homes. Men of education, character, ability, industry. Fathers and mothers, of every two guns leveled at your sons, slavery kept one, and slavery fired both. I lifted your sons; some to bury, some to send home. It was slavery that killed them all.

I saw, on another day, that same regiment undaunted in the fiercest battle of this continent. One fourth of its number came out. Its good men, how they fell. One of the noblest, who cared not for his life if victory was ours, hated slavery as I do. Of every two guns at Antietam, slavery kept one, and slavery fired both. I saw countless maimed men there. Slavery maimed them. I saw countless bleeding men. Slavery pierced them. I saw countless dead there. Slavery killed them.

The product of slave labor doubles every gun the South could without it put into the field. To sustain slavery the South keeps both guns there – without slavery they could keep none there. And shall any man tell me that the system which killed these gallant comrades is one whose continuance, it is his comfort, is sure, whether we succeed before January 1st or whether we fail finally, -- and I not loathe him as I would a snake? Is Massachusetts sunk so low as to breed such reptiles?

Therefore, as the South has made slavery the great test, the great object of this war, as the only grievance of which the South complained was interference with slavery; as they call us all abolitionists; we say, let that be the test.

I hope and believe that the President will stand by his Proclamation. We never had a doubt of his honesty, his patriotism, his conscientious firmness. He will be sustained. The country will sustain, God will help him.

That it will have no effect is absurd. That the slaves will not hear of it is absurd. That the blacks will rush North is absurd. That the South has feared it as the hardest blow, Southerners have repeatedly told me.

It is a *right* step. There is but one more, universal emancipation. I have now but one article of faith on this point: *no man can own another*; no, not for a moment. All laws saying he can, are, of right, void. It is only a question of the best way now to treat them as void. But void they are, and cursed with a curse. This is the simple platform on which every man can stand; no man can own another.

A. H. Q.

December 12, 1862

Letter from Chaplain Quint
Near Sharpsburg, Md., Dec. 5, 1862

"All quiet on the Upper Potomac." Two rebel brigades at Winchester. Constant reconnoissances from Harper's Ferry, and more noise about them than is profitable. Waiting for news from Fredericksburg, where the remarkable rapidity of advance shows some hidden strategy.

So we read the President's message, and ponder over it. And the Secretaries' reports, and ponder over them.

Of the President's message I am puzzled to say what impression it makes. Its honesty, its earnestness, strike us at once. Renewed and strong determinations that the South must and shall be conquered, would have suited well, I think. Of the matter of "compensated emancipation," I believe nobody cares. Our way would be to carry out the proclamation by force of arms; hang all men at home who dared to proceed to "give aid or comfort to the enemy;" and reply to any rebellious cities of northern rowdies by infantry, cavalry, and artillery.

So, as it is a delicate matter to discuss a President's message, -- especially as our assistant surgeon was "dismissed" according to the papers, for "absence without leave," whereas he was not absent a day without leave, although for weeks prostrated by malarious fever, and placed in charge of a surgical ward at Washington while hardly able to walk, -- and as another officer was "dismissed" after he was dead.

I began, in a former letter, to say something about gifts for the religious and moral improvement of the army, and for general reading. I feel impressed with the need of some public utterance, in view of the sums which the large-hearted friends of soldiers are making. It is due to them that they should be informed of the best methods. They are not alone in this benevolence. I have in my possession a little religious tract, one of a series printed at the South for distribution in the rebel army. I remember, also, seeing, the morning after the battle of South Mountain, a large number of Testaments which had been taken from the bodies of killed or wounded at the rebel road-side hospital, with letters and other papers. So far as I can learn, the Southern army is quite well supplied with chaplains; nor has their congress cut down their pay to so low a rate (as ours has) that no man from an expensive place of residence can support his family upon it unless – as some of the nine months' chaplains have parishes rich enough to allow – the home salary of the pastor is continued.[203]

Of all the organizations which minister to the comfort of the soldiers, the Sanitary Commission is, beyond all comparison, the most useful. I think I could point out some evils connected with it: I think it has some defects in itself. But it has done, it is doing, a vast amount of good. The expense is great, the waste considerable; but the work is great, and would not otherwise be done at all. Its facilities for forwarding supplies instantly in the emergency, as after the battle of Antietam, form its great excellence in my opinion. Government could furnish the same necessaries, but while requisitions were going the round of the circumlocution office, a thousand men might die. Government is not much to blame for such slowness; for, a certain amount of formalities is essential to a proper regulation of expenditures. The Sanitary Commission is bound by no such official routine, inasmuch as its business is in one board, able to act instantly. Of the donations of the Commission I have seen but little indeed. But the character of the men constituting it, is a perfect guarantee of integrity.

---

203 Quint qualifies his complaint about pay by adding the phrase "from an expensive place of residence," but in fact the Congress of the Confederate States of America had initially authorized the pay of an Army Chaplain to be $85 per month, but that was lowered by amendment to $50 per month. The Congressman who proposed the amendment complained "all a chaplain has to do is to preach once a week." When you consider the rampant inflation throughout the South, the pay for a Confederate chaplain was very low. Brinsfield; *Faith in the Fight: Civil War Chaplains*.

The recent recommendations of the Commission as to the sending of articles direct to soldiers, are in the main good. They make the exception of such articles that can be sent by mail, which is also good. Socks, and even boots come through our mail. When our first Colonel was applied to by a benevolent association in Boston and vicinity, for information as to the best articles to send to soldiers, he replied, "The same things that government furnishes, only of better quality." All such save the cost to the soldiers. Our regiment is very generally supplied in this way, with excellent effect. Care is taken to have the boxes sent only when and where we are likely to be stationary. A bright official at Hagerstown, indeed, stopped a box of clothing the other day, on the ground of its suspicious appearance, not opening it, but keeping it back for days. It is seldom, however, there are such fools as officials, and such matters come safely. To recommendations to make the Sanitary Commission the sole medium of donations, I advise our friends to pay no attention. The Society for the Relief of Massachusetts soldiers, located at Washington, is a specialty worthy of support.[204]

As to other departments of general benevolence, it is a little unfortunate, in some respects, that there is a multiplicity of organizations doing substantially the same work. The Christian Commission,[205] and the Tract Societies[206] occur to me, besides some minor agencies. The different mediums must of course dis-

---

204 The Society for the Relief of Massachusetts Soldiers was a short-lived association of interested parties, largely made up of members of the Massachusetts Congressional Delegation, their employees and other Massachusetts-born Federal employees who formed, in April of 1861 an association for the relief of those soldiers of Massachusetts who are wounded or needed care. Benjamin Perley Poore was its first President. By 1863, most of its work had been taken over by the Massachusetts Relief Agency being conducted by Gardner Tufts, State Agent commissioned by Governor Andrew. Schouler; *A History of Massachusetts in the Civil War*; and, "Report of a Meeting of the Massachusetts Soldiers' Relief Association."

205 The U. S. Christian Commission was organized in November of 1861 as an off-shoot of the YMCA to provide supplies, medical services and religious literature. During the war, they would utilize five thousand volunteers, many Protestant clergy, and expended more than $6,000,000 worth of goods and supplies. Moss; *Annals of the United States Christian Commission*

206 There were many "Tract Societies" whose existence pre-date the Civil War and they were responsible for helping to spread bibles, testaments and other religious and educational works throughout America and around the world. The largest of these during the Civil War was the American Tract Society, which was an amalgamation of the New York Tract Society and the New England Tract Society. They maintained offices in both Boston and New York. Burrows and Wallace; *Gotham*.

tract attention in some places. But as they probably operate on different fields, and so differ in some particulars of working, perhaps they will not interfere with each other; and some ground may be occupied which would otherwise be neglected.

It is to be remembered that chaplains are the authorized officers charged by government with care for the religious and moral condition of regiments. For posthospitals, other chaplains are appointed specially. There remain, therefore, only the temporary assemblages of sick and wounded after a battle. Even these are cared for by regimental chaplains, except when the forces move on, in which case voluntary efforts like that of the Christian Commission in its plans, (if I understand their plans) is invaluable. Even then, one or two workers, remaining while the temporary hospital remains, are better far than twenty men volunteering for a week or two, to be replaced then by twenty more. There is everything in having a system in such a place; in knowing the entire ground, and arranging accordingly. If government had extra chaplains – as they have surgeons – to be detailed for such special duty, it would be a far better plan than any voluntary organization can supply. Until they do, the efforts of outside friends are at such times indispensable.

Beyond such extraordinary emergencies, there are some regiments without chaplains, the number of which is, in our vicinity, diminishing.

But wherever there are chaplains, it should be always remembered that the work is in their care, however great it may be. They will always welcome all suitable help; but doing their work is an irregularity which would prove disastrous. In a well-regulated regiment, it would not be allowed; no more than to allow voluntary surgeons to prescribe to the sick. If a chaplain tries to do his duty, he will be glad of all help in a legitimate way. If he does not try to do his duty, there is ample field for usefulness in interesting him in his duty. If I remember correctly, Dr. Nettleton[207] once directed a person who came from a particular parish for spiritual advice, to go to his own minister, notwithstanding the fact that that minister was uninter-

---

207 Asahel Nettleton (1783 - 1844) was a graduate of Yale (1809) and is considered one of the greatest influences of the Second Great Awakening. Nettleton preached an evangelical Calvinism, moving from community to community, frequently filling empty pulpits where there had been a lack of a regular minister. It is claimed by some that Nettleton was personally responsible for the conversion of more than 30,000 people. Tyler; *Memoir of the life and character of Rev. Asahel Nettleton, D. D.*

ested in such cases. The Doctor judged that such a call would interest the pastor. The minister was aroused, and with him his whole church; and vastly more good was accomplished than if Dr. Nettleton had tried to do the pastor's work. If a man wants to work a mill, he will do rather better to put water in the boiler, and fire in the furnace, than try to work the crank himself. A systematic, kindly, visitation of chaplains by a Christian Commission would be a capital plan. The idea is novel; but don't start another society to do it. Come, agents of some old one, and we will be delighted. Come, see just what we need – as the agents of the Sanitary Commission do in the sister work – whose ministrations have saved many a life. Come, and we will tell you what we do and how we do it, and how we are crippled for want of help. Employ some minister of experience, and ripe, genial, piety, and send him to visit, in a brotherly way, every chaplain in some one corps; to see his privations, perhaps, and cheer him with Christian fellowship.

Gifts – we come to that – are sometimes useless. I have before me a lot of tracts addressed to sellers of ardent spirits; that business is not carried on by our men. I have had a quantity addressed to distillers; but we have no distillers. And tracts to Sunday school children, on their behavior in Sunday school; which is of another meridian. And tracts to Sunday school teachers on the preparation of their lessons, or how to greet their classes, and on visiting their pupils; which is a work adapted to places where there are children. And tracts on dancing; a fault to which there is little liability – as I remember but one instance, and was glad when that took place – on the ground, closing at tattoo. I could multiply the list, but you have specimens. What do we want of the unsaleable lumber taken from cobwebbed shelves of some institution glad to be rid of it – *but reckoning it at the usual price* in their demands for more contributions? Or of bundles of worn out Sunday school books? Or of piles of volumes of some Christian truth adapted to certain states of mind, of which ten copies are enough for a year? Or of tracts attacking Catholicism, to distribute which, even by chance, would effectually destroy all influence with many men, even if a chaplain was fool enough to suppose it his business to try to make Protestants – which tracts I have carefully put into the fire?

Again, many bundles of good reading are mere heaps of duplicates of what has already been widely circulated. Societies cannot tell what has been distributed, and they glut the market with some particular work. Or volumes come to be thrown away the first march.

Or works which excite only ridicule. For instance, here is a little book entitled "Valuable Hints to Soldiers," issued in Cornhill.[208] It tells what a soldier needs: A "Bible;" no he doesn't; he needs a Testament. A "cheap portfolio of _____;" won't any other portfolio do? "a filter;" of which he disengages the tube to smoke through. "Three flannel undershirts, ditto shirts, ditto drawers, four or five pairs of woolen socks!" I wish the man who wrote this had to march the 800 miles our men have, with such a load on his back. Then it tells us that the soldier "should never sleep at night in the flannel shirt, drawers or socks work during the day." How, when off on picket duty, one night in two or three? How, when, at the close of a march he is too tired to do *anything*? "No one should on any account be in wet clothing." Suppose he bivouacs in the rain as we have over and over again? Suppose he changes, and gets out again immediately? "Blankets must be aired in the morning." Of course, when up before daylight to march on, with just time enough to pack one's knapsack. "Soup may be omitted at one dinner, and beef at another." How many courses do soldiers have? They are glad enough to get *one* article, even if they get down to green corn, as we all did on the Rappahannock. "Never be afraid of good beef." No, nor of turtle soup or blanc mange. "An entire meal should never be made of beans." What *will* he eat then, when beans are the only dish. In certain cases "increasing" the quantity "of vegetables." He *can't* increase it, especially as two-thirds of the time in marching he does not have any. Soldiers laugh at such directions. It may be a very good book, but it doesn't suit the latitude of a regiment that has been out a year and a half.

Now, when people have money they wish to pay for reading matter to be sent to a regiment, the best thing to do is this. Write to the chaplain first. Tell him how much money you will spend. If you wish it to go to any particular publishing house, tell him so, and send the catalogue of their publications. Ask him to say if he has any choice, what he can use the best advantage. You will thereby avoid sending useless matter or heaps of works already distributed. If you have a particular fancy for sending some one book, mention it. The chaplain will be glad enough to reply. Then send the publications – paying express charges, in which from an expensive experience, I have a feeling interest. And remember that some of the best minds

---

208 *Valuable Hints to Soldiers* was compiled for the Forty-fifth Regiment Massachusetts Volunteers, from *Hints on Health in Armies* by J. Ordronaux, M.D. and published by the American Tract Society at 28 Cornhill, Boston. It was only 16 pages long.

of the whole land are in the army; that there are educated men in the ranks as privates; that soldiers are men of common sense. In reading some of the books got up for soldiers, I am reminded of a good brother who, happening to preach at the Mariner's Church in Boston, got along very well until in describing a storm in the middle of the Atlantic, asked, when attention was intent, "What would you do?" and himself replied, "You'd instantly let go the anchor!" Just as many occasional preachers think they must "talk sailor" to sailors, so man writers "talk soldier" to soldiers, with as much accuracy as letting go the anchor where the water is any number of miles deep. I am aware that I didn't know an adjutant from a company cook eighteen months ago, but the books are just as ridiculous where men do know; just as that most excellent book the "life of Adjutant Stearns,"[209] which I have read with the deepest liking, has one rank for him in the volume, and another on the shoulder-straps in the likeness – a very slight matter in a volume of such touching interest and so admirably written. Such a book soldiers will read.

If any one wants to feel sure that what he gives for reading will be used, let him subscribe for such number as he pleases of some good religious newspaper, which he can usually get at half the usual rates, and have the copes mailed direct to the chaplain for distribution. These will be read eagerly. For myself, I never have a quarter enough. With the *Christian Banner*,[210] I never get over one third through the regiment. I have had copies of various papers, religious and secular; some donors have become weary in well doing, for which I am sorry. It is the readiest and steadiest way of supplying good reading matter.

A. H. Q.

---

209 Frazer Augustus Stearns (1840 – 1862), the son of the President of Amherst College, was Adjutant in the 21ˢᵗ Massachusetts Infantry when he was killed at the Battle of New Bern in March of 1862. One of the cannons captured by Stearns and his regiment permanently resides at Amherst as a war memorial. His father published a memorial of the young man's life and according to the annual report of the Sabbath School Union the book "proved one of the most beneficial and popular" in the army. "Massachusetts Sabbath School Union;" *Boston Traveller*; and, "Presentation of a Rebel Cannon to Amherst College;" *Springfield Republican*.
210 There was a *Christian Banner* published in Fredericksburg, VA from 1848 – 1862, but being a pro-slavery paper, Quint probably means the *Christian Banner*, a monthly 8"x11" non-sectarian periodical produced by the American Tract Society in Boston. The periodical was printed especially for the soldiers and sailors in service and was filled with engravings, music for worship in camp and letters from chaplains. "Religious Intelligence – Miscellaneous;" *Springfield Republican*.

December 26, 1862

Letter from Chaplain Quint.
Fairfax Station, Va., Dec. 15, 1862.

Suddenly we were turned out of our anticipated quarters. We were tumbled into the "winter campaign." We did not know of the movements on the Rappahannock, but we were modestly satisfied that if anything was to be accomplished, they would want the Second Massachusetts of course!

We had built huts. Some had log houses. The Surgeon and myself were building an elegant log cottage. We were satisfied that the capacities of logs for ornamental building had not been developed, and we intended a model. Our logs were straight. They lay close. The corners went up vertically. We had the foundations of an elegant stone fireplace – already having a brick one.

But, on Tuesday afternoon orders came. So on Wednesday morning we started. Our house was left. For no fault; the owner, being about to leave town, had no further use for it. Camp was hardly left when the place swarmed with people to search for goods. A deserted camp is wealth to many a Marylander.

We were ordered to be at Antietam Iron Works at 9 A.M., -- a mile and a half from camp. We were there ten minutes early. At fifteen minutes past an orderly came with a document certifying that we need to be at the Iron Works until *noon*, -- which was very comforting, considering that we were there, and had only three hours to wait on a cold morning. The change was made – too late – because other regiments had miles to move, and the 3d Wisconsin had not had orders at all at 9 o'clock. Was the fact known the night before – that the other regiments could not possibly be there until 12 M.? Of course, but what matters it that the soldiers must have reveille [sic] at 4 A.M., leave a comfortable camp in winter, and lay three hours uselessly in the road?

Twelve o'clock came, and one, and half past one; and then we moved on. We had studied the history of the dilapidated Iron Works – disused four or five years since – whose pig iron, accumulating at Harper's Ferry, had repaired the ford there. We had inspected a capital stone bridge, and an arched channel for the canal. And the men snow-balled.

About 5 P.M. we went into a light wood about five miles from Harper's Ferry, for a bivouac; built our fires; made excellent beds by piling on the snow some cornstalks, and topping off with pine branches; and, wrapped in blankets, slept well.

Reveillée at half past three, to start at five. Orders came at half-past six. What mattered it that we were deprived of an hour and a half's sleep uselessly?

The horses slipped badly on the icy roads, and we had to "wait for the wagon." Early we were at Harper's Ferry, and crossed into Virginia for the *fourth* time. Three times driven out – the fourth should be a better advance. The pontoons passed over the Potomac, and over the Shenandoah, into Loudon county, round the base of Loudon Hights, – and resting in a field whose fences fell suddenly. Out came the owner; he tried to stop it, but in vain. Then he came to the commander: "Your men are taking my fences." "Yes." "Isn't it hard," said he, excitedly, "for me to lose my fences?" "Yes," said our sensible Lieut. Col. Cogswell, "but it would be a good deal harder for my men to be cold. Government will pay you."

So we waited five or six hours. Then we were ordered to move, -- which resulted in several rods. Then a halt of half an hour, in the road, waiting for orders which started several regiments but did not reach the regiment next before us. That regiment finally started without orders, and as our business was to follow them, we followed. Soon it was dark, but we kept on – on – through half frozen brooks, half frozen mud, over rocks and ruts, for several hours of darkness, and then bivouacked. We had very gloomy views of public affairs, until after supper, when, with good fires, we became altogether more hopeful. Orion watched us going to sleep. What mattered it that we had waited hours in the middle of the day, and stumbled on in the darkness?

Reveillée at three A. M.; to be ready to move at half past four. We were ready, and of course waited until half past one. Then, orders to fall in; in less than five minutes, orders *not* to fall in; in five minutes more, orders again to fall in, -- whereupon our commander sent a lieutenant to ascertain which orderly[211] was *the* one; "the last," and we went on. We had waited because "the brigade train was not up;" but the Second's train was up close, and the man responsible for the other ought to be broke, -- only, what matters it that soldiers are up at three A.M., and wait ten hours needlessly.

Through the pretty little stone-built hamlet of Hillsborough, which is beautifully located in a cleft of the "Short Hills," and a mile on. Then, some guerrillas, only half an hour before we reached that point, had daringly captured a wagon. A party of cavalry trotted off and re-captured it, and we went on, having waited only two hours, which would take three of horrible stumbling with sore-footed men over a wet, rocky road at night. Three miles from Leesburg we bivouacked, on the western slope of the Kittoctan. What mattered it that two hours of daylight had been wasted?

The first day we had made six miles; the second fourteen and a half; the third, ten and a half.

The fourth day reveille at four; to start at half past five. At half past, a message *not* to fall in immediately, as the brigade would not start as early as expected. The orderly could not help smiling, respectfully, as he delivered the order. We did start, to our astonishment, at half past six; climbed the Kittoctans, wound round the hight still crowned with a former rebel earthwork, passed through the shabby Leesburg, -- which has one pretty house, which I thought I recognized as copied from a plan in Godey's Ladies' Book;[212] saw lots of fellows who we knew would mount as guerrillas as soon as we were gone; and reached Gum Spring, a "shoddy" village of nine houses, a spring (whether "gum" or not I don't know,) and a church,

---

211 Quint means to say here "which order was *the* one."

212 *Godey's Ladies Book* was a magazine published in Philadelphia and edited by Sarah Josepha Hale and was geared, as the title rightly suggests, towards the women of America. Its pages were filled with poetry, articles, music, engravings, and fashion plates, as well as drawings of the latest and fashionable residences. Hale was among the first to insist on the magazines' copyright (to prevent its articles and poetry from being pirated) and the cost was $3 per year. Its circulation was about 150,000 in 1860. Greenberg; "Publication History."

probably a Dunker, Tunker, Dunkard, or Tunkard,[213] whether these names denote one, two, three, or four denominations, I don't know; reached the turnpike to Fairfax – turned into a wood; found a good wood; discovered Straw, and had glorious beds in front of splendid Log Fires; having accomplished seventeen miles and a half. Wagons attacked in the rear; guerrillas beat off.

Reveillée at four o'clock, to start at five. Fancy our intense astonishment when we found that the foremost regiment actually took the road at that hour! It seemed like old times when our own Brigadier Gen. Gordon (now sick) was with us. Trains were up also, -- which reminded us of the same commander, who would have dressed down somebody handsomely for such delays and hitches as had disgusted us for the several days gone, -- only such delays don't often occur where he is. Nor will we be bored by the yellings of some of our neighbors when he gets back.

Next day was pleasant. Indeed all were good marching days, if decently used. Saturday threatened to be wet, but the storm was "postponed on account of the weather." Sunday morning we over took the bulk of the corps, which had a day's start of us, and we entered Fairfax (Court House) in the afternoon. There we learned, indefinitely of the fight at Fredericksburg. But no newspapers, no really satisfying news.

Fairfax is in a terribly injured condition. Roads cut up. Ditches everywhere. We left it, over a most horrible corduroy road, for Fairfax Station, five miles away. That road I traversed with sick, last summer, when it was a smooth, well fenced, well shaded, pretty road. Now it is corduroy, fences gone, wood cut down. Only one fence remains – that around a graveyard, which stands entire, though large armies have camped all around and passed on. Near Fairfax Station we bivouacked, in a pine wood, where trees are lying in every direction, utterly defying order. And we sleep very sound. Rations are, however, given out at night, which were needed. Before leaving Sharpsburg, there had actually been delivered, *flour*, for a march! It reminded us of the night before the battle of Antietam, when for the first time for a long while the coffee was sent to us in the *berry*, to men without the possibility of burning and grinding it, and who were to go into battle the next morning. On this

---

213 The Dunkards or Dunker Congregation were a branch of German Baptists descended from the denomination founded in Wittenberg, Germany in 1708. Church members began to arrive in Pennsylvania in 1719 and spread south and west. The name derives from the German word "tunken" which means "to immerse." Jackson; "Religion in Louisiana."

march, too, we had to pick up forage for horses as best we could, although entitled to a supply. It is not strange, of course, on a march, and nobody could complain. It was worse when, in camp, receipts had to be given for two hundred and five pounds while the actual weight was one hundred and sixty. Don't think I blame the government for such hitches – as to flour, coffee, or forage; there never was a government which lavished so much on its armies, or which was more ready to punish fraud or incompetency; but some of its intermediate officials are – well, not angels.

We had a new illustration, in this movement, of the stupidity of the new ambulance arrangement. It was necessary to send all the sick to the Smoketown hospital, before starting.[214] The senior medical officer of the brigade made a requisition for ambulances. It was not answered until *next day*. Men got sick on the road; we had one; no ambulances within *nine miles*. Our surgeon had to put him in a house and leave him, but he was, fortunately, brought on afterwards. The whole of this much praised system is a perfect humbug. The officer in charge of the brigade ambulance train is under nobody's orders except the Medical Director. Our Medical Director at Sharpsburg was eleven miles off. Have a brigade train, but let the regiments have, each, three or four ambulances, subject to the Colonel's orders, in care of the surgeon. On the march of Saturday they had to come down a little, and gave each regiment one, which was a farce.

I am glad to see my notions as to the military position of medical officers corroborated by those of Senator Hale,[215] who advocates just what I did in the *Congregationalist*. If he would go farther, and put every general hospital into the hands of physicians in civil life, he will accomplish a great work. There is too much "authority" about the hospitals. I know, for I have visited them much, and have acted as chaplain temporarily by request of a Major General. I know that coffee, (without milk) and bread for breakfast; bread, boiled potatoes and boiled meat

---

214 The Smoketown Hospital was near the Antietam battlefield, two and a half miles north of Sharpsburg, Maryland. The "town" consisted of only two or three houses, but the hospital held over 600 men at one point and was the last of the Antietam hospitals to close, which occurred in May of 1863. Richards; "War Memories – LIII, Smoketown Hospital;"

215 John Parker Hale (1806 – 1873) was a lawyer and politician and was a graduate of Phillips Exeter Academy and Bowdoin College (1827). Hale was a member of the House of Representatives from 1843 to 1845 from New Hampshire and a member of the Senate from 1847 – 1853 and 1855 – 1865. Hale's daughter Lucy was betrothed to John Wilkes Booth. "John Parker Hale;" *Springfield Republican*.

for dinner; and coffee and bread for supper, are not precisely the suitable diet for men just able to sit up, -- particularly when government allows most liberally for support – means to purchase milk, eggs, chickens, &c., being at hand, besides such portions of the army ration as may be asked for, -- rice, molasses, vegetables, &c. I was told, a day or two since, by a chaplain of high character, of a hospital he had often visited lately, for which chickens and the like are *paid for* by government, but which he could never find a patient who had seen.

Ask some of the "civil" surgeons from Massachusetts about their visits to various places, and they will tell you how *gladly* they were welcomed!

The root of the evil is the "military command" of those in charge. Sick men should be treated as such in hospitals, not as mere soldiers.

I am afraid I am grumbling, but I do not mean to. Indeed, I presume that the majority of the hospitals are well managed. I have seen most excellent ones. At Frederick, the one organized by our present surgeon was admirably conducted. But at Sharpsburg the surgeon in charge (whether subordinate or not I don't know) of one building, showed himself a pig, and a brutal pig at that. A fierce "I order!" was his natural, grunt. He absolutely refused a sick man left there one night by his comrades through mistake, bed, supper, breakfast, nurse or medicines, though entreated by a surgeon who had a heart, -- the man being low the typhoid fever. But such swine are rare; I never saw but one who was his equal – the pompous pig at Antietam.

--- Still on our march.

A. H. Q.

December 26, 1862

Letter from Chaplain Quint
Fairfax Station, Va., Dec. 18, 1862.

Though dating from the same place as at last writing, we have not been here in the intermediate time.

On Monday we left the Station. Reveillée was at five A. M., but as we were the rear regiment, to guard the brigade supply train, we had to wait until a train came in with supplies to be loaded into wagons. It was therefore near two P.M. before we started. The last previous regiment had over five hours' start, but at Occoquan Creek it was but an hour ahead.

But such a road! Mud, ruts, corduroy, holes, -- such a mixture was never known to me before. A mile and a half an hour was handsome progress. About sunset we reached the Occoquan, which we had forded, a few miles above, last August; forded it anew six miles and a half from Fairfax Station, climbed the opposite hills still crowned with last winter's rebel earthworks, moved on a mile, and bivouac in a tangled wood.

The stars cheated us. The clear sky promised fair weather. But towards morning it rained; it blew; it poured. We pulled our rubber blankets over us, and went to sleep again. Reveillée at five, in a cold drenching rain. The men stood it good-naturedly, however. At seven we moved on, one regiment in advance.

The roads the day before were the worst possible. That day they beat possibility. Mud, mud, mud. The road was ascertained to be fordable in several places, however; but men who could not swim staid on the banks. By noon the column had made three miles, but it took till night for the wagons to get so far. At noon, orders came from below to halt, -- nobody knew why. The halt was turned into camp, -- which means, on the march, building fires and siting down on the ground. The wind blew the clouds off, and it came warmer too. We had luxurious quarters – *we* did. A young pine thicket with the interior cut out and the walls thickened up with pine branches; a bed of pine boughs fit for a king, and a huge fire in front. There we slept – five of us in one enclosure, soundly.

Up at five again. Two days' cooked rations in haversacks. Soon on the road – for Dumfries? No, northward! Then we knew that fifteen hundred rebel cavalry, and nobody knew how many infantry, were at Brentsville, threatening Fairfax Station, and our division was to march back to defend that depot of rations. So we did, yesterday, nine miles and a half. Nothing special occurred save a snow squall, -- and a little trouble by reason of a brigade running into us, and trying to get ahead of us, as we were ordered to bring up the rear of ours next behind the wagons. I did not know who the officer was that made the trouble, but he showed importance enough to be Lieut. General, at least, if not President of the United States (what is left of it.)

It seems to us very queer that a whole division should be sent back merely to guard Fairfax Station, a place of no consequence except from its deposit of rations – two thirds of which are kept in cars for fear of accidents. Needed so much elsewhere, it looks strange to see our armies scattered in petty service. So we suppose it presages a general backward movement.

The defeat at Fredericksburg we now learn of, with sadness. The papers do not say "defeat," but what else is it, where the army, having crossed the Rappahannock, is three times repulsed in its attempt to carry the enemy's works – repulsed with terrible loss – retires across the river in a dark and rainy night, and pulls back all its pontoons to destroy communication? It is simple defeat – that is all. Call it so. Look at it as it is. Give the rebels credit for using, in fortifying, the time in which our army lay quiet in front of Fredericksburg. Their army is no braver than ours. They are miserably deficient in supplies of which we have abundance. They are no *better* armed, have no *more* nor *better* artillery; but our only late success is Antietam. We have forces scattered everywhere, enough, if concentrated, to annihilate the rebel armies. We reverse the old rule, "divide and conquer;" we divide our own forces, and let the enemy conquer. That fathers at home should clamor against what their sons here unitedly consider their best interests, is, however, one of the hardest things to bear.

Eight days we have been on the road. The weather has generally been wonderfully favorable for this season. But we have had cold and wet, toil and sleepless hours. We try the winter campaign under pleasant circumstances, and we do it cheerfully. But we often wish that the wise people at home, demanding a winter campaign as they sit by their comfortable firesides, with their well cooked food to eat, their warm beds to sleep in when they are tired of urging on the army – could try a week of march and bivouac even before the snows come. We are willing to do what is needful; but, wise men, let those control the campaign who knows enough to do it.

Yet I do not wonder that civilians are astonished at the results of this war. Who is not? With such an army, so large, so brave, always equal, in an open fight, to Southerners, man for man, it is humiliating to see such failures.

A Baltimore paper just comes to us with the statement that *Gen. McClellan* is recalled to command. We do not know who true it is. But I wish you could have seen our faces and heard our shouts. Every countenance, before despondent, brightened up. Cheers broke out instantly. From company to company, the sound spread. Regiment after regiment in sight and out of sight, rolled up their shouts. Ready to march in mud or storm, ready for winter campaigning, ready to fight – only one feeling existed.

A. H. Q.

Index

Abbott Grays, 3
Abbott, Edward G., 192, 224
Abbott, Fletcher M., 150, **150**, 192, 223
Abercrombie, General John J., **13**, 104, **138**, 170
abolition, 43, 70
abolitionists, 130, 237
Alexandria, VA, 46, 206
Allegheny Mountains, 144, 158
Alvord, Reverend John W., 39, **39**
ambulance corps, 229
ambulance drivers, 58
ambulance train, 250
ambulances, 57, 70, 150, 192, 198, 201, 202, 204 – 206, 219, 236, 250
Andover Theological Seminary, **39**, **53**, **88**, **93**, 111, **156**, **186**, **230**,
Andrew Light Guard, 3
Andrew, Governor John A., **33**, 236, **236**, **241**,
Andrews, George L., 3, 122, **122**, 149, 153, 158, 224, 227, 228

Andrews, Major General Samuel, 4
Antietam, **14**, **32**, **52**, 73, **122**, **182**, **190**, **209**, **210**, 220, 222, 237; battle of, 73, **97**, **102**, **104**, 214, **217**, 223, 228, 229, **232**; night before the battle of, 366
Antietam Creek, 73, 214
Antietam Iron Works, 246
anti-slavery, 41, **104**, 128
army camp, wickedness in, 10
army chaplains; character of, 185; different denominations of, 8; reduction of pay and subsistence, 230; uniform and dress, 337
army generals, character of, 187
Army Hymn, 20, **20**
Army of the Potomac, 12, **13**, **14**, 17, 79, 88, **98**, 101, 102, **121**, **166**, 170, **182**, **196**, **198**, **200**, **208**, **217**, newspaper reporters excluded, 201; Post Office, 141; regimental chaplains, 81

255

army rations, 251
army surgeons 49, 113, 116, 188, 205, 218, 228 - 230, 235, 242; uniform and dress, 230
Articles of War, 18, 173
artillery 7, **12**, **14**, 19, 21, 34, **34**, 65, 69, 70, 72, 73, 98, 103, 114, 115, 121 - 124, **121**, 127, 128, 133, 135, 144, 149 - 152, **149**, 170, 192, 194, 197, 203, **208**, 209, **209**, 210, 215, **218**, 239, 253; units without chaplains, 178
Ashby, Turner, 113, **113**, 114, 121, 127, 140
Associated Press, 145, **145**
Atlanta, GA, **79**, **121**, **171**, **217**, **232**
AtlanticMonthly, 47
Bacon, Reverend Leonard, xxvi
Baker, Edward D., 31, **31**, 32, 33, 35, 46
Ball's Bluff, 5, 12, 14, **29**, **31 – 35**, 38, 46, **90**, dead and wounded, 91
Baltimore and Ohio Railroad, 58, 80, 101, **109**, 208
Baltimore, MD, 45, 48, 85, 94, **97**, **148**, 183, **229**, 254
Banks, General Nathaniel P., 12, **12**, 19, 29, **30**, 46, 69 – 73, 76, 77, 81, **88**, 102, 103, **105**, 106, 121, **122**, 124, **134**, 142, 147, 148, **148 – 150**, 153, 157 - 159, 170, 177, 182, 184, 191, **191**, 196 -198, 203, 204, 211, 212, 223, 224, 226, 227, 232; respect for religion, 184; retreat of, 214
Banks, Mary T. (Palmer), 75, 77, **77**
Baptist, 8, **20**, 64, 128, 139, 185, **249**
Barbarism of Slavery Charles Sumner's speech on, 160
barracks, 75, 81, **81**
Bartonsville, VA, 71, 165
baseball, 52
battalion drill, 7, 17, 18
Baylor, Robert W., 109, **109**, 110
Bealeton, VA, 196, 197, 201
Beecher, Reverend Henry Ward, xxvi
Benjamin, Judah P., 79, **79**
Berryville, VA, 103, 104, 109, 232
Best, Clermont L., 149, **149**
bible-class, 9
bivouacking, 72, 120, 144, 157, 165, 190, 195, 196, 208, 215, 223, 247 - 249
blasphemy, xxii
Bonney, Wallace, 69, 123
Boonsboro', Md, 207, 214, 215
Boston Journal, xxvii, **93**, 214, **214**, **217**
Boston Latin School, **33**, **91**, **151**, **192**, **202**, **216**
Boston, MA, xxi, xxiv, xxx, 3, 5, 7, **14**, **39**, 40, **49**, **52**, 85, 86, 91, 102, **108**, 111, **123**, 125, **152**, 162, 163, 186, **186**, **187**, 188, **191**, **202**, **205**, **208**, **224**, 241, **241**, **244**, 245
bounties, 173 – 175, 179, 180
Bowdoin College, xx, **156**, **185**, **250**

Bramhall, Walter M., 34, **34**
Bristow Station, VA, 198, 203
Brook Farm, xxi, 3, 4, **30**, 147,
Brookes, Reverend Benjamin F., **110**
Brown University, **49**, **53**, **151**, **186**, **217**
Brown, John, 21, 23 - 28, 95, 100, **100**, 105, **113**, 128
Bull Run, **12**, **14**, **20**, **104**, **107**, 110, **138**, 139, **166**, 180, **182**, 194, **197**, **202**, 204, 208, **236**; 2nd Battle of, **20**, 73, **79**, **97**, **210**
Bunker Hill, WV, 103, 157, 165
Burke, Redmond, 73, 233, **233**
Burns, Anthony, xxi
Burns, Robert, xviii
Burnside, General Ambrose E., xxiii, **97**, **98**, 182, **182**, **196**, **198**, 208 - 211
Butler, General Benajmin F., 187
California, Infantry, 1st, **31**, 32, **32**, 33
Camp, duties, 92; hygiene, 48; life, 17; liquor in, 81; routine, 14
Camp Andrew, xxi, 3 – 5, 147, **147**, 162, **217**, 225,
Camp Hicks, 56, 66, 75, 80, 85, 90
cantonment, 75
Carey, Thomas, 72
Carman, Ezra, **217**
Carver, Reverend Robert, 186, **186**
Cary, Richard, 3, 91, **91**, **92**, 193, 223, 224
Cedar Creek, 72, 120
Cedar Mountain, **20**, **49**, 72, 73, **92**, **104**, **134**, **149** – **151**, **166**, 190 – 193, 194, 195, 220, 223, **224**, 229; battle of, 190 - 193
censorship of mails, 194
Centerville, VA, 132, 195, 197, 198, 201, 203, 204, 211
Chalmers, Reverend Thomas, 40, **40**
Chapel, Dr. Artemus, **229**
chaplain, xvii, xxi, xxii, xxvii - xxviii, 7 - 10, 15, 19, **20**, 39, 51, 60 - 62, 64, 65, 72, 81, 84, **88**, 100, 140, 159, 161, 168, 169, 178, 184, 185, **186**, 193, 202, 205, 212, 220, 225, 230, 240, **240**, 242- 245, **245**, 250, 251
chaplains, in hospitals, 81; in the army, 169; Post Hospitals, 242; uniform, 60; work, 7
Charlestown, WV, 24, 25, 28, 40, 69, 88, 97 – 99, **100**, 102, 112, 127, 206, 232
Choate, Rufus, 5
Christian Banner, 245, **245**
church call, 9
Clark, Reverend Edward L., **53**, 186, **186**
Clark, Reverend Jonas B., 186, **186**
Clarke, James Freeman, xxi, 4, **147**,
Cleaveland, Reverend John P., 185, **185**
Coffin, Charles C., 214, **214**
Cogswell, Milton, 34, **34**, 35
Cogswell, William, 3, 150, **150**, 152, 224, **224**, 233, 247,
Collins, Sergeant Edward, 4, **4**
company drill, 18

compulsory colonization, 167
Confederate army, condition of, 253; negroes in the service of, 172
Confederate chaplains, 240
Confederate civilians, treatment of, 157
Confederate currency, 99, 101
Confederate guerrillas, 73, **233**, 248, 249
Confederate prisoners, 203
Confiscation Act, 42
Congregational Quarterly, xxx, xxxi, 39
Congregationalist, xviii, xxii, xxviii, xxx, xxxi, 97, 101, **151**, 165, **186**, **187**, 235, 250
Congregationalists, xxvi, 185
Connecticut, Infantry, 5th, 20, 134, **140**, 152; chaplain of, 20, **20**
Conrad's Ferry, Md, 29, 62
conscription, xxv, 174, 175, 179
conservative politicians, on the outcome of the war, 173
Cook, John Edwin, 100, **100**
Copeland, R. Morris, 30
Corthren, George W., 121, **121**, 124, 149, 196
Couch, Darius N., 208, **208**
Crawford, General Samuel W., 72, 190, **190**, 217
Cromack, Reverend Joseph C., 187, **187**
Cromwell, Oliver, xxi
Crowninshield, Francis W., 11, 71
Culpepper Court House, VA, 72,
Culpepper, VA, 72, 177, 180, 190, 195, 196
Curtis, Greely S., 3

Cushing, Reverend Christopher, 39
daguerreotypes, 54, 63
dancing, 243
Darnestown, MD, 5, 12, 17, 19, 21, 23, 29, 38, 56, 58, **60**, 62 – 65
Dartmouth College, xvii, xx, xxxi, **186**
Democratic party, 128, **156**, 184, **221**
deploying the regiment, 122
deserter, 228
Devens, Charles, 56
Dickens, Charles, xviii
discipline, 13, 48, 52, 54, 75 - 77, 81, 88, 92, 101, 122, 153, 155, 212, 236, **236**
Diven, Alexander S., 180, **180**
Division hospital, 81
Dodge, Mary A., 187, **187**
Donelly, Dudley, 134, **134**, 140, 148
Dover Herald, xxx
Dover, NH, xvii
draft, 174, 179, 180
dress parade, 9, 18
drunkenness, xviii, xxiii, **20**, 54, 55
Dunkard church, 249
Dunkards, **249**
Dwight, Wilder, xx, xxiii, 3, 51, **51**, 71, 73, 122, 135, 150, 154, 158, 163, 218, 219, **219**, 223, 225; death of, 223; funeral of, xxiii
Edinburgh, VA, 69, 120, 124, 131
Edwards Ferry, 5, **14**, 35, 36
emancipation, 42, 43, 167, 238, 239
Emancipation Proclamation, xxvii, **235**,
Enfield rifles, 4, 12, 65, 123

England's abolition of slavery, xxvii
Episcopal, 108, 128
Episcopalians, 185
evening parade, 18
Ewell, General Richard S., 69, 191, **191**, **208**
Fairfax, VA, 198, 249
Fairfax Court House, VA 205, 206, 249
Fairfax Station, VA, 205, 246, 249, 252, 253
Faneuil Hall, xxiii, 202
Fast Day, 19
flankers, 69, 99, 121, 150
Floyd, John B., 28, 79, **79**
forage, **169**, 184, 250
foraging, 163, 183, 184,
Forestville, VA, 135
Fort Lafayette, 89
Fourth of July, 168
Fowle, George W., **205**
Fowle, John A., 204, 205, **205**
Franklin Academy, xvii
Frederick, MD, 56, 58 – 60, 66, 75, 77, 78, 80, 81, **81**, 82, 85, 88 – 90, 97, 98, **98**, 102, 106, 163, **182**, 208, 209, 211, 214, 232, 251
Fredericksburg, VA **32**, 239, **245**, 253; battle of, **33**, 73, **198**, **208**, **210**, **232**, 249, 253
Free-Mason, 128
Fremont, General John C., 41, 71, 145, 159, 163, 172, 226, 233
Front Royal, VA, 69, 70, 148, **148**, 155, 157 – 159, 162, 165

Fugitive Slave law, xxi, 28, 43, **108**, 112, 236
furlough, xxiii, **49**, 85, **98**
Gainesville, VA, 197, 201 - 203
games, 53
Gaylord, Reverend Noah M., 20, **20**, 186. **186**
Geary, General John W., 103
General Hospital, **24**, 48, **49**, 78, 81, **229**, 250
gifts to soldiers, 234, 240, 243
"Glory, Hallelujah," 23, 100
Godey's Ladies Book, 248, **248**
Goodwin, Richard C., 4, 192, **192**, 22, 224
Gordon, George H., xviii, xxi, 3, 4, 13, **13**, **27**, 70, 72, 73, 99, 102, 103, 107, 113, 121, 123, 134, **134**, 148 - 150, 152, 153, 157, 158, 165, 166, 171, 201, 217, **217**, 233, 249
Gorman, General Willis A., 104, **104**
government clerks, 205
Grafton, James I., 151, **151**
Grand Army of the Republic, xxviii, xxix - xxxi,
Quint Chaplain-General of, xxvii
Grand Masonic Lodge of Massachusetts, xxxi
Greene, General George S., 170, **170**
grog sellers, 82
grogshop, 81, 88
guerrilla, 146, 233
"Hail Columbia," 40

Hale, John P., 250, **250**
Halleck, General Henry W., 105, 170, 170, 172
Hamilton, Gail, 187, **187**
Hamilton, General Charles S., 105, **105**, 107, 170
Hancock, MD, 76, 80, **90**
hand grenades, 153, 154
handkerchiefs, 54
Hardee's Tactics, 53, **53**
Harper's Ferry, WV, 14, **20**, 25, 37, 38, 40, 41, 46, 63, 69, 73, 88, 98, 100, **100**, 102, **103**, 109, **109**, 113, 132, 157, 158, 177, 223, 227, **233**, 236, 239, 247
Harper's Weekly, 46
Harrisonburg, VA, 69, **113**, 138 – 140, 142, 143, **143**, 148, 158, 177, 227
Hartsuff, General George L., 218, **218**
Harvard, **24**, **32**, **33**, 49, **51**, 150, **151**, **192**, **202**, 216, 217, **224**; Law School, **33**, **150**; Medical School, **24**, **49**, 150
Hatch, General John P., 70, 148, **148**, 149
Havelock, Gen. Henry, xxi, 13
Havre-de-Grace, MD, 85
Heath, Dr. William H., 119, 229
Heintzelman, General Samuel P., 107, **107**, **198**
Hill, General Ambrose P., 191, **191**
Hillard, George, 5
Holmes, Oliver Wendell, **21**

Hooker, General Joseph, 73, 198, **198**, **208**, 211, **212**, 215, 216
hospital(s), 64, 72, 78, 81, 83, 84, 88, **88**, 92, 113, 115, 116, 133, 141, 159, 160, 169, 185, 192, 201, 202, 205, **205**, 211, 218, 233, 234, 240, 242, 250, 251; after a battle, 113; flags, 133, 202; Medical Director of, 82; Hospital Steward, 116
"I wish I was in Dixie," 105, 120
"I'm bound for the land of Canaan," 105
Illinois, Infantry, 39th, 111, **111**
India, British robbing of, xxvi
Indiana, Infantry, 2nd, **232**; 12th, 14, **14**; 13th, **143**; 14th, **232**; 16th, 14, **14**, 60; 27th, 70, 140, 149, 150, 152, 153
intemperance, xxii
Ireland, British plundering of, xxvi
Jackson, General Thomas J. "Stonewall", 61, 69 – 72, 90, 105, 106, 113, 114, 121, 127, 132 – 135, 139, 142, **143**, 147, 148, **148**, 158, 191, **191**, 192, 195, **196**, 197, **198**, 199, 201, **208**, 227, 232, 233, 236, **249**
Jamaica Plain, MA, xix, xxii, xxiv, 125, 219
James, Reverend Horace, 186, **186**, 220
"John Brown's body," 95, 105

Kabletown, WV, 103
Kendall, Dr. Albert A., 218, **218**
Kenley, John R., 69, 148, **148**, 162
Kentucky, 21, 88,
Kernstown, VA, **49**, 70, 105, 151, **232**; battle of, 105
Kimball, General Nathan, 232, **232**
King, Dr. James B., 219, **219**
Lander, General Frederick W., 90, **90**, 103, 232
Lasher, Reverend George W., 20, **20**
leave of absence, 85, 181
Lee, General Robert E., **33**, **140**, **170**, **208**, 227, 233
Lee, William R., **32**, **33**, **33**
Leesburg, VA, 31, 33, 34, 46, 104, **104**, 248
Leland, Dr. Francis, **24**, **49**, 119, 154, 159, 163
Letcher, Governor John, 146, **146**
Lincoln, President Abraham, xxvii, **31**, **44**, 103, 105, **121**, **170**, **182**, **235**
liquor, 81, 89, 108, 237
Little Washington, VA, 71, 190
log houses, 75, 246
Longfellow, Henry Wadsworth, *Evangeline*, 167, **168**
Loudon Heights, VA, 247
Lutheran, 108, 135, 139
macadamized road, 143, **143**, 152
Manassas Gap railway, 142
Manassas railroad, 134, 142, 148; destruction of, 134

Manassas, VA, 43, 72, 76, 101, 102, 134, 142, 145, 195, 197, 198, 202, 203, 227, 233, 236
Mansfield, General Joseph K. F., 73, 211, **211**, 215 - 218
Mariner's Church, Boston, 245
marking graves, xxix, 133, 193
Marryatt, Frederick, 183, **183**
Martinsburg, WV, 76, 153, 157, 165
Maryland, Infantry, 1st, 69, 148, **148**; 2nd, 97, **97**; Potomac Home Brigade, 103, **103**
Maryland Heights, 26, 73, 223
Masanutten Range, 143, 144
Mason, James M., 108, **108**, 180
Massachusetts, Infantry, 2nd, xvii, xviii, xxi, xxvii, 3 - 5, **13**, 20, 25, 36, 47, **49**, 66, 69-73, 100, **122**, **149**, **151**, 152, **192**, 193, **217**, 228, 233, 234, 246; baggage reduced, 166; captures a Confederate flag, 216; casualties at Antietam, 73; casualties at Cedar Mountain, 190; color bearer, 228; discipline of, 13; horses stolen by NY Cavalry, 166; leave Massachusetts, 5; pioneers, 135; preparedness of, 13; receive national & state colors, 5; regimental band, 40, 53, 81, 91, 95, 184; regimental library, 92; soldiers fit for duty, 163; soldiers on detached service, 163; Sunday church

service, 9; Wednesday prayer meeting, 9; 7th, **208**; 12th, 14, **14**, **53**, 60, **186**, 202, **218**; surgeon killed, 218; 13th, 20, **20**; 15th, 32, **32**, **33**, **34**, **187**; 19th, 32, **32**, **187**; 20th, 32, **32**, **33**, 34, 35, **236**; 21st, **245**; 22nd, 95, **187**; 23rd, **186**; 25th, **186**; 30th, **185**; 33rd, **152**; 45th, 244; 54th, **24**, **49**; Cavalry, 1st, **49**

Massachusetts soldier uniforms, 65

Massachusetts Bay Colony, xxiv

Massachusetts Historical Society, xxx, 100

Massachusetts Legislature, xxviii,

Massachusetts Soldier's Relief Association, 205

Massachusetts, General Association of, xix, xxiv, xxx

Mather Church, xix

Mather, William L., **88**

Maulsby, William P., 103. **103**

McClellan, General George B., 12, 35, 46, 73, 92, **97**, 98, 99, **105**, **121**, **143**, **148**, 159, 161, 163, 164, **166**, 170, **170**, 172, 175, **182**, **191**, 195, 198, 199, 206, 207, **208**, 209, **212**, 216, **217**, 221, 222, 226, 227, 254; criticism of, 222; restoration to command, 207

McDowell, General Irvin, 182, **182**, 191, 196 - 198, **197**, 201 - 203, 226

McReading, Reverend Charles S., 111, **111**

medical department, 219, 229, 230

Memorial Day, xxix, xxx

men for the army, Confederate vs. Union, 164

Methodist, 8, **20**, 108, 110, **111**, 117, 128, 139, 185, 187

miasma, 46

Michigan, **79**, Cavalry, 97, 98; 1st, **97**

Middletown, VA, 70, 149, 158

Middleway, VA, 40

military concert, 81

militia, 4, **12**, **20**, 30, **31**, 34, **53**, 77, **79**, **113**, **138**, 228, **236**

ministers, xviii, xix, xxii, xxviii, 98, 112, 140, 164, **186**; their role in supporting the war, 164

Minkins, Shadrach, xxi

mittens, 54

Monday Chaplains' Meeting, 7, 140

Monocacy river, 60, 209

Morrell, General George W., 223, **223**

Motley, John Lothrop, 5, 216, 216

Mt. Vernon Church, xxv

Muddy Branch, MD, 38, 46, 56

Mudge, Charles R., 3, 71, 224, **224**

mutilation of union corpses, 110

National Council of Congregational Churches, xxiv - xxvi

negro ambulance drivers, 236

Nettleton, Reverend Asahel, 242, **242**

New Bedford, MA, xxiv, xxvii - xxx

New England Historical and
  Genealogical Society, xxx
New Hampshire Historical Society,
  xxx
New Jersey, Infantry, 13th, 73, 217,
  217
New York, xxiv, xxvii, 8, 47, 65, **171**,
  180, **186** 208, **217**, **218**, **221**,
  223, 229; Artillery, 1st Light,
  121, **121**, ; 6th Independent
  Battery, **34**; Battery M.,
  121; Cavalry, 5th, 166, **166**;
  Infantry, 2nd, **34**; 9th, 20, 34;
  28th, 134, 149, **149; 42**nd, **32**,
  34; ; 82nd, **32**; 83rd, **20**; 107th,
  180, 217, **217**;
New York, NY, 5, 23, 85, 92, 94, 95,
  145, **236**, **241**
New York World, 156
Newmarket, VA, 132, 135, 136, 142 - 144
newspapers, xxiii, xxiv, 3, **15**, **20**, 45,
  142, 184, 187, **217**, 249, ;
  advertising, 188
Newtown, VA, 700, 149, 150, 155
North Congregational Church, xxiv,
  xxx
nurses, 48, 57, 58, 82, 113, 116, 163
Nutting, Joseph W., 49, **49**, 116
obscene literature, 81
Occoquan creek, 198, 204, 252
Old South Meeting House, xxv
outpost duty, 120
Palmer, Mary T., **77**

Patterson, General Robert, 17, 138,
  138, 170
peace, xxi, xxix, xxx, **19**, 94, 100, 133,
  160, 230, 234,
Pennsylvania, 8, 15, **103**, 124, 158, **187**,
  219, **249**, ; Artillery, 1st, ; 1st
  Battery, 14, **14**, ; Infantry, 2nd,
  103 – 104, 138; 14th, **15**; 15th,
  14, **15**; 28th, **104,** 29th, 20, **20**,
  152, 153; 30th, 20, 60, **60**; 46th,
  134; 66th, **60**; 71st, **32**; 73rd,
  60; 99th, **60**;
Pennsylvania Reserves, **190**, **219**;
Pennsylvania, University of, **108**;
Perkins, Stephen G., 223
Perkins, William E., 11
Philadelphia, PA, **14**, **20**, **31**, **32**, **60**,
  85, **145**, **168**, **248**
Phillips, Reverend Benjamin T., 20, **20**
picket, xviii, 19, 27, 29, 50, 64, 85, 99,
  103, 106, 114, 120, 127, 140,
  146, 152, 153, 192, 202, 203
picket duty, 223, 227, 244
Point of Rocks, 46, 58
pontoon bridge, 98, 247, 253
Poolsville, MD, 30, 63
Pope, General John, 71, 72, **79**, **97**, **149**,
  166, **166**, 170 – 172, 177,
  182 – 184, **182**, 191, 195, 197,
  200, 204, 209
Port Royal, SC, 45, **45**
Post, Reverend Truman M., xxv
"Praise to God, the great Creator," 51

prayer meeting, xxiii, 9, 10, **39**, 65
Presbyterian, 8, **20**, 64, 65, 108, 110, 128, 139, **140**, 141, 185, 186
professional soldiers versus militia officers, 228
promotions, 76, 158
Putnam, Allen, xx
Quincy, Samuel M., 224, **224**
Quint, Alonzo H., animosity towards England, 181; birthplace, 141; furlough, xxiii; letters to the Congregationalist, 165; opinion of England, 169; opinion on General Banks, 212
Quint, Clara Gadsden, xx
Quint, George, xvii
Quint, George Putnam, xx
Quint, John Hastings, xx
Quint, Katherine Mordannt, xx
Quint, Rebecca Page (Putnam), xx
Quint, Sally (Hall), xvii
Quint, Wilder Dwight, xx
rebel chivalry, 140
rebel prisoner, 203
rebel scouts, 121
Reed, Reverend Benjamin F., 37, **37**
regimental bands, 95, **95**, **169**
discharge of, 95
regimental supplies, 231
regiments without chaplains, 242
Reno, General Jesse L., 196, **196**
Republican party, xx, 12, 94, 112, 168, 180, 184, 221
Reynolds, General John, 219

Rhett, Robert B., 79, **79**
Ricketts, General James B., 197, **197**
Roanoke, NC, 90,
Rodman, William Logan, xxviii
Rohr, George, 109, **109**, 110
Roman Catholic, xix, xxiii
Sabbath service, xxiii, 9, 178
Sargent, Dr. Lucius M., **49,** 119
Sargent, Moses H., 91
Savage, Jr., James, 3, **151**, 223, 224,
Scandlin, Reverend William G., 187, **187**
Scott, General Winfield, **12**, 46, 53, **53**, 61, **182**, 198
Scott's Tactics, **53**
Sedgwick, General John, 73, 102, **102**
Seneca, MD, 45, 46, 55, 56, 62, 92, 95, 103
sentries, 19, 30, 57, 63, 81, 120
sermons, xviii, xxi, xxii, xxviii, 86, 125, **156**,
Sewell, Reverend Benjamin T., **20**
Sharpsburg, MD, 73, **197**, **208**, **212**, **218**, 220, 226, 232, 239, 249 – 251; **250**
shelter tents, 162, **162**
Shenandoah River, 16, 135, 139, 142, 161, 247
Shenandoah Valley, 14, 69, 711, **103**, **138**, **148**, **166**, **191**, **197**
Shepardstown, VA, 73, 233
Shields, General James, 103, **103**, 105, 114, 116, 132, 134, 142, 148
Sibley tents, 47, **47**, 75

Sigel, General Franz, 157, 182, **182**, 191, 192, 196, 197, 201, 202
singing, xxi, 9, 10, 23, 51, 52, 65, 100, 105, 144, 234
Sisters of Charity, xxii
skirmishers, 35, 69, 99, 121, 122, 124, 150 - 153, 192, 196, 215
slavery, xx - xxii, xxvii, 21, 28, 41 - 44, 94, 112, 128 - 130, 154, **157**, 160, **160**, 165, 167, 173, 181, 184, 235 - 237
slaves, xxvii, 28, 38, 42, 43, **44**, 112, 128, 130, 137, 139, 166 - 168, 172, 183, 184, 236 - 238
unfit for liberty, 168
Smithsonian Institute, 103, **208**
Smoketown Hospital, 250, **250**
Snicker's Ferry, 120, 130
Snickers Gap, 69
Society for the Relief of Massachusetts soldiers, 241
soldier burial, 15, 58
soldiers, amusements, 234; bounties, 173 - 175; burial, 15, 133, 178, 193; for gunboats, 91; funeral, 14; leaving the battlefield, 228; life, 81; mail, 241; picking cherries, 163; picking flowers, 145; rations, 249; reading material, 231, 244; snow ball fight, 247; wedding, 62
Sons of Temperance, xxii
South Carolina, 42, 45, 79, 110, 133, 160

South Mountain, 351; battle of, **149**, **196**, 210, 222, 240
Southern chivalry, 79, 88, 176
Southern honor, 79, 117
Sperryville, VA, 177, 181, 182, 191
Springfield Rifles, 65
"Star-Spangled Banner," 40, 91
Staunton, VA, 142, 143, **143**
Stearns, Frazer A., 245, 245
Stone, Dr. Lincoln R., 24, **24**, **49**, 82, 119, 154, 218, 229
Stone, General Charles P., 12, **12**, 30, 38, 46, **90**, 102
Strasburg, VA, 69, 70, 113, 118, 120, 142, 143, 148, 149, 158, 159, 227
Sturgis, General Samuel D., 210, **210**
Sullivan, General Jeremiah C., 143, **143**
Sumner, Charles, 5, **30**, 160, **160**
Sumner, General Edwin V., 208, **208**, 211
surgeons, 49, 81, 82, 113, 116, 188, 205, 218, 219, 228 - 230, 235, 242, 251
surgery, 82
sutler, 18, 58, 94, 95
target shooting, 52
tattoo, 18, 54, 55, 105, 203, 243
telegrams, 192
telegraph, 13, 14, 42, 63, 91, 184, 194, 201
Tennallytown, MD, 12, 207
Tennessee, 88, 90, 101, **182**, **198**, **210**, **217**

Thanksgiving, 50 - 54, 234
The Civil War, a holy crusade, 164
"The Star Spangled Banner," 40, 91
Thoroughfare Gap, 197, 202, 203
Tolman, Reverend Samuel H., 93, **93**
Tract Societies, 241, **241**
tracts, 66, 243
Train, Charles R., 217, **217**
transport by railroad, 162
Trask, Reverend George, 156, **156**
Tucker, Francis H., 3
turnpike, 70, 73, 88, 134, 143, 249
U. S. Christian Commission, xxii, **39**, 241 - 243, 241
U. S. Congress, **12**, **31**, 42, 46, 76, 80, 84, 88, 94, 95, 109, 157, 168, 169, 173, 217, **221**
U. S. Sanitary Commission, xxii, **20**, 47, **47**, 183, **186**, **187**, 231, 240, 241, 243
Underwood, Adin B., 4, 151, **151**, **152**
Union Army, XII Corps, **79**, **104**, **198**, **212**, 217
Unitarian, 187
United Brethren in Christ, 128
United States, Artillery 4th, **149**, **218**
United States Military Academy at West Point, **3**, **12**, 13, **13**, **33**, **34**, **102**, **105**, **107**, **122**, **148**, **149**, 156, 163, **166**, **170**, **182**, **191**, **196** – **198**, **208**, **210**, **211**, **218**, **223**, 228
United States Naval Academy, **143**
Universalists, 186

Vermont, Cavalry, 1st, 140, **140**
Verne, Jules, xviii
Virginia, 29, 33, 40, 42, 46, 50, 69 – 71, 73, 76, 88, 93, 94, 101, 108 – 112, 117, 126, 132, 133, 139 - 141, **146**, 159, 161, 162, 165, 168, 170 - 172, 175, 181, **182**, 183, 184, **191**, 200, 207, 222, 223, 233, 247
volunteer surgeons, 230
volunteers for the army, the end of, 174
Ward Master, 48, 49, 58, 202
Warrenton, VA, 77, 162, 163, 165, 176, 177, 197, 201
Washington, DC, 12, 46, 56, 60, 63, 71, 73, 75, 77, **102 - 104**, **107**, 143, **149**, **152**, 158, 159, 161, 167, 170, 173, 176, 177, 181, **182**, 183, 190, 194, **196**, 197, 199, 201, **202**, 204 – 206, **205**, **212**, **223**, 230, 235, 239, 241
Washington's birthday, celebration of, 97
"We are Coming Father Abraham," 177
Webster, Fletcher, **14**, 201, **202**
Wheaton, Jr., Charles, **27**
whiskey, 58, 63, 100
white flag, 109, 117
Williams, General Alpheus S., xix, 79, **79**, 132, 142, 170
Williams, William B., 150, **150**, 192, 223
Williamsport, MD, xxi, 46, 71, 147, 153, 157, 158, 165,

Wilson, Henry, 94, **94**
Winchester, VA, 24, 69 – 71, 101 – 110, 113, **123**, 132, 138, **143**, 151 – 154, 156 – 159, 163, 165, 172, 177, 223, 232, 236, 239; 1st Battle of, **49**, 115, **224**; Battle of, casualties, 154
Winslow, Reverend Horace, 140, **140**, 184, 185
winter campaign, 76, 221, 222, 246, 254
winter huts, 246
Wisconsin, xxvi, 8, 58, **186**; Infantry, 3rd, 88, **88**, 98, **105**, 152, 153, 246
Woodstock, VA, 123
Woodville, VA, 181
wounded soldiers, removal of, 192
Yale University, **272**
"Yankee Doodle," 91, 136
Young Men's Christian Association, xxii, 110, **241**
Young People's Meeting, 10
Zacharias, Daniel, 98, **98**

www.ingramcontent.com/pod-product-compliance
Lightning Source LLC
Chambersburg PA
CBHW070635160426
43194CB00009B/1469